DEPRESSION FREE

DEPRESSION FREE

A 12-WEEK SELF-HELP GUIDE TO OVERCOME DEPRESSION

Dr. Dave Ferruolo

Dr. Dave Books

Dr. Dave Books
Laconia, NH
drdavebooks.com

DEPRESSION FREE: A 12-Week Self-Help Guide to Overcome Depression

ISBN: 9781963834031 (paperback)
ISBN: 9781963834055 (ebook)

Printed in the USA
0 9 8 7 6 5 4 3 2 1

First Printing, 2024

Disclaimer

DEPRESSION FREE is a structured self-help guide to illuminate a path out of depression, offering insights, strategies, and hope. It is important to emphasize that although *DEPRESSION FREE* is rigorously grounded in the psychological and mental health practice evidenced-based, it is not a substitute for professional medical, psychological, or psychiatric help. *DEPRESSION FREE* provides supportive self-help strategies that are effective for addressing depression and it is an excellent complement for healthcare professionals.

We strongly encourage every reader to seek a comprehensive evaluation by medical, psychiatric, and mental health professionals. Overcoming depression requires a multifaceted approach; professional guidance is essential for navigating this complex issue.

Contents

PART IV
APPENDIX   **361**

Forward

DEPRESSION FREE is more than a self-help guide. It is the culmination of years of dedication, shaped by my experiences, triumphs, setbacks, and an unwavering commitment to excellence and rigorous study.

My path to writing *DEPRESSION FREE* began in the trenches of community mental health, where I served as both a psychotherapist and a counselor for individuals battling alcohol and substance use. Despite a solid academic background and high-achieving success in graduate school, I quickly realized that the real-world demands of a psychotherapist were far more complex than I had anticipated. Faced with a caseload that ranged from mild to severe, from situational to chronic, pervasive mental illnesses, I found myself grappling with a daunting array of challenges right from the start.

Feeling inadequately prepared for the enormity of the task and driven by a personality that confronts issues head-on, I plunged into the depths of evidence-based practices. This wasn't just about filling gaps in my knowledge; it was about building a fortress of understanding and skills to navigate the intricate challenges of mental health care.

I started chronicling my learning journey in a humble notebook, which quickly grew into a comprehensive binder. This binder was more than just paper and ink; it became a treasure trove of psychotherapeutic treatments, skills, exercises, coping mechanisms, strategies, and processes. I delved deeply into the *Diagnostic and Statistical Manual of Mental Disorders* and an extensive array of psychology and counseling books, participated in countless counseling workshops, became certified in many evidenced-based therapies, and earned multiple licenses. My goal was clear: to amass the broadest possible skill set and enhance my ability to make a meaningful difference in the lives of those I served.

Over a decade, this binder earned its place on the corner of my desk, etching its significance into the fabric of my professional identity. It symbolized everything I had learned, struggled with, and overcame along the way. This binder, filled with the distilled essence of countless hours of study, practice, and reflection, laid the groundwork for *DEPRESSION FREE*.

DEPRESSION FREE is thus born out of a relentless personal journey through the world of mental health, a journey marked by uncompromising pursuit, profound insights, and the desire to convey hope and empowerment to others. It's a narrative that intertwines my experiences, successes, failures, and the lessons learned through rigorous study and practice, all aimed at helping others find their path to healing. Through this book, I aim to share the knowledge and strategies that have proven effective over years of practice, offering readers a proven path out of the darkness of depression.

PART I

Depression Free

1

Welcome to Your Journey

You stand at the threshold of a significant journey—a deeply personal and resonantly universal path. *DEPRESSION FREE* will be your guide through the intricate, often misunderstood terrain of depression. It is a compassionate, understanding, and steadfast commitment to support you at every step toward a life emancipated from the shadows of depression.

Embracing this journey reflects your strength, a clear signal of your resolve to reclaim your life and well-being from the clutches of depression. This condition, characterized by its dense fog of sadness, isolation, and fatigue, can make one feel alone even amidst a sea of people, disconnected from the world's vibrancy. Yet, as you turn these pages, we will embark on this path together, discovering avenues of healing and the rekindling of joy that seemed lost.

Embarking on this journey is neither a quest for a quick fix nor a promise of an effortless path. It demands bravery, patience, and unwavering perseverance. However, hold on to the belief that you are never alone. This book's collection of pages is a companion that offers light in the darkest times and strategies to alleviate the burden of depression. Together, we will methodically traverse this journey toward a horizon filled with brightness and hope. But I must emphasize the importance of professional help. Navigating the world of depression is complex, and the use of a professional can significantly increase successful outcomes.

The Nature of Depression

Depression is more than just a bad day or a fleeting feeling of sadness; it's a complex mental health condition that affects every facet of an individual's life. It can distort your perception of the world, yourself, and your future, often leaving you feeling trapped in a cycle of despair. However, understanding depression is the first step in overcoming it. This condition wears many faces, affecting people differently. Depressive symptoms include, persistent feelings of sadness, loss of interest in enjoyable activities, and a range of physical and emotional problems that can interfere significantly with daily functioning.

Depression is not a sign of weakness or a failure of willpower. It is a health condition as real and treatable as any physical ailment. Just as someone with a broken leg would seek medical treatment, addressing depression may require professional intervention and support. By demystifying depression, this book aims to dismantle the stigma surrounding it, encouraging a more open and supportive dialogue about mental health.

A Journey of Healing

Healing from depression is a journey of rediscovery—a process of learning to understand and manage your emotions, thoughts, and behaviors in ways that lead to a healthier, more fulfilling life. This book introduces a plethora of beneficial evidence-based therapies and practices, including Cognitive Behavioral Therapy (CBT), Acceptance and Commitment Therapy (ACT), and mindfulness, to name a few. These approaches offer practical tools to challenge and change the negative thought patterns and behaviors that fuel depression.

Moreover, healing is not a solitary journey. This book emphasizes the importance of building a support system, including friends, family, and, as mentioned, mental health professionals, who can offer encouragement and understanding. Healing also involves self-care, from ensuring proper nutrition and sleep to engaging in activities and hobbies that bring joy.

Navigating the Journey Together

As your guide, *DEPRESSION FREE* does not merely instruct; it walks beside you. Each chapter is structured to gradually build understanding, skills, and confidence. The exercises and insights within these pages are designed to be integrated into your daily life, providing a practical framework for managing depression. This guide also complements professional psychotherapy, enhancing the therapeutic journey with additional resources and support.

Your journey through depression to healing is uniquely yours, but you do not have to walk it alone. This book serves as a bridge to understanding, a tool for change, and a source of hope. Through its pages, you will find strategies to confront and overcome the challenges posed by depression, fostering resilience and a renewed sense of purpose.

As you embark on this journey, remember that moving toward a life free from depression is a process filled with challenges and triumphs. It requires courage to face the unknown and the commitment to keep moving forward, even when the path seems daunting. Let *DEPRESSION FREE* be you guide and a companion on this journey, offering insights, encouragement, and practical strategies every step of the way.

Your journey begins now. With each step, with every page turned, you move closer to a life defined not by depression but by hope, resilience, and joy. Welcome to your journey toward becoming Depression Free.

2

How to Use this Book

This book, designed as a 12-week guidebook, is your companion in navigating the path out of depression. Within these pages, you will find a structured program that combines knowledge, practical exercises, and self-reflection to foster resilience and well-being. Whether you're exploring these tools on your own or as an adjunct to psychotherapy, this chapter will outline how to maximize the benefits of this guidebook.

Understanding the Structure

At the heart of this guidebook lies a meticulously designed 12-week self-help guide, each segment devoted to unraveling and addressing a different facet of depression. This structured approach is not arbitrary; it mirrors the journey from understanding the depths of depression to cultivating recovery and resilience. The progression through these weeks is akin to navigating through chapters of your evolving story, where each adds a layer of understanding, skills, and self-awareness.

Weekly Themes

Each week is anchored around a theme that is critical to the multi-faceted nature of depression. These themes have been selected based on their relevance and impact on mental health, ensuring a holistic approach to recovery. For instance, one week may focus on Cognitive Behavioral Therapy techniques, offering insights into how to identify, challenge, and change negative thought patterns that fuel depression. Another week might delve into Emotional Intelligence, enhancing your ability to understand and manage your emotions and those of others. This thematic approach ensures that by the end of the program, you will have explored a broad spectrum of topics essential for overcoming depression.

Daily Exercises

Central to each week are the daily exercises that will deepen your understanding of the week's theme and facilitate the application of this knowledge in your life. These exercises blend reflective questions, practical tasks, and mindfulness practices, each designed to engage you in active learning and self-exploration. For example, a day's exercise might involve journaling about a particular thought pattern, practicing a relaxation technique, or performing an act of kindness for oneself or others. The variety and depth of these exercises ensure that each day offers a new opportunity for growth and healing.

Evolution into Weekly and Monthly Practices

As you progress through the book, specific exercises are intended to evolve beyond their daily format, becoming weekly and eventually monthly practices. This progression builds a sustainable foundation of habits that promote mental health and well-being. For instance, a daily exercise focused on gratitude might evolve into a weekly ritual of writing gratitude letters or a monthly practice of volunteer work. This evolution reflects the natural progression of healing, where initial steps lead to more significant, impactful actions over time.

The Rationale Behind the Structure

The structure of this book reinforces the principle that overcoming depression requires understanding and action. The thematic weekly focus educates and enlightens, while the daily exercises encourage active engagement with the material. This combination ensures a comprehensive approach to tackling depression, addressing it from cognitive, emotional, and behavioral angles.

By the end of the 12 weeks, you will have gained a deeper understanding of depression and how to combat it and also developed a repertoire of skills and habits that support your mental health. This journey is about transformation—transforming understanding into action, challenges into opportunities for growth, and ultimately, depression into a state of well-being and joy.

Complementing Psychotherapy

Embarking on this 12-week journey with the guidance of a therapist can be an incredibly enriching and transformative experience. We wholeheartedly encourage incorporating this book into your psychotherapy sessions, as it offers a wealth of structured themes and exercises that can significantly enhance the therapeutic process. Engaging with a mental health professional while working through the book provides a unique opportunity to deepen your understanding of depression and to tailor the recovery process to your individual needs.

Each week's focus within this guide presents an opportunity to explore specific aspects of depression in a structured manner with your therapist. This approach allows for an enriched dialogue where you can share personal reflections, tackle challenges, and celebrate insights gained from the exercises. Your therapist can offer professional insights, help you navigate the complexities of your experiences, and apply the book's teachings in the most beneficial way.

Moreover, this guide's daily, weekly, and monthly exercises facilitate self-discovery and healing. Your therapy homework extends the therapeutic work beyond the confines of the therapy room, allowing you to apply and practice new skills in real-world settings. This continuity of care and practice fosters a more meaningful therapeutic journey.

Seeking the support of a therapist while engaging with this book is not merely a recommendation; it is a pathway to unlocking a more profound level of healing and growth. The dual approach of professional guidance and self-led exploration can synergistically infuse you with more significant momentum and insight. We strongly advocate for this collaborative approach, viewing it as an optimal strategy for confronting and overcoming depression.

Remember, reaching out for professional help is a sign of strength and an essential step in your journey to wellness. While a comprehensive tool for addressing depression, do not overlook the expertise and personalized care that a therapist can provide. Together, they form a powerful alliance against depression, illuminating the path to healing and resilience.

Practical Tips for Integration

Integrating the practices and insights from this book into your daily life is a journey that requires commitment, understanding, and self-compassion. By embracing this guide as a companion on your path to healing, you can unlock its full potential and pave the way for a transformative experience. Here's how to weave the teachings and exercises from this book into the fabric of your everyday life, creating a tapestry of growth and recovery.

The first step in this process is to carve out specific moments in your day dedicated solely to engaging with the book. This could be a quiet morning period where you reflect on the day's exercise over a cup of coffee or a nightly ritual where you review the day's experiences and plan for the next. The key is consistency; establishing a routine creates a space for engagement and reflection, allowing the principles and practices outlined in the book to become a natural part of your daily rhythm.

Embarking on this journey is a deeply personal endeavor, yet the support of those around you can significantly enrich the experience. Share your journey through this book with close friends or family members. Their encouragement and understanding can provide a layer of support that enhances your journey, offering motivation and accountability as you work through the exercises. Knowing that others are aware of and support your efforts can make the path less daunting and more filled with shared joy and understanding.

Journaling is a powerful tool for self-discovery and reflection, serving as a mirror to your inner world. Keeping a dedicated journal for your experiences, thoughts, and feelings as you progress through the book can enhance your self-awareness. This journal can be a safe space to express yourself freely, explore your exercise responses, and track your progress. It becomes a companion on your journey and a tangible record of your growth and insights gained along the way.

The path to healing and growth is rarely straight and often filled with challenges. It's essential to approach this journey with patience and kindness. Celebrate every step of progress, no matter how small, and recognize that difficult days are part of the process. Self-compassion is a powerful ally in healing, encouraging you to treat yourself with the same kindness and understanding you would offer a friend.

While this book provides a structured approach to addressing depression, there may be times when professional guidance is needed. If topics or exercises stir up strong emotions or if you find yourself struggling significantly, reaching out to a mental health professional can provide the support and expertise necessary to navigate these challenges. Professional help can offer personalized insights and strategies, ensuring that your journey through the book is both safe and effective.

Integrating the practices from this book into your life is an act of self-care that can lead to profound personal growth and healing. By dedicating time, creating a supportive environment, journaling your journey, practicing patience and self-compassion, and seeking professional guidance when needed, you set the stage for a transformative experience. This book is your guide, but the journey is uniquely yours, filled with potential for discovery, recovery, and renewal.

As we conclude Chapter 4, reflect on the journey you are about to undertake. This chapter has outlined a roadmap for effectively using this book as a tool in your fight against depression. It has provided you with practical strategies for integrating the book's teachings into your daily life, emphasizing the importance of dedication, support, self-reflection, patience, and the pursuit of professional guidance when needed.

Embarking on this 12-week program will enhance your understanding and support overcoming depression. It requires commitment, but remember, you do not walk this path alone. This book serves as your guide, offering daily exercises and insights to help you navigate the complexities of depression. But beyond its pages lies a world of support —from friends, family, and mental health professionals—all rooting for your success.

Remember, healing is a journey, not a destination. There will be days of progress and days of challenge. Embrace each day with kindness, knowing that every step forward, no matter how small, is a victory. This journey is as much about discovering your resilience and strength as it is about overcoming depression.

3

Recognizing Depression

Recognizing depression is about spotting a set of symptoms. It's about understanding that it's a deeply personal experience that can profoundly affect life. In this chapter, we shed light on those symptoms. We do this whether we are looking inward at our feelings or outward at the experiences of those close to us. Acknowledging depression shows the shift from suffering and uncertainty. It shows the potential for healing and hope.

Depression often masks itself within the ebb and flow of life's usual ups and downs. This makes it challenging to discern when it's addressable or if it is time to seek assistance. Recognition is the cornerstone of initiating a transformative recovery process. The aim is to give you the knowledge and insight to navigate this complex terrain. It will help you see beyond mere sadness or passing moods. It will help you understand the deeper, lasting depression that needs attention.

Through encouraging self-awareness, we guide you to explore self-discovery. This chapter connects symptoms to recognizing a condition beyond usual emotions. It creates a space where seeking help is empowering.

By diving into depression symptoms, we highlight the need to spot them early. This is important for oneself and for others, as recognizing it early helps treatment. It also lessens depression's long-term impact on a person's life. We will explore what it means to live with depression. We will show how to spot its subtle signs. Our goal is to give you the clarity and courage needed to take the first, crucial step.

Embarking on this journey of recognition does not happen alone. It invites a dialogue. It's a shared understanding between those with depression and those who can offer support. We will demystify the symptoms and impacts of depression. This will foster a supportive network. It will encourage seeking help as an act of self-care and self-respect.

As you read through this chapter, you'll gain insights into the details of depression. You'll learn how to tell the difference between the normal ebbs and flows of emotions. You'll also learn to spot the more serious, long-lasting waves of depression. This understanding is vital. It lays the groundwork for seeking and getting the help needed.

Understanding the Nature of Depression

Depression goes beyond occasional sadness. It is also more than the temporary challenges of being human. It represents a mental health condition that affects every part of a person's life.

At its core, depression affects emotions. It leads to a sense of despair, hopelessness, and often, emptiness. Sadness after a bad day is fleeting. But, depression's emotional turmoil lingers. It also ruins an person's ability to feel joy, excitement, and satisfaction. This feeling affects the person inside. It shows in how they relate to others. It often makes them leave social events. They also disconnect from relationships that once made them happy.

Physically, depression can be just as debilitating. It often brings about significant changes in sleep patterns—either insomnia or hypersomnia (excessive sleeping)—and can alter appetite, leading to weight loss or gain. The physical exhaustion associated with depression is not merely a result of poor sleep or nutrition; it's a profound fatigue that persists regardless of rest or diet, making everyday tasks and responsibilities feel insurmountable.

The impact on one's quality of life is substantial. At work, depression can sap productivity, concentration, and motivation, making it challenging to meet deadlines, complete tasks, or even maintain regular employment. At home, it can strain relationships, diminish one's role in family life, and erode the pleasure in hobbies and interests that once brought joy. The cumulative effect of these changes often leads to a decrease in overall life satisfaction and can exacerbate the symptoms of depression, creating a vicious cycle.

Recognizing the signs of depression is thus not merely about identifying a set of symptoms; it's about acknowledging a pervasive change in one's emotional and physical well-being. Acknowledgment requires an understanding that depression is a genuine and treatable medical condition, not a weakness or a failure of character. By recognizing the multifaceted nature of depression—its emotional, physical, and life-altering dimensions—we open the door to seeking the necessary support and intervention.

Understanding depression in its entirety helps demystify the condition, making it easier to recognize in oneself or others. This foundational knowledge is essential, not only for those experiencing depression but also for their loved ones and caregivers, enabling them to provide the understanding and support needed to navigate the path.

Signs of Depression in Yourself

Depression unfolds like a slow, creeping fog. Subtly at first. Then the symptoms become so integrated into daily life they seem almost normal. It's a gradual shift where the joy and color of life start to fade, leaving behind a persistent gray.

Imagine waking up day after day to a profound sense of sadness or despair. A feeling so deep and enduring that it clings to you, even in moments that used to sparkle with happiness. This isn't just a fleeting sorrow but a blanket of hopelessness that smothers joy and interest in life. The hobbies and social activities that once filled your evenings and weekends, the intimacy that connected you to your partner all begin to lose their appeal. It's like watching the world through a glass, disconnected and disinterested.

Changes in appetite or weight might also signal this inner turmoil. Perhaps you find yourself skipping meals without thought. Or, eating without hunger. This leads to noticeable weight loss or gain. It's a physical sign of the mental battle within. Sleep, too, becomes a battleground. Nights are restless, spent chasing sleep that darts away, or mornings come too early, leaving you feeling exhausted when you awake. Alternatively, you might sleep too much yet never feel rested.

Fatigue sets in, a relentless drain on your energy, making even the most minor tasks feel Herculean. This isn't the tiredness from a long day's work or lack of sleep but a bone-weary exhaustion that doesn't recede with rest. You might also notice a creeping sense of worthlessness or undue guilt over past actions or failures. You may criticize yourself. It can be harsh and unforgiving, far beyond what the situation warrants.

Your mind, once sharp and clear, now seems fogged. Concentration falters. Decisions that should be simple become insurmountable challenges. Memories slip through your fingers like water. Physical symptoms can emerge without any apparent medical cause. These might include aches and pains, digestive issues, a constant discomfort that no treatment seems to alleviate.

And in the quiet moments, thoughts of death or suicide might whisper in the back of your mind, a dangerous undercurrent that signals the depth of the despair. These thoughts are the most alarming signs of depression, a red flag that immediate help is needed.

Recognizing these symptoms in oneself isn't easy. It requires a moment of clarity, an acknowledgment that what you're experiencing isn't a normal part of life's ebb and flow but an indication of a more enduring condition. This realization is the first step to seeking help and finding your way back to a life filled with color and joy.

Recognizing Depression in Others

Recognizing depression in others is a delicate process that necessitates keen observation. You need a deep sense of empathy, and a willingness to support someone through their struggles. It's about noticing the subtle and sometimes not-so-subtle shifts in behavior, mood, and personality that might indicate a friend, family member, or colleague is experiencing more than just a bad day or a temporary setback. This task involves attunement to changes suggesting a deeper, more persistent issue.

One of the first signs might be a noticeable withdrawal from social interactions. Someone who once enjoyed gatherings, participated in regular outings, or simply cherished spending time with loved ones might suddenly seem distant, preferring isolation over companionship. This shift could be gradual or abrupt, but the contrast in their social engagement can signify their inner turmoil.

Closely related is the neglect of personal appearance. Depression can sap the energy and motivation required for routine self-care, leading to noticeable changes in how a person dresses or maintains their hygiene. These changes might seem minor but can indicate a loss of interest in self-presentation, a hallmark of declining mental well-being.

Performance at work or school can also suffer significantly. Tasks once handled with competence and enthusiasm may now seem overwhelming or receive less attention, leading to a stark drop in quality and productivity. This decline is often accompanied by difficulties in concentration, memory, and decision-making, further impacting their professional or academic life.

Listening is equally necessary in recognizing depression in others. Pay attention to expressions of hopelessness, overwhelming guilt, or a pervasive lack of interest in the future. These verbal cues can be explicit or hidden in casual conversation, revealing a deep-seated sense of despair or a feeling that their situation will not improve.

Increased irritability is another symptom overlooked or misattributed to stress or being overworked. However, when this irritability becomes a consistent part of someone's demeanor, it might be reflective of the frustration and emotional pain associated with depression.

Substance use can escalate as individuals try to cope with their feelings or numb the pain. An increase in alcohol consumption or the use of drugs as a form of self-medication can be a sign that someone is struggling to manage their emotional state.

Lastly, any mention of self-harm or suicide, no matter how offhand it may seem, should be taken seriously. These are the most alarming signs of psychological distress and require immediate attention and action to ensure the person's safety.

Recognizing depression in others is not about making a diagnosis but about noticing when someone might be in pain and needing support. It's about opening a dialogue, offering a listening ear, and encouraging them to seek professional help. By being observant and empathetic, you can play a crucial role in someone's journey, reminding them that they are not alone and that help is available.

The Importance of Early Recognition

The importance of early recognition of depression is paramount. It serves as a critical juncture in the road, acting as a preventative measure against the deepening of the condition and enhancing the efficacy of treatment strategies. This early detection and subsequent intervention are pivotal, not only in halting the progression of depression but also in setting the foundation for a more favorable response to therapy and medications.

Early recognition of depression involves a keen awareness of its signs and symptoms, coupled with the understanding that these indicators point to a genuine and treatable health condition. This understanding can significantly empower individuals, encouraging them to step forward and seek the professional assistance they need. By identifying depression at its onset, individuals can access treatment options sooner, which may be less intensive and more effective than if the condition had been allowed to progress unchecked.

Moreover, early intervention in depression can significantly mitigate its impact on one's personal, professional, and social life. By addressing the condition promptly, individuals can preserve their relationships, maintain their productivity at work or school, and continue to engage in activities they enjoy. This improves their quality of life during treatment and contributes to a more robust support network and a more resilient sense of self.

Furthermore, early recognition and treatment of depression can reduce the risk of co-occurring conditions, such as anxiety or substance use disorders, which often complicate or exacerbate depressive symptoms. It can also decrease the likelihood of recurrence, setting the stage for long-term management and recovery.

Educating the public, healthcare providers, and individuals about the importance of recognizing the early signs of depression is crucial in creating a society that supports mental health and encourages timely and effective treatment. Empowerment through knowledge and understanding can transform the way we approach depression, moving from a reactive to a proactive stance that prioritizes early detection and intervention.

In essence, early recognition of depression is not just a critical step for the individual affected but a collective goal that society should strive toward. It encapsulates the hope that, with prompt action and the proper support, recovery is not just possible but probable, allowing individuals to reclaim their lives from the clutches of depression.

Taking the First Step

Addressing depression is fundamental. It signifies a readiness to seek support and engage in the healing process. Acknowledging the need for help is an act of courage and self-compassion, marking the beginning of a transformative process. Several avenues are available for assistance, each offering a unique form of support.

While this book serves as an informative and supportive first step in recognizing and understanding depression, it is crucial to remember that it is not a substitute for professional help. This guide will provide you with knowledge, strategies to overcome a wide rage of depression and its causes. But engaging with a healthcare professional is essential for a comprehensive assessment and personalized treatment plan. Professional treatment may include therapy, medication, lifestyle changes, or a combination of these approaches tailored to your needs.

Your primary care provider is often the most accessible starting point for seeking help. They can perform an initial evaluation, offer support, and provide referrals to mental health specialists. Depending on the severity and specifics of your condition, this may include therapists, counselors, or psychiatrists. Primary care physicians can also assess the wide range of physical health issues that might be causing or contributing to depression.

The internet is a valuable resource for finding mental health support. Numerous websites and online platforms can help you locate therapists and psychiatric prescribers in your area. Many online resources have search tools that filter professionals by location, specialty, and insurance acceptance. For those considering medication as part of their treatment plan, similar resources are available to find psychiatrists or psychiatric nurse practitioners skilled in diagnosing mental health conditions and prescribing appropriate medications.

Support groups, both in-person and online, offer a sense of community and understanding that can be incredibly comforting. These groups provide a platform to share experiences, coping strategies, and encouragement with others facing similar challenges. Online forums and social media groups dedicated to mental health awareness and support can provide comfort and information.

Professional help offers a level of personalized care and expertise that is critical for effectively treating depression. Mental health professionals can work with you to identify the root causes of your depression, develop effective coping strategies, and monitor your progress over time. They can adjust treatment plans as needed, ensuring you receive the most effective care possible.

Depression is a pervasive condition that affects many aspects of an individual's life, but with recognition comes the power to seek change. By understanding and acknowledging the signs of depression in oneself or others, individuals can advance in the direction of recovery and to a healthier, more joyful life.

The Critical Role of Medical and Psychiatric Evaluations

When addressing depression, it is important to recognize the need for medical and psychiatric evaluations. These evaluations are not merely formalities; they are essential processes that can significantly influence your path to healing.

First, let's talk about why a medical evaluation is indispensable. Depression, while often viewed solely through a psychological lens, can often have its roots in physical health issues. Conditions such as thyroid disorders, vitamin deficiencies, or hormonal imbalances can mimic or exacerbate symptoms of depression. A comprehensive medical evaluation helps rule out these and other medical reasons for mood and affect dysfunctions. It's crucial to understand that if such underlying medical issues exist, addressing them might be the key to alleviating depressive symptoms. Ignoring potential medical causes and focusing solely on psychological aspects could hinder your depression-free progress.

Encouragingly, most general practitioners are well-equipped to perform an initial screening for common conditions that could be contributing to your depression. Specific tests might be recommended based on your symptoms and medical history. This proactive approach ensures that any treatable medical conditions are identified and managed appropriately, laying a healthier foundation for addressing the psychological components of depression.

Parallel to the medical evaluation, a psychiatric evaluation provides a detailed understanding of your mental health, offering insights crucial for formulating an effective treatment plan. This evaluation focuses on assessing your mental state, exploring the presence of depressive symptoms, and determining their impact on your daily functioning. Importantly, it also evaluates the need for and appropriateness of psychotropic medication.

Psychotropic medications can play a significant role in managing depression, especially when biological factors are at play. These medications can help correct chemical imbalances in the brain, facilitating significant improvements in mood and well-being. However, the decision to use medication should be made carefully, considering factors such as the severity of symptoms, the presence of co-occurring mental health conditions, and your personal preferences regarding treatment.

It's vital to acknowledge that while active self-help and professional psychotherapy are powerful tools for overcoming depression, they may not fully address the biological aspects of the condition. For some individuals, a combination of medication and therapy offers the best chance for recovery. A thorough psychiatric evaluation, conducted by a psychiatrist or a qualified mental health professional, ensures that any recommendations for medication are tailored to your specific needs, enhancing the overall effectiveness of your treatment plan.

Seeking both medical and psychiatric evaluations underscores a holistic approach to treating depression, recognizing the complex interplay between physical and mental health. This integrated path respects the multifaceted nature of depression, ensuring that all potential contributing factors are considered and addressed.

We strongly encourage you to pursue these evaluations as early as possible. Doing so not only enhances your understanding of your depression but also maximizes the effectiveness of your treatment plan. Remember, uncovering and treating any underlying medical conditions, alongside the appropriate use of medication and counseling, significantly increases your chances of successfully overcoming depression.

In your pursuit of becoming depression-free, embracing the dual approach of medical and psychiatric evaluations is not just a step but a courageous leap. It's a commitment to thoroughly understanding and addressing all aspects of your well-being, setting a solid foundation for your path to healing and resilience.

As we close Chapter 3, it's crucial to reflect on the journey of recognizing depression in oneself and others. This chapter has illuminated the paths through which we can identify the signs of depression, emphasizing the critical distinction between transient sadness and the more severe, enduring nature of depressive states. By fostering self-awareness and understanding, we've explored how to acknowlede depression and seek the support necessary for healing.

Understanding the nature of depression, recognizing its signs, and appreciating the importance of early recognition are foundational elements in addressing this complex condition. We've discussed various avenues for seeking help, from reaching out to healthcare professionals to utilizing online resources and underscored the importance of professional intervention in effectively managing depression.

Seeking help is a courageous act of self-care that sets the stage for recovery. This book aims to serve as a supportive guide in your journey, offering insights and encouragement. However, it's essential to remember that this guide is a starting point, not a substitute for professional help. The path to overcoming depression is unique for each individual, and professional support is paramount in navigating this path successfully.

Chapter 3 has armed us with the knowledge to recognize the often subtle signs of depression, highlight the critical nature of early intervention, and provide guidance on how to seek help. As we move forward, let's carry with us the understanding that reaching out for support is decisive and often necessary. It's a step filled with hope, signaling the beginning of a journey out of the shadows of depression and into the light of understanding, healing, and resilience.

4

Understanding Depression

Many people oversimplify depression as brief sadness. But, it's much more complex and severe in clinical terms. This misunderstanding exemplifies the need to look deeper. We need to look into what is clinical depression verses feeling down. It goes far beyond the occasional sadness or blue moods that everyone feels at times. Clinical depression is also called major depressive disorder. It includes a complex set of symptoms. When these symptoms persist, they affect a person's thoughts, feelings, and physical health. They also impair the ability to fully function and engage in life.

This chapter will provide a clear, full understanding of depression. It's crucial to recognize that depression is not a sign of weakness. Nor can one simply "snap out of" or "push through" it through willpower or positive thinking. Instead, it is a condition that requires understanding, compassion, and appropriate treatment.

We will delve into the many parts of depression. We want to distinguish the difference between temporary sadness and the despair that marks clinical depression. This distinction is critical for several reasons. Firstly, recognizing when you need professional help is important. Second, understanding the depth and breadth of depression's impact can lead to a more empathetic and supportive approach. This helps regarding those who are struggling. It also reduces the societal stigma of this condition.

Addressing and challenging the widespread misconceptions about depression is an essential part of this process. Myths such as the belief that depression is the result of a poor attitude or a lack of gratitude contribute to the stigma and can prevent people from seeking the help they need. By fostering a more profound understanding of depression as a complex interplay of genetic, biochemical, environmental, and psychological factors, we can collectively move toward a more informed and compassionate society that supports mental health and wellness.

As we transition into discussing the symptoms and impact of depression, it's important to keep in mind that recognizing these signs is the first step toward healing. The journey from understanding to action is vital, not only for individuals directly affected by depression but also for their loved ones and society as a whole. By demystifying this condition, we empower ourselves and others to seek the necessary support and treatment to lead healthier, more fulfilling lives.

Symptoms and Impact

The symptoms of depression, while commonly summarized as persistent sadness or a chronic low mood, encompass a far broader and more complex range of experiences that can affect an individual's mental, emotional, and physical well-being. These persistent and multifaceted symptoms can drastically impair one's capacity to engage in daily activities and experience life's pleasures. Beyond the hallmark signs of enduring sadness and diminished interest in activities once found enjoyable, depression manifests in various ways that are elusive and are hard to recognize as symptoms of the condition immediately.

Individuals battling depression might encounter significant changes in appetite, leading to notable weight loss or gain unrelated to dieting. Sleep disturbances are also common, manifesting as insomnia or excessive sleeping. Physical symptoms such as chronic fatigue, even after sufficient rest, muscle aches, headaches, and digestive issues can be prevalent, further complicating the ability to function normally. Emotional manifestations might include pervasive feelings of worthlessness or disproportionate guilt over minor matters, difficulties in concentrating or making decisions, and recurring thoughts of death or suicide, highlighting the condition's severity.

Cognitive symptoms of depression, such as pervasive feelings of hopelessness and worthlessness, significantly impact an individual's mental state and perception of self. Among the more alarming symptoms are thoughts of self-harm or suicide, which necessitate immediate action. If you or someone you know is experiencing serious thoughts of suicide, it is critical to seek help without delay. Contact emergency services or a crisis hotline immediately to get needed support and intervention. Remember, reaching out for help is a sign of strength and the first step towards recovery.

The impact of these symptoms extends well into every facet of an individual's life. Socially, the overwhelming sense of despair and isolation can lead to withdrawal from friendships, family relationships, and social activities. This isolation not only exacerbates the feelings of loneliness and worthlessness but also deprives the individual of potential sources of support and joy. Professionally, depression can severely hinder performance and productivity. The inability to concentrate, loss of motivation, and physical symptoms like fatigue make maintaining regular work responsibilities a formidable challenge, potentially leading to job loss or significant career setbacks.

Physically, the neglect of self-care routines is a critical concern. Individuals suffering from depression may find even basic self-care—such as personal hygiene, eating, and exercise—overwhelmingly tough. This neglect can precipitate a vicious cycle where physical health deteriorates, further impacting mental health. The physiological effects of depression, including changes in neurotransmitter levels and hormonal imbalances, can exacerbate existing health conditions or lead to new health issues, underscoring the interconnectedness of mental and physical health.

The pervasive impact of depression underlines the necessity of understanding its underlying causes. Recognizing that depression results from a complex interplay of genetic, biological, psychological, and environmental factors is central to addressing and treating the condition effectively. As we explore these causes, it becomes evident that depression is not a sign of weakness or a condition to overcome through sheer willpower. Instead, it requires comprehensive and compassionate treatment approaches that address the multifaceted nature of the disorder. This holistic understanding paves the way for more effective interventions and supports healing and recovery, emphasizing the importance of recognizing the signs and seeking professional help.

Understanding the Causes

Understanding the intricate causes of depression requires delving into the myriad factors that contribute to its onset, illustrating that the roots of this condition are as individualized as the people it affects. At the heart of depression lies a complex interplay of biological, psychological, and environmental factors, each intertwining to influence the risk and experience of depression in unique ways.

Biologically, the dance of neurotransmitters within the brain—such as serotonin, norepinephrine, and dopamine—plays a pivotal role in mood regulation and, consequently, in the development of depression. These chemicals, responsible for transmitting signals in the brain, can become imbalanced, leading to the symptoms of depression. Genetics also weigh heavily in the equation, with a family history of depression significantly raising one's risk, pointing to the inheritable nature of vulnerability to this condition.

Beyond the biological blueprint, an individual's physical health and bodily functions exert a considerable influence. Chronic conditions, from persistent pain to hormonal imbalances and specific disorders like thyroid issues or diabetes, can predispose someone to depressive symptoms, blurring the lines between physical and mental health.

The cognitive and emotional landscapes of the mind also offer fertile ground for depression to take root. How one perceives and interacts with the world—shaped by negative thinking patterns, low self-esteem, and ineffective coping mechanisms—can profoundly affect one's susceptibility to depression. These internal dialogues and beliefs can shield us from or expose us to the harsher impacts of life's challenges.

Environmental and social factors further complicate this picture, with life's upheavals, such as trauma, loss, or significant life changes, serving as potential catalysts for depression. The context of one's life, including the stress of socioeconomic challenges, social isolation, and a lack of a supportive network, plays a crucial role in either mitigating or exacerbating the risk of developing depression.

This multiplicity of biological causes, personal health, cognitive processes, and environmental factors highlight the complex nature of depression. It underscores the importance of a nuanced approach to understanding and treating this condition, paving the way for discussing the necessity of professional evaluation. Recognizing the diverse origins of depression not only aids in its diagnosis and treatment but also fosters empathy for those affected, encouraging a more compassionate and comprehensive response to their needs.

The Importance of Professional Evaluation

As mentioned in the previous chapter, the necessity of professional evaluation in diagnosing depression cannot be overstated. This nuanced process transcends mere symptom checklist completion, diving deep into symptoms' context, duration, and severity to truly understand the individual's experience. Such a comprehensive approach is vital for several reasons, not least because depression can often be a chameleon, mimicking other conditions or co-existing with them, thereby complicating the diagnostic landscape.

A psychological evaluation delves into the cognitive and emotional realms, assessing thought patterns, emotional responses, and behaviors that may be indicative of depression. This involves a conversation and a structured assessment using various tools and techniques to uncover underlying issues such as negative thinking, low self-esteem, or ineffective coping mechanisms. Understanding an individual's psychological state is crucial for distinguishing depression from other mental health disorders and for tailoring treatment to address both the symptoms and their root causes.

Environmental factors also play a significant role in the onset and progression of depression. A thorough professional evaluation, therefore, extends to understanding the individual's social context, including relationships, work environment, and life events. This holistic view allows mental health professionals to consider factors such as trauma, loss, or significant life changes in their diagnosis and treatment plan, recognizing that the environment can both trigger and sustain depressive episodes.

Medical evaluation is equally critical, given the potential for physical health problems to precipitate or exacerbate depressive symptoms. A comprehensive medical assessment can identify conditions like thyroid disorders, hormonal imbalances, or nutrient deficiencies, which may contribute to or mimic the symptoms of depression. This underscores the importance of a collaborative approach to diagnosis, involving mental health and medical professionals, to ensure proper evaluation of all potential causes.

Psychiatric evaluation specifically addresses the need for and appropriateness of psychotropic medication. This step is indispensable for determining whether medication should be part of the treatment plan, which medications are most likely effectual, and proper medication management. Considering the individual's health history, other conditions, and potential interactions between medications, this evaluation ensures that any prescribed treatment is safe, effective, and personalized.

The importance of professional evaluation in diagnosing and treating depression lies in its ability to integrate these diverse assessments into a coherent understanding of the individual's mental health. By considering the full spectrum of biological, psychological, environmental, and medical factors, professionals can develop a treatment plan that addresses each person's unique needs, offering the best chance for effective treatment and recovery. This comprehensive approach not only aids in accurately diagnosing depression but also in crafting a multifaceted treatment strategy that encompasses the entirety of the individual's experience.

Medications

For many individuals, medication can be an integral part of the treatment plan for depression. Antidepressants work by altering the brain's chemical balance to help improve mood and alleviate some of the physical symptoms of depression. However, the decision to use medication should always follow a thorough psychiatric evaluation.

This evaluation is critical to determine the most appropriate type of medication based on the individual's specific symptoms, health history, and other factors. It also involves discussing potential side effects, the expected timeline for improvement, and the importance of adherence to the prescribed treatment plan.

Medications are not a one-size-fits-all solution, and finding the right medication or combination of medications can require patience and close collaboration with a healthcare provider. Furthermore, medications are often most effective when used in conjunction with other treatments, such as psychotherapy, lifestyle changes, and supportive interventions.

Understanding depression is the first step to demystifying this complex condition and moving toward effective treatment and recovery. By recognizing the multifaceted nature of depression—encompassing biological, physiological, cognitive, and emotional factors—we can approach its treatment with the nuance and specificity it demands.

Professional evaluation and the careful consideration of all treatment options, including medications, are paramount in crafting a comprehensive, individualized approach to overcoming depression. Through increased awareness and understanding, we can reduce stigma and support those affected by depression in their journey toward healing.

PART II

12-Week Depression-Free Self-Help Guide

5

The Bridge to a Depression-Free Life

A depression-free life often involves exploring uncharted territories of self-awareness and healing. Unlike the other traditional empirical approaches in this book, this chapter invites you to engage in an intuitive tracking process. This method centers on your feelings and perceptions about where you are on your path, recognizing that the destination of a depression-free life might be something you can't fully envision until you arrive.

Intuitive tracking moves beyond concrete symptoms and goals, diving into how you *think* and *feel* about your journey. It acknowledges that the landmarks of progress are not always visible or measurable in conventional terms but are felt and experienced deeply within. This approach allows you to chart your progress in a way that resonates with your personal experiences and emotional landscape, even if the exact contours of a depression-free life remain undefined.

We will use the metaphor of the bridge to visualize your journey. Imagine a bridge spanning across a calm river. The bridge representing your path from the throes of depression to the hopeful banks of a depression-free life. Unlike a bridge marked by clear signs and measurements, this bridge's progression is guided by your inner sense of movement and growth.

Each week, you'll be encouraged to reflect on where you *think* and *feel* you are on this bridge. It's a moment to pause, look around, and sense your position in the emotional landscape of your journey. Ask yourself:

- How do I feel about my progress this week?
- Do I sense that I've moved forward, back, or stayed stagnant, and if so, how?
- What part of the bridge do I believe I'm currently on?

There are no right or wrong answers. Attune to your intuition and emotional truths and chart your journey authentically.

Keep a journal of the bridge (or use the bridge image in these pages) and after each weekly reflection, mark where you are on it. This could be a simple dot, a symbol, or even a color that you associate with your current state. Over time, this visual representation will become a map of your emotional journey, filled with the unique markers of your progress.

Navigating Uncertainty with Hope

It's natural to face moments of doubt or uncertainty about where you are on the bridge. You might even feel like you've taken a step back some weeks. Remember, the path to healing is non-linear, and every emotion forward and back, is part of the journey. These moments are not detours but integral parts of your path, offering insights and depths to your understanding of healing. Each week's place on the bridge offers an opportunity to learn and grow, regardless of where you are.

As you continue to engage with this intuitive process, you'll gradually build a richer, more refined map of your journey. While the destination might not be clearly in sight, your sense of progress and movement will the guide. The bridge metaphor serves as a reminder that, step by step, you are moving toward a life where depression's hold lessens, making room for new experiences, emotions, and a sense of well-being that may currently be beyond imagination. Trust in this journey, for each step on the bridge, guided by your intuition and feelings, is a step closer to discovering what a depression-free life means for you.

As you turn the page, you will begin the 12-Week Self-Help Guide to Overcome Depression! Remember to track your progress on the *bridge* as you venture to create your depression-free life.

6

Defense Mechanisms and Cognitive Distortions

Let us now delve into the complex topic of defense mechanisms and cognitive distortions. This topic helps to comprehensively understand the inner world. These ideas are like undercurrents in a vast ocean. They are often invisible on the surface but powerful enough to direct our thoughts, emotions, and behaviors. They shape our reality. Sometimes they protect us, but more often they keep us anchored to bad patterns.

Defense mechanisms are our psyche's guardians. They step in when we face threats to our self-esteem or emotional well-being. They work in the shadows, ensuring our immediate psychological survival. However, overuse can leave us blind to the truths we need to confront and address. Cognitive distortions are the close relatives of defense mechanisms. Cognitive Distortions twist our thinking. They lead us down paths of irrationality and negativity, where our perceptions and interpretations of the world and ourselves are skewed.

This chapter aims to reveal these dark parts of the mind. It will guide you in finding them within yourself. By learning to recognize these patterns, you embark on a path of self-discovery that is both challenging and deeply rewarding. Understanding that defense mechanisms and cognitive distortions hold us back and misguide us will help us navigate skewed inner landscapes. It will keep us aware, objective, and grounded.

As we unpack these concepts, we'll explore their definitions and provide examples of their profound impact. More importantly, we will offer strategies for recognizing these mechanisms and distortions and practical steps for addressing them head-on. This is about moving beyond mere recognition, aiming for a place where you can gently but firmly guide your thoughts and emotions in directions that serve your well-being and growth.

As we navigate this chapter, remember that the journey of healing and self-understanding is ongoing. Each step and insight is a puzzle piece of who you are and who you can become. Armed with the knowledge and tools to recognize and transcend the unseen forces shaping your thoughts and behaviors, you are better equipped to move forward on a depression-free path and a life of greater authenticity, resilience, and joy.

Defense Mechanisms

Defense mechanisms are our psyche's unseen guardians, operating beneath the surface of our conscious awareness. They serve a protective function, shielding us from painful or unacceptable feelings such as anxiety, guilt, or shame. These mechanisms are triggered when we encounter situations that threaten our self-esteem or evoke stress, acting as psychological safety valves to manage emotional overload.

However, while defense mechanisms can temporarily relieve distress, their overuse or misapplication can distort reality, fostering unhealthy patterns and behaviors that can impede personal growth and well-being. Let's go deeper into how these mechanisms work, the common types we engage in, and the implications of their operation in our lives.

At their core, defense mechanisms are psychological strategies that deny, distort, or manipulate reality to reduce or avoid distress. Sigmund

Freud initially proposed the concept, to describe how individuals cope with conflict and stress. These mechanisms operate unconsciously, meaning we're often unaware of their activation.

Below is a partial list of common defense mechanisms. You'll find a comprehensive list of defense mechanisms in the appendix at the end of this book.

1. **Denial**: Refusing to accept reality or facts, thereby avoiding painful feelings. For example, someone may deny they have a problem with alcohol despite clear evidence to the contrary.

2. **Projection**: Attributing one's unacceptable thoughts, feelings, or motives to another. This can manifest as accusing someone else of being angry or jealous when, in fact, it is the accuser who harbors these feelings.

3. **Rationalization**: Justifying behaviors or feelings with seemingly logical reasons, even if these are not true. An individual might rationalize procrastination by claiming they work better under pressure.

4. **Displacement**: Redirecting emotions or reactions from the source to another, safer target. A classic example is taking out frustration on a family member after a bad day at work.

5. **Regression**: Reverting to an earlier stage of development in the face of unacceptable thoughts or impulses. For instance, an adult throwing a temper tantrum when things don't go their way.

6. **Sublimation**: Channeling unacceptable impulses into socially acceptable or beneficial activities. Aggressive people might take up a sport to vent their frustration constructively.

While defense mechanisms can cushion us against the immediate impact of stressors or emotional pain, their prolonged use can lead to significant issues. They can obscure the root causes of our distress, preventing us from addressing and resolving underlying problems. Over time, reliance on these mechanisms can stunt emotional growth, strain relationships, and contribute to the perpetuation of negative patterns of thought and behavior that are characteristic of depression.

Overcoming the limitations imposed by defense mechanisms involves fostering self-awareness, practicing mindfulness, and seeking to understand the origins of our emotional responses. By acknowledging and confronting our use of these mechanisms, we can face our realities more directly and foster healthier ways of coping with distress.

This process is not about eliminating defense mechanisms, as they can effectively manage short-term stress. Instead, it's about achieving a balance, recognizing when we're using them in unhelpful ways, and learning to engage with our emotions and experiences more openly and constructively.

Understanding and addressing defense mechanisms is foundational for mental wellness. By demystifying these processes and learning to navigate them with awareness and intention, we empower ourselves to lead richer, more authentic lives marked by deeper connections with ourselves and others.

Cognitive Distortions

As we delve further into the psyche's undercurrents, we encounter cognitive distortions: the skewed thought patterns that distort our perception of reality. Much like defense mechanisms, cognitive distortions operate beneath our conscious awareness, yet they directly shape our emotional landscape, often leading to feelings of distress, anxiety, and depression. By identifying and addressing these distortions, we can begin to clear the murky waters of our thoughts, leading to healthier perceptions and interactions with the world around us.

Cognitive distortions are irrational or exaggerated thought patterns that convince us of a reality that is far from accurate. They are the mind's biases and are particularly pervasive in shaping negative thinking. Aaron T. Beck, the father of Cognitive Behavioral Therapy, identified these patterns as central to depression and anxiety disorders.

A partial list of distortions are below. A comprehensive list is included in the Appendix.

- **All-or-Nothing Thinking**: Viewing situations in black and white categories, with no middle ground.
- **Overgeneralization**: Making broad interpretations from a single or few events.
- **Mental Filtering**: Focusing solely on the negatives and discounting positives.
- **Jumping to Conclusions**: Interpreting things negatively without evidence.
- **Magnification and Minimization**: Exaggerating negatives and understating positives.
- **Emotional Reasoning**: Believing that because we feel a certain way, it must be true.

To navigate the landscape of cognitive distortions, we must first become adept at recognizing them. This requires mindfulness and an active engagement with our thought patterns. Here's how you can begin to identify and correct distorted thinking:

- **Self-Monitoring**: Keep a journal of your thoughts, particularly those that lead to strong emotional reactions. Note the situation, the thought, and the feeling associated with it.
- **Identifying Distortions**: Look at your thought journal and identify patterns. Are there common distortions that emerge? Label these thoughts according to the type of cognitive distortion they represent.
- **Challenging Distorted Thoughts**: For each distorted thought, ask yourself, "Is this thought based on facts or a feeling? What evidence do I have to support or refute this thought?" This process of questioning can help you see the thought for what it is—a distortion.

- **Reframing Thoughts**: Once you've identified and challenged a distorted thought, aim to reframe it into a more balanced and realistic thought. This doesn't mean replacing it with overly positive or false optimism but rather adjusting it to reflect a more accurate view of reality.
- **Practice and Patience**: Like any skill, recognizing and correcting cognitive distortions takes time and practice. Be patient with yourself as you learn to navigate your thought patterns more healthily.

As you become more proficient in identifying and addressing cognitive distortions, you may notice a significant shift in your emotional well-being. Thoughts that once led to spirals of negativity can be seen for what they are, reducing their impact on your mood and behavior. This doesn't mean you won't encounter negative thoughts or emotions, but rather that you'll be better equipped to handle them constructively.

Correcting cognitive distortions is akin to cleaning a lens through which we view ourselves and the world. It allows for a clearer, more balanced perspective, fostering emotional resilience and a greater sense of control over our mental health. By integrating these strategies into your daily life, you move closer to a path of authenticity, resilience, and joy, untethered by the distortions that once held sway over your perceptions.

The Impact on Our Lives

Defense mechanisms and cognitive distortions can significantly impair our lives. They can lead to misunderstandings, damaged relationships, and missed opportunities. More critically, they can fuel and exacerbate depression, trapping us in a cycle of negative thinking and emotional turmoil.

Recognizing the psychological barriers of defense mechanisms and cognitive distortions is crucial for overcoming them. This process requires a blend of mindfulness, self-reflection, and a willingness to confront uncomfortable truths about ourselves and our interactions with others.

Defense mechanisms are subconscious strategies our minds employ to protect us from feelings of anxiety or guilt. To recognize them:

- **Reflect on Your Reactions**: Notice how you respond to stress, conflict, and criticism. Do you find yourself denying the significance of stressful events, rationalizing your behavior to avoid guilt, or projecting your feelings onto others?
- **Identify Patterns**: Be mindful of recurring behaviors that may serve as defense mechanisms. Common examples include denial, projection, rationalization, and displacement.

To identify cognitive distortions in yourself:

- **Identify Your Patterns**: Pay attention to recurring themes in your thoughts, especially those that provoke a strong emotional response. Look for patterns such as all-or-nothing thinking, overgeneralization, and catastrophizing.
- **Use Journaling**: Keep a thought diary to track thoughts that precede emotional distress. This can help you identify specific distortions.
- **Question Your Thoughts**: Challenge the accuracy of your thoughts. Ask yourself if there's factual evidence or if another interpretation is possible.
- **Practice Mindfulness**: Stay present with your thoughts without judgment. Reflect on their validity and helpfulness.

Recognizing these patterns in others:

- **Listen for Absolutes**: Phrases like "always" or "never" indicate all-or-nothing thinking.

- **Notice Overgeneralization**: Statements like "I'm always unlucky" suggest a tendency to overgeneralize.
- **Detect Emotional Reasoning**: Phrases expressing feelings as facts, such as "I feel like a failure, so I must be one," reveal emotional reasoning.
- **Observe Catastrophizing**: Expecting the worst or exaggerating the significance of adverse events can indicate catastrophizing.

Strategies for Both:

- **Education**: Learning about defense mechanisms and cognitive distortions increases your ability to recognize them.
- **Compassion and Support**: Approach self-recognition and recognition of others with compassion. Offer support instead of judgment.
- **Seek Professional Help**: A therapist can provide valuable insight and strategies for addressing these psychological barriers.

Recognizing defense mechanisms and cognitive distortions in ourselves and others is pivotal. It's not about assigning blame but fostering growth and understanding. By becoming more aware of these patterns, we can see the world more clearly, challenge our distorted thoughts and behaviors, and cultivate healthier ways of interacting with the world around us. This awareness and intentional action pave the way for a more positive outlook and fulfilling relationships, contributing significantly to our journey out of depression.

Overcoming Defense Mechanisms and Cognitive Distortions

Overcoming ingrained patterns of defense mechanisms and cognitive distortions is essential for mental wellness. This journey requires patience, self-awareness, and a commitment to personal growth. Below, we outline a comprehensive approach to navigating and transcending these psychological barriers.

1. Awareness: The Foundation of Change

- **Cultivating Mindfulness**: Practice mindfulness to enhance your awareness of the present moment. This can help you notice when using defense mechanisms or experiencing cognitive distortions.
- **Self-Observation**: Pay close attention to your thoughts, feelings, and reactions. Notice patterns that might indicate the use of defense mechanisms or the presence of cognitive distortions. Awareness is the first step toward change.

2. Question and Challenge: The Path to Clarity

- **Critical Inquiry**: When you identify a potential defense mechanism or cognitive distortion, question its validity. Ask yourself, "Is this thought or behavior truly reflective of reality, or is it a way for me to avoid discomfort?"
- **Evidence-Based Thinking**: Look for evidence that supports or contradicts your thoughts. This can help challenge and dismantle distortions and the need for certain defenses.

3. Replace: Fostering Healthier Thought Patterns

- **Identifying Alternatives**: Once you've challenged a distorted thought or recognized a defense mechanism, seek healthier, more realistic ways of thinking or responding.
- **Skill Development**: Develop emotional regulation and stress management skills to reduce your reliance on defense mechanisms. Practice more adaptive thinking strategies to counter cognitive distortions.

4. Seek Feedback: Gaining External Perspectives

- **Engaging Your Support System**: Sometimes, our perceptions can be biased. Trusted friends, family, or therapists can offer valuable perspectives on our behaviors and thought patterns.
- **Openness to Feedback**: Approach feedback with an open mind. It can provide insights into how your defense mechanisms and cognitive distortions manifest in ways you might not have realized.

Integrating New Insights: The Ongoing Journey

- **Continuous Practice**: Overcoming these psychological patterns is not a one-time task but an ongoing process. Regularly practicing awareness, challenging distortions, replacing them with healthier thoughts, and seeking feedback can lead to profound changes over time.
- **Compassion and Patience**: Be compassionate with yourself throughout this process. Change takes time, and self-compassion is a critical component of healing.

Overcoming defense mechanisms and cognitive distortions requires a multifaceted approach, incorporating self-awareness, critical thinking, developing healthier coping strategies, and the willingness to seek and accept feedback. This journey is deeply personal and can significantly impact your mental health and overall quality of life. Remember, this process is not about achieving perfection but striving for a more authentic, balanced, and fulfilling way of living.

How to Not Be Triggered by Others

Navigating social interactions without being emotionally triggered by others involves a deep understanding of your psychological patterns and those around you. When we recognize that the defensive actions or words of others are reflections of their internal struggles rather than personal attacks, we can shift our response from one of defensiveness to one of empathy. Here's how to deepen this understanding and respond more constructively:

Understanding that the behaviors triggering you often stem from the other person's defense mechanisms or cognitive distortions can provide significant relief and perspective. These behaviors might include projecting their insecurities onto you, rationalizing their actions to avoid accountability, or engaging in all-or-nothing thinking. Recognizing these as their coping strategies rather than truths about you is the first step in not being triggered.

Increasing your self-awareness can help you identify why certain behaviors trigger you. Often, they might touch on your insecurities or reflect your unresolved issues. By understanding your reactions, you can differentiate between what is truly about you and what is about the other person.

Emotional intelligence (EI) is crucial in managing how we react to others. EI involves recognizing our emotions, understanding what they tell us, and realizing how emotions affect others. By developing your EI, you can better manage your emotional reactions to triggers, choosing responses that align with your values rather than reacting impulsively.

Mindfulness can help you stay centered and calm, even in the face of triggering behavior from others. It allows you to observe your thoughts and emotions without reacting immediately. This pause can give you the space to choose how to respond rather than being swept up in an emotional reaction.

Try to see the situation from the other person's perspective. They might be acting out of pain, fear, or misunderstanding. Empathizing with their situation can help you respond with kindness and understanding rather than defensiveness or anger.

While understanding and empathy are important, setting healthy boundaries is crucial. If someone's behavior is consistently hurtful or toxic, limiting your exposure to that person or assertively communicating your needs is okay.

Talking to a friend, family member, or therapist about your experiences can provide you with perspective and strategies for dealing with triggers. External support can help validate your feelings and offer new ways of understanding and responding to challenging situations.

Not being triggered by others is a skill that requires practice, patience, and self-compassion. By recognizing the root of triggering behaviors, increasing our self-awareness, and responding with empathy and understanding, we can foster healthier interactions and maintain our emotional balance. Remember, the goal isn't to avoid ever being triggered but to manage how we respond to those triggers in a way that supports our well-being and respects our boundaries.

As we wrap up our exploration of defense mechanisms and cognitive distortions, it's vital to recognize that this understanding forms the bedrock upon which our forthcoming journey is built. This chapter, positioned at the threshold of our 12-week guide, serves as a foundational piece, preparing you for the transformative path ahead.

The insights gained here about cognitive distortions and defense mechanisms will be instrumental throughout the weeks to come. As we delve into various self-help and therapeutic approaches, you'll find that recognizing and addressing these psychological patterns is integral to effectively applying the strategies and techniques we will explore. Each week, as we introduce new concepts and practices, from Cognitive Behavioral Therapy (CBT) to Mindfulness and beyond, this foundational knowledge will enhance your ability to engage with these methods meaningfully and effectively.

Understanding how our minds may distort our perceptions or shield us from discomfort is crucial for breaking free from these constraints. As we progress through each week, we will revisit and build upon this understanding, applying it in new contexts and deepening our insight into moving beyond automatic thoughts and reactions toward a more deliberate and empowered way of being.

This journey is not just about learning techniques; it's about fostering a deeper understanding of ourselves and the unseen forces that shape our experiences. By starting with a clear grasp of defense mechanisms and cognitive distortions, we set the stage for a more profound and lasting transformation.

As you step into the weeks ahead, remember that this chapter is not just a starting point but a continuous reference. The awareness and skills you develop here will be tools you carry with you, refining and relying upon them as we navigate the diverse landscape of self-help and therapeutic strategies. Together, we will embark on this journey of healing, growth, and a life free from the shadow of depression, using our newfound knowledge as a guiding light.

As we draw this chapter closed, it's important to understand that the insights gained about defense mechanisms and cognitive distortions will serve as a foundational layer for our journey. Positioned now at the beginning of our exploration, this chapter sets the stage for a deeper, more informed engagement with the therapeutic approaches and self-help strategies we will encounter in the upcoming 12-week guide.

In the coming weeks, we will continuously refer to the concepts of cognitive distortions and defense mechanisms, integrating them into our learning and applying various therapeutic techniques. This understanding will enhance our ability to recognize and address the underlying patterns that contribute to depression, enabling a more effective and personalized application of the self-help cycle and therapeutic approaches.

Embarking on this journey, equipped with a keen awareness of how our minds can distort reality and protect us from perceived threats, empowers us to navigate the healing process with greater clarity and purpose. As we progress through each week, remember that the knowledge and skills you develop here will be pivotal in transforming your relationship with yourself and the world around you.

Week 1 Self-Help Guide

This first week you will only have two individual assignments; however, you are encouraged to do these two assignments each day for the next seven days. Set some time aside each day so that you can reflect and journal about any identified cognitive distortions that occurred or defense mechanisms that were triggered.

Week 1 Day 1

Recognizing and Addressing Defense Mechanisms

Objective: Increase awareness of personal defense mechanisms and develop strategies for addressing them.

Instructions:

1. **Reflection and Identification:** Spend a week observing and journaling about instances where you notice potential defense mechanisms at play. This could be during moments of stress, conflict, or emotional discomfort.
2. **Analysis:** Review your journal entries at the end of the week and identify patterns or recurring defense mechanisms. Note the triggers and the feelings you were trying to protect.
3. **Strategy Development:** Choose one defense mechanism you frequently use. Develop a plan for addressing this mechanism when it arises. This might involve confronting the underlying feelings directly, seeking alternative coping strategies, or discussing your feelings with a trusted friend or therapist.
4. **Implementation and Reflection:** Over the following week, implement your strategy whenever you notice the defense mechanism. Journal about your experiences, noting any challenges and successes.

Integration: Incorporate mindfulness practices to enhance your awareness of defense mechanisms as they occur. Practice self-compassion and patience, recognizing that change takes time.

Week 1 Day 2

Recognizing and Addressing Cognitive Distortions

Objective: Enhance the ability to identify cognitive distortions and practice reframing them into more balanced thoughts.

Instructions:

1. **Daily Monitoring:** Keep a daily log of thoughts that evoke strong emotional responses. Identify any cognitive distortions present in these thoughts.
2. **Challenge and Reframe:** Choose one or two distortions each day to focus on. Write down evidence that challenges the distorted thought and then reframe the thought in a more balanced and realistic way.
3. **Reflection:** At the end of each day, reflect on the process of challenging and reframing your thoughts. Consider how the reframed thoughts impacted your emotions and behaviors.
4. **Long-Term Application:** Identify one cognitive distortion that you struggle with consistently. Create a detailed plan for addressing this distortion moving forward, including specific strategies for challenging and reframing.

Integration: Practice these techniques regularly, integrating them into your daily routine. Pay attention to how your emotional responses change as you adjust your thought patterns.

Bridge Week 1

As you conclude this week, take a moment to connect with your journey across the bridge. Reflect on the experiences, emotions, and insights you've gathered. Here's a gentle reminder to track your progress on the bridge, an essential practice that will accompany you through each week of this transformative journey.

- **Visualize the Bridge**: Recall the image of the bridge that represents your path from the current challenges towards a brighter, depression-free horizon. Each section of the bridge symbolizes a part of your journey, with the far side representing your goals and aspirations for healing and happiness.
- **Reflect Intuitively**: Ask yourself where you "think" and "feel" you are on the bridge right now. This isn't about precision but about your inner sense of progression and change. How has this week influenced your position on the bridge?
- **Mark Your Spot**: On your visual representation of the bridge (whether it's a drawing, a printed image, or a journal entry), mark where you feel you currently stand. Use a symbol, color, or word that captures your state at this moment. This act of marking your progress is a powerful affirmation of your journey and growth.
- **Embrace Your Feelings**: Remember, there's no 'right' place to be on the bridge. Whether you've moved forward, stayed in the same spot, or even taken a few steps back, each position tells a part of your story. Embrace where you are as a valid and valuable part of your journey towards healing.
- **Look Ahead with Hope**: As you mark your place on the bridge, take a moment to look forward across it. Allow yourself to feel

hope for the journey ahead. Each week brings new opportunities for progress and insight.

7

Cognitive Behavioral Therapy

This week in *DEPRESSION FREE*, we delve into the transformative world of Cognitive Behavioral Therapy (CBT). This marks the beginning of an empowering exploration into how your thoughts, feelings, and behaviors create your emotional well-being. CBT offers practical strategies and insights that have significantly advanced the field of mental health. This therapeutic approach is meticulously researched and proven highly effective in treating depression and a wide range of emotional and psychological challenges.

The essence of CBT lies in its focused, problem-solving approach, aiming to transform how you perceive and interact with your world. It encourages a deep introspection into your cognitive processes, helping you to identify and challenge the negative thought patterns that often lay the groundwork for depressive feelings. By understanding the core principles of CBT, you will gain the tools to dismantle these harmful patterns and construct a foundation for lasting positive change.

This chapter will guide you through the fundamentals of CBT, breaking down complex concepts into understandable segments. As we progress, you will learn to recognize the cognitive distortions that cloud thinking. You will understand the impact of behavioral patterns, and discover how to reframe thoughts to promote resilience and emotional health. The journey through CBT is a step closer to reclaiming control over your mental landscape, opening the door to a life characterized by greater joy and fulfillment.

As we transition into the understanding of Cognitive Behavioral Therapy, keep an open mind and be ready to engage with the exercises and reflections provided. This is more than just an educational endeavor; it is a practical toolkit for transformation. Let's embark on this journey with curiosity and enthusiasm, ready to embrace the changes.

Understanding Cognitive Behavioral Therapy

Understanding Cognitive Behavioral Therapy (CBT) is akin to learning how to untangle a complex web of thoughts, feelings, and behaviors that influence our mental health. The foundational premise of CBT rests on the idea that these three elements—thoughts, feelings, and behaviors—are interconnected. This means that one change can lead to significant shifts in the others. For instance, altering our thought patterns can transform our emotional responses and lead to healthier behaviors.

Let's break it down with a simple example: Imagine you're preparing for a presentation at work. If you think, "I'm going to mess this up, and everyone will laugh at me," this thought is likely to stir up feelings of anxiety and fear. As a result, you might avoid preparing adequately, which could lead to a less successful presentation. This cycle of negative thinking, emotional distress, and unhelpful behavior is what CBT aims to address.

CBT teaches you to identify these negative thought patterns, often referred to as cognitive distortions, and challenge them. For example, the thought "I'm going to mess this up" is an example of *catastrophizing*, where you anticipate the worst possible outcome. CBT strategies would encourage you to examine the evidence for and against this thought, consider alternative outcomes, and develop a more balanced perspective, such as, "I've prepared well, and while I might make some mistakes, I can handle it."

By focusing on the present, CBT emphasizes practical strategies for dealing with current problems rather than exploring the deep-seated origins of these issues. It's a structured, time-limited approach that provides clear goals and measurable outcomes. This makes CBT efficient and effective, offering specific tools and techniques for individuals to apply daily.

An essential aspect of CBT is its empowering nature. It equips you with the skills to become your therapist, enabling you to apply CBT principles outside therapy sessions independently. This self-help aspect ensures that the benefits of CBT extend far beyond the therapy room, providing you with lifelong tools for managing thoughts and behaviors. For instance, learning to identify when engaging in *all-or-nothing thinking* (viewing situations in only two categories, like success or failure) and then challenging this by recognizing the nuances and grey areas in real-life situations can significantly reduce feelings of failure and enhance resilience.

As we delve into "The Mechanics of CBT: Cognitive Distortions and Schema," in the next section, we'll explore the specific types of distorted thinking that CBT targets. We'll examine how recognizing and reevaluating these thoughts can change the emotional and behavioral patterns contributing to depression. This journey through understanding and applying CBT principles is about transforming how you think, feel, and act to navigate life's challenges more effectively and with a healthier mindset.

The Mechanics of CBT: Cognitive Distortions and Schemas

Cognitive distortions are biased ways of thinking about ourselves and the world around us. They act like flawed lenses, distorting the reality of our experiences with negativity that can significantly impact our emotional well-being. These distortions come in various forms. They warp our perception in unique ways and contribute to the cycle of depression and emotional distress.

Imagine you're on a path to improving your health through better eating habits. *Black-and-White Thinking* might make you see this journey in extremes: any deviation from your diet, no matter how minor, feels like a complete failure. This *all-or-nothing* perspective overlooks the progress you've made, focusing solely on the imperfections.

Or consider the times you've felt out of place at a social gathering. *Overgeneralization* can take this discomfort and paint your entire social persona with the same brush, leading you to believe, "I'm always awkward at parties." This broad stroke ignores the complexity of social interactions and the moments you've felt connected and engaged.

Catastrophizing amplifies our fear of negative outcomes, convincing us that the worst scenario is not only possible but likely. A minor disagreement with a friend isn't just a bump in the road of your relationship. It's seen as the end of the friendship entirely, ignoring the strength and resilience built over time.

Personalization involves taking responsibility for things beyond our control, such as when a friend is having a bad day, and we blame ourselves for their mood. This distortion places an unreasonable burden on us to manage the emotions and reactions of those around us, disregarding the myriad of factors that influence others' feelings.

Cognitive Behavioral Therapy (CBT) offers a pathway through this maze of distorted thinking. It begins with identifying these patterns, illuminating how our thoughts can skew our perception of reality. Understanding the negative impact these distortions have on our mood and behavior is the next step, acknowledging our thoughts' power in shaping our emotional landscape.

The final and perhaps most empowering stage of CBT is the process of challenging and reframing these thoughts. This doesn't mean dismissing our feelings but examining our thoughts critically, asking ourselves if they're truly accurate and serve us well. We can construct a more constructive and supportive internal dialogue by adjusting our thought patterns to be more balanced and realistic.

Through CBT, we learn to question the validity of our negative thoughts and actively reshape them. This process of transformation doesn't erase challenges or difficult emotions; it provides us with tools to approach them more healthily and constructively, paving the way for a more balanced and fulfilling emotional life.

Schemas: The Root Beliefs

Schemas, the bedrock of our cognitive architecture, are the entrenched beliefs that shape how we view ourselves, others, and the broader world. These foundational narratives significantly influence our perceptions and reactions. They are not static but dynamic, shifting in prominence and influence depending on our context and specific circumstances. Understanding schemas requires delving into the three primary categories: schemas about the self, schemas about the world, and schemas about the self in relation to the world.

Schemas About the Self:

Our understanding of ourselves and the world around us isn't set in stone; it shifts along a spectrum, shaped by our life experiences. This spectrum encompasses our beliefs about ourselves, ranging from our sense of competence and worth to feelings of inadequacy. How we view these beliefs can change depending on different situations in our lives, such as work, hobbies, or family interactions.

At one end of this spectrum, positive beliefs about oneself, such as feeling competent, intelligent, resilient, and lovable, can boost confidence and promote well-being. For instance, taking joy in hobbies like painting or music can reinforce a positive self-image, contributing to feelings of fulfillment and happiness.

On the other side, negative beliefs about oneself, including feelings of inadequacy or unlovability, can significantly affect mental health, leading to lower self-esteem and a skewed perception of one's abilities and value. These negative beliefs can turn constructive criticism at work into perceived evidence of incompetence, overshadowing achievements.

Our sense of self and the value we place on our abilities can fluctuate, particularly influenced by the support and recognition from those around us. Positive reinforcement from family and friends can bolster our self-esteem, whereas professional challenges or negative experiences at work can trigger self-doubt, affecting our overall self-perception.

This duality underscores the fluid nature of our self-beliefs and the significant role context plays in shaping them. It also highlights the potential for change and growth. By recognizing the shiftability of our beliefs, we can work towards transforming negative perceptions into more positive and adaptive ones, using strategies from cognitive behavioral therapy (CBT). For example, by acknowledging achievements at work, seeking balanced feedback, and engaging in positive self-talk, individuals can begin to see themselves in a more favorable light, illustrating the malleable nature of self-beliefs.

Through understanding and addressing the spectrum of our self-beliefs, we can navigate the complexities of self-perception, learning to foster a more positive self-view across all aspects of life, thereby enhancing self-esteem and overall well-being.

Schemas About the World: Schemas about the world are the filters through which we interpret our experiences, shaping our expectations, interactions, and sense of security within our environment. These embedded schemas are not merely passive reflections but active filters that significantly influence our perception of reality. They encompass a broad spectrum, from viewing the world as a place of opportunity and kindness to seeing it as fraught with danger and hostility.

At one end of this spectrum, positive world schemas might imbue an individual with a sense of optimism and trust. For example, someone with a belief in the fundamental goodness of people might approach interactions with openness and generosity, expecting similar goodwill in return. This schema can lead to a reinforcing cycle of positive experiences, where trust begets trust and kindness reciprocated, fostering a sense of connection and community.

Conversely, negative world schemas, such as the belief that the world is dangerous or that people are inherently untrustworthy, can lead to a defensive and isolated stance. An individual holding these beliefs might interpret ambiguous situations as threats, overlook acts of kindness as ulterior motives, and generally expect adverse outcomes. This can create a self-fulfilling prophecy, where the expectation of hostility leads to withdrawal or aggression, provoking the responses they feared reinforcing their negative view of the world.

As with self-schemas, specific contexts and experiences can activate and influence world schemas. A person who generally feels safe and optimistic might encounter a situation—such as a personal experience of crime or exposure to sensationalized media reports—that temporarily activates a schema of the world as dangerous. This activation can skew their perception, leading to heightened fear and caution even in previously perceived safe environments.

Conversely, positive experiences or deliberate exposure to counter-narratives can challenge and soften negative world schemas. Volunteering, traveling, or engaging in community events can reveal people's kindness, generosity, and commonality, fostering a more nuanced and optimistic view of the world.

Understanding the malleability of world schemas helps foster a more balanced and realistic worldview. By recognizing that our schemas can change and are influenced by our focus and interpretation, we can consciously seek experiences and information that broaden our perspective. For someone prone to seeing the world as dangerous, actively seeking out positive news, engaging in trust-building activities, or simply spending time in nature can provide evidence that challenges this schema, gradually leading to a more balanced view.

This does not mean naively ignoring the real dangers and injustices of the world but rather adopting a more complex and nuanced understanding that acknowledges both the beauty and the brutality of human existence. By doing so, individuals can navigate the world with a sense of realism that is neither blindly optimistic nor despairingly pessimistic, leading to a more fulfilling and engaged life.

Schemas About the Self in the World: Schemas about the *self in the world* represent a intricate intersection of our inner beliefs and our understanding of the external environment. These multifaceted schemas reflect how we see our place and purpose in the broader context of society, relationships, and the world at large. They encompass our perceived roles, sense of belonging, and beliefs about our ability to influence our surroundings and be influenced in return.

The spectrum of beliefs within this category can range from feeling like an integral, valued part of a community to sensing an insurmountable disconnect from the societal fabric. On the positive side, an individual might strongly believe in their capacity to effect positive change, feeling deeply connected to their community and valued for their contributions. This schema fosters engagement, activism, and a sense of purpose, driving individuals to participate actively in social and community affairs, believing in the impact of their actions.

Conversely, negative schemas in this category might include feelings of alienation or the belief that one's actions are inconsequential. An individual harboring a schema of perpetual outsider status might view every social interaction through a lens of exclusion, interpreting even inclusive gestures as patronizing or insincere. This belief system can lead to withdrawal, passivity, and a diminished sense of agency, reinforcing the person's perceived detachment from the societal web.

These schemas are not uniformly activated but vary significantly depending on context, environment, and recent experiences. A person may feel competent and appreciated professionally, contributing meaningfully to their workplace and enjoying collegial relationships. However, the same individual might feel like an outsider in more personal settings, such as neighborhood gatherings or family reunions, where they struggle to find common ground or feel their contributions are undervalued.

Similarly, someone might see themselves as a change-maker in specific contexts, perhaps within a volunteer organization or a social movement, yet feel powerless and overlooked in other areas of their life, such as in bureaucratic or institutional settings. These contrasting experiences highlight the complexity of self-in-world schemas and the variable nature of our social identities.

Recognizing the malleability of these schemas offers pathways for transformation and growth. By understanding that our sense of belonging and influence is not fixed but subject to change, we can seek out experiences, relationships, and environments that affirm our value and enhance our sense of connection. Engaging in community service, pursuing collaborative projects, or simply fostering open dialogues within our social circles can challenge and expand our perceptions of our role in the world.

Moreover, cognitive behavioral strategies can be instrumental in reframing negative self-in-world schemas. Challenging the evidence for beliefs of exclusion or powerlessness, actively seeking out counter-examples, and setting small, achievable goals for social engagement can gradually shift these schemas to a more positive and inclusive self-concept.

In sum, schemas about the self in the world are dynamic and shaped by an interplay of personal beliefs and societal interactions. By actively engaging with and reflecting on these schemas, individuals can navigate their social worlds with a more nuanced understanding and a greater sense of purpose and belonging.

Schema Activation and Cognitive Flexibility: Schema activation and cognitive flexibility are integral to understanding how we navigate the complexities of our internal and external worlds. Schemas, while foundational to our perceptions and reactions, do not operate in isolation. They interact dynamically with our experiences and triggers and are influenced by varying events, leading to many cognitive and emotional responses that define our unique human experience.

Schema activation refers to the process by which certain events or experiences trigger specific schemas, bringing them to the forefront of our consciousness and influencing our thoughts, feelings, and behaviors. This activation is not random but tied to our experiences and the context in which we find ourselves. It underscores the situational nature of our cognitive processes, highlighting how our reactions to similar events can vary widely depending on the underlying schemas activated at the time.

For instance, encountering a demanding project might activate a schema of self-efficacy in one context, driving an individual to tackle the challenge with vigor. In a different setting, however, the same project might trigger a schema of doubt or fear of failure, leading to procrastination or anxiety. This variability illustrates the contextual nature of schema activation and its profound impact on our behavior and emotional state.

Cognitive flexibility is the ability to adapt our thinking in response to changing circumstances and information. It involves recognizing when a particular schema is activated and consciously choosing how to respond. This capacity is crucial for mental health, allowing us to step back from automatic thoughts and behaviors and consider a broader range of responses.

Cognitive Behavioral Therapy (CBT) plays a major role in enhancing cognitive flexibility. Through techniques such as cognitive restructuring, CBT helps individuals identify when a schema is influencing their perception and guides them in challenging and modifying these automatic thoughts. By questioning the validity of activated schemas and considering alternative viewpoints, individuals can develop a more nuanced understanding of themselves and their environment.

Achieving greater cognitive flexibility and schema adaptation is challenging and rewarding. It involves a continuous process of self-reflection, learning, and growth. By becoming aware of the triggers that activate certain schemas and understanding their impact, individuals can experiment with new ways of thinking and responding. This might include actively seeking out situations that challenge negative schemas or practicing mindfulness to remain present and engaged, even in the face of schema activation.

CBT offers a structured approach to this exploration, providing tools and strategies to dismantle unhelpful schemas and build new, more adaptive ways of viewing the world. Through this therapeutic process, individuals can achieve greater control over their thoughts and emotions, leading to improved mental health and a more fulfilling life.

The Path Forward: From Distortion to Clarity: Recognizing cognitive distortions and challenging negative schemas can make a profound and lasting change in your life. CBT equips individuals with the tools to dismantle the mental habits that feed into depression, replacing them with thought patterns that support well-being and resilience.

As we transition into the next section, *Negative Cognitions and Their Impact*, we'll delve deeper into how these distortions and schemas manifest in everyday thoughts and behaviors. We'll explore the direct link between negative cognitions and emotional distress, highlighting the importance of CBT's techniques in not only understanding but actively altering the landscape of our mental health for a brighter, more hopeful future.

Negative Cognitions and Their Impact

Negative cognitions and worldviews profoundly influence our mental health and daily functioning. These cognitive patterns, often deeply rooted in our schemas and life experiences, color our interpretation of events, interactions, and self-perception, leading us to distorted judgment and maladaptive actions.

At the heart of this cycle, as previously discussed, are negative beliefs about ourselves, others, and the world. For example, an individual harboring a schema of failure may view a minor mistake at work not as an opportunity for learning but as concrete proof of their perceived incompetence. This interpretation overlooks objective evidence of their skills and successes, further entrenching the belief in their inadequacy.

Such distorted perceptions have a tangible impact on emotions, fostering feelings of worthlessness, anxiety, or depression. These emotions, in turn, influence our behaviors—perhaps leading someone to avoid challenging tasks or to withdraw from social interactions, thereby missing opportunities for growth and connection.

Cognitive Behavioral Therapy (CBT) addresses these issues by focusing on the intricate relationship between thoughts, emotions, and behaviors. By identifying and examining the accuracy of negative cognitions, CBT helps individuals to challenge these harmful thought patterns. This process involves dissecting the evidence for and against negative beliefs, exploring alternative interpretations of events, and testing these new interpretations through behavioral experiments.

CBT also emphasizes the development of coping strategies that can be used in response to the activation of negative schemas. These strategies might include problem-solving techniques, assertiveness training, or mindfulness practices designed to reduce the emotional distress associated with negative cognitions and promote more adaptive responses to challenging situations.

Changing these deep-seated cognitive patterns can significantly alter the trajectory of an individual's emotional well-being. By reshaping their thought processes to be more balanced and reality-based, individuals can begin to see themselves and their environment in a new light. This shift can lead to a reduction in symptoms of depression and anxiety, as well as improvements in self-esteem and overall life satisfaction.

Moreover, as individuals learn to challenge and change their negative cognitions, they often discover a greater sense of agency and control over their lives. This empowerment fosters resilience, enabling them to navigate future challenges with increased confidence and adaptability.

The journey from being ensnared in a web of negative cognitions to achieving a state of mental clarity and resilience is central to the therapeutic process of CBT. It requires patience, effort, and the willingness to confront and modify long-held beliefs. It can be very challenging; however, the rewards of this journey—a life characterized by elevated mental health, fulfillment, and a deeper understanding of oneself and the world—are immeasurable.

As we continue to explore the dynamics of cognitive therapy, it becomes evident that altering our thought patterns is about reducing symptoms and fundamentally enhancing our capacity for joy, connection, and growth.

The Role of Actions in CBT

As an integral component of Cognitive Behavioral Therapy (CBT), behavioral therapy addresses the impacts and behaviors have on thoughts and emotions. CBT focuses on how behaviors impact mental health. Behaviors are powerful determinants of psychological well-being.

Behavioral activation, a strategy within behavioral therapy, is designed to counteract the inertia that often accompanies depression. The premise is straightforward yet profound: by systematically engaging in activities that are rewarding or fulfilling, individuals can disrupt the downward spiral of depression. This approach is based on the theory that depression can lead to a decrease in rewarding experiences due to withdrawal and avoidance behaviors, which, in turn, exacerbates the depressive state.

Implementing behavioral activation involves identifying activities that are meaningful or enjoyable, regardless of their current mood. These activities might range from social interactions, physical exercise, hobbies, or work-related tasks. The goal is to increase the frequency of these rewarding activities, thereby enhancing mood and reducing depressive symptoms.

The process often starts with small, achievable goals to build momentum and confidence. For example, someone withdrawn from social activities might start by reaching out to a friend for a brief conversation, gradually increasing social engagements as their comfort level improves.

As individuals engage more with the world around them, the positive experiences from these activities challenge and shift negative thought patterns. Even small successes can provide evidence against feelings of worthlessness or hopelessness. They can lead to more positive thoughts and beliefs about oneself and one's capabilities.

Moreover, behavioral activation can lead to a cycle where increased activity levels improve mood, which in turn motivates further engagement in activities. This positive feedback loop stands in contrast to the vicious cycle of depression, where negative thoughts lead to inactivity, which then worsens mood.

This focus on behavior illustrates the dynamic interplay between our actions, thoughts, and emotions. It highlights the principle that while our thoughts can shape our actions, our actions can also powerfully influence our thoughts and feelings. This bidirectional relationship is a cornerstone of CBT, emphasizing the importance of a holistic approach that addresses both cognitive and behavioral aspects for effective depression treatment.

Behavioral therapy within CBT provides a concrete, action-oriented pathway for improvement, demonstrating that we can significantly impact our mental state by changing our behaviors. It reinforces the message that taking active steps, however small, can lead to meaningful changes in our psychological well-being.

Applying CBT Principles: Applying the principles of Cognitive Behavioral Therapy (CBT) is a transformative process that requires understanding and action. Throughout this week, you'll learn and use a series of practical exercises specifically designed to illuminate the cognitive distortions and negative schemas that often underpin depressive thoughts and feelings. The objective is to identify these patterns and actively challenge and replace them with more adaptive, constructive ways of thinking and behaving.

The exercises you'll encounter are grounded in real-life applications, ensuring that the insights and strategies you learn are not confined to theory but are deeply relevant to your daily life. For example, you might begin by keeping a thought diary, a tool that helps you track negative thoughts as they occur, analyze the situations that trigger them, and identify the cognitive distortions at play. This practice encourages a heightened awareness of how specific thoughts contribute to your emotional responses and behaviors.

As you become more adept at recognizing these patterns, you'll be guided through the process of challenging their validity. This might involve examining the evidence for and against your automatic thoughts, considering alternative interpretations of events, and testing new behaviors in response to these insights. For instance, if you frequently find yourself caught in a cycle of self-criticism following minor mistakes, you'll learn strategies to reframe these experiences, recognizing that errors are opportunities for learning rather than proof of inadequacy.

The overarching goal of this week's exercises is not to eradicate negative thoughts—a common misconception—but to cultivate a more balanced and realistic perspective on your experiences. This shift in thinking lays the groundwork for positive mental health and a life characterized by greater satisfaction and resilience. It's about developing the skills to navigate life's ups and downs with competence and stability.

As we conclude this introductory phase and prepare to dive into the practical application of CBT principles, we stand at the threshold of meaningful change. The upcoming seven-day self-help guide is designed to take the foundational knowledge you've built this week and translate it into daily practices and reflections. Each day will focus on a specific aspect of CBT, providing structured exercises that encourage you to apply what you've learned in a focused, reflective manner. This hands-on approach is crucial for internalizing CBT's strategies, ensuring you're not just passively absorbing information but actively integrating it into your life.

Remember, the journey through CBT is one of growth and discovery. As we move into the next segment of our program, keep an open mind and be prepared to engage deeply with the exercises. Your work in the coming days will be instrumental in building the skills and insights necessary for a more positive outlook and a more fulfilling life.

Week 2 Self-Help Guide

Creating an ongoing Depression Free journal, including a "positivity log," is a powerful tool for overcoming depression and fostering a more positive outlook. This journal serves as a personal space for reflection, tracking progress, and celebrating successes, however small they may seem. It's a place to document your thoughts, feelings, and insights, facilitating a healthier mindset. Here's how to create and maintain this valuable resource:

Setting Up Your Depression-Free Journal

1. **Choose Your Medium:** Decide whether you prefer a digital journal (using an app or document) or a traditional notebook. Consider privacy, convenience, and personal comfort in your choice.
2. **Divide Your Journal:** Allocate sections for your daily entries, positivity log, insights gained from exercises, and general reflections on your progress.
3. **Personalization:** Customize your journal to make it inviting and personal. This might include decorating it, choosing a specific pen for writing, or creating a digital template that appeals to you.

Maintaining a Positivity Log

Your positivity log will be a key component of your journal. It's designed to help shift your focus from negative to positive, reinforcing cognitive therapy principles.

Morning Routine

- **Date Your Entry:** Start with the date at the top of your new entry.
- **List What's Good:** Write a short list of good things about you and your life. This could be personal strengths, something you're looking forward to, or aspects of your life you're grateful for.
- **Set a Positive Intention:** Conclude your morning entry with a positive intention for the day. This could be an attitude you want to adopt or a small goal you wish to achieve.

Evening Routine

- **Reflect on the Day:** In the evening, reflect on your day and list what was good about it. Focus on positive experiences, moments of joy, achievements, and steps toward your goals.
- **Acknowledge Your Efforts:** Highlight what you did well. This includes efforts to challenge negative thoughts, engage in positive activities, or progress made using CBT exercises.

Tips for Effective Journaling

- **Consistency is Key:** Try to write in your journal every morning and evening. Regular reflection enhances the benefits of this practice.
- **Be Honest and Kind:** Approach your entries with honesty and self-compassion. This journal is a judgment-free zone.
- **Review Regularly:** Set aside time weekly or monthly to review your journal. This can provide insights into your progress, patterns in your thoughts and behaviors, and areas for further growth.

Using Your Journal for Growth

- **Track CBT Exercises:** Use your journal to track exercises, insights, and any cognitive distortions or negative schemas you're working on. Reflect on how these patterns shift over time.
- **Celebrate Successes:** No success is too small to celebrate. Use your journal to acknowledge and celebrate progress, reinforcing your commitment to a positive mental state.

Your Depression Free journal, with its internal positivity log, becomes a powerful ally in your journey out of depression. It's not just a record of your journey; it's an active tool for reshaping your thoughts, celebrating your progress, and recognizing the beauty in your life. By dedicating daily time to this practice, you manifest a more positive and fulfilling life.

Week 2 Day 1

Objective: The goal of today is to foster self-awareness by closely monitoring and understanding your thought patterns, especially those that are negative. This awareness is crucial for recognizing how your thoughts influence your mood and overall mental well-being.

Information: Becoming aware of your thought patterns is the first step in cognitive restructuring, a key component of Cognitive Behavioral Therapy (CBT). By identifying negative thoughts and their impact, you can begin to challenge and change them, paving the way for a more positive outlook on life.

Instructions:

1. **Morning Reflection:**
   - **Purpose:** To set a mindful tone for the day ahead.
   - **Activity:** Upon waking, take a moment to quietly reflect on how you're feeling. Identify your current mood and any predominant thoughts, especially those that are negative or worrisome.
   - **Recording:** In a journal or digital note, briefly document your mood and the thoughts you're experiencing. This can be as simple as a few words or a sentence.

2. **Throughout the Day: Thought Diary**
   - **Purpose:** To track the occurrence of negative thoughts in real time.
   - **Activity:** Carry a small notebook or use a digital app to record any negative thoughts that arise throughout the day. Note the situation in which the thought occurred,

how you felt at the moment and the exact nature of the thought.

- ○ **Tips for Success:** Keep your recording tool easily accessible. The more detailed your entries, the better you'll understand your thought patterns.

3. **Evening Review:**
   - ○ **Purpose:** To reflect on and analyze the day's thoughts.
   - ○ **Activity:** Set aside some quiet time in the evening to review the thoughts you've recorded. Look for patterns or recurring themes. Are there specific situations that trigger negative thoughts? Do you notice common distortions in your thinking, such as "all-or-nothing" or "catastrophizing"?
   - ○ **Recording:** Summarize your findings in your journal, noting any insights or patterns you've observed. This will help you identify areas for growth and change.

Reflection: Reflect on this process of monitoring your thoughts. How did it make you feel? Were you surprised by the frequency or nature of your negative thoughts? Consider how this awareness can be the first step in changing your thought patterns.

Integration: Begin integrating this practice into your daily routine. Even beyond Day 1, continue to use your thought diary to track your thoughts. Over time, this ongoing awareness can become a powerful tool for identifying and altering negative thought patterns improving mental health and well-being.

Week 2 Day 2

Objective: Today's focus is on deepening your understanding of cognitive distortions, often automatic thoughts that can be misleading or inaccurate and significantly impact your mood and behavior. By recognizing these patterns, you can start to challenge and change them.

Information: Cognitive distortions are skewed perspectives about ourselves and our world. They are often rooted in our upbringing or past experiences and can lead to negative thinking, exacerbating feelings of depression and anxiety. Common distortions include all-or-nothing thinking, overgeneralization, and catastrophizing, among others.

Instructions:

1. **Morning Reflection: Identifying Relevant Distortions**
   - **Purpose:** To begin recognizing the recurring cognitive distortions influencing your thinking.
   - **Activity:** Review a comprehensive list of cognitive distortions. Reflect on your thought diary entries from the previous day, identifying which distortions appear most often in your thoughts.
   - **Recording:** Jot down the distortions you identify as most relevant to you in your journal or note-taking app.
2. **Activity: Exploring a Distortion in Depth**
   - **Purpose:** To analyze how a specific cognitive distortion affects your interpretation of events.
   - **Activity:** Choose one cognitive distortion that you identified in the morning reflection. Write about a recent situation where this distortion played a significant role.

Describe the situation, the thoughts that went through your mind, and the outcome.

- **Recording:** Document your analysis, focusing on how the distortion shaped your perception of the event and its impact on your emotions and actions.

3. **Evening Exercise: Practicing Reframing**
   - **Purpose:** To begin the process of challenging and changing your distorted thoughts.
   - **Activity:** Reflect on your day, identifying one negative thought influenced by a cognitive distortion. Practice reframing this thought by questioning its accuracy and attempting to view the situation from a more balanced perspective.
   - **Recording:** Write down the original thought, the identified distortion, and your reframed, more rational thought. Note any changes in how you feel after this exercise.

Reflection: Spend some time reflecting on today's exercises. How did it feel to identify and challenge your cognitive distortions? Do you notice any shifts in your mood or outlook as you practice reframing your thoughts?

Integration: Integrate today's learning by continuing to be mindful of cognitive distortions as they arise in your daily life. Practice challenging and reframing distorted thoughts regularly, noting any patterns or situations that frequently trigger these distortions. This ongoing awareness and adjustment can lead to more accurate and constructive thinking patterns, contributing significantly to your journey out of depression

Week 2 Day 3

Objective: Today aims to actively challenge the negative thoughts you've identified, applying a critical analysis to test their validity. This process is essential for weakening the hold that automatic negative thoughts have on your mood and behavior.

Information: Challenging negative thoughts is a core aspect of Cognitive Behavioral Therapy (CBT). This technique involves scrutinizing the thoughts for evidence of truthfulness and considering alternative, more balanced viewpoints. This method helps to develop a more realistic perspective on situations, reducing the emotional distress associated with negative thinking.

Instructions:

1. **Morning Exercise: Evaluating a Negative Thought**
   - **Purpose:** To practice assessing the accuracy of your negative thoughts.
   - **Activity:** Select one particularly pervasive negative thought from your thought diary. Write down any evidence supporting this thought, then list evidence contradicting it.
   - **Recording:** Use your journal to document the thought, supporting and contradicting evidence. This side-by-side comparison will help you see the thought more objectively.
2. **Throughout the Day: Questioning Negative Thoughts**
   - **Purpose:** To cultivate a habit of critically evaluating the validity of negative thoughts as they arise.

- **Activity:** Whenever a negative thought enters your mind, pause and ask yourself, "What evidence do I have for this?" Consider both for and against the thought's accuracy.
- **Tips for Success:** If possible, keep a small notepad or digital note-taking device handy to jot down these instances and your evaluations.

3. **Evening Reflection: Assessing the Impact of Challenging Thoughts**
    - **Purpose:** To reflect on how the practice of challenging your thoughts has influenced your emotional state.
    - **Activity:** Spend some time in the evening contemplating the day's efforts to challenge your negative thoughts. Consider whether this practice has changed how you feel about the situations that prompted these thoughts.
    - **Recording:** In your journal, note your observations about this process and its effects on your mood. Did challenging your thoughts alter your emotional response? How did it feel to question the validity of your negative thoughts?

Reflection: Reflect on the experience of actively challenging your negative thoughts throughout the day. What did you learn about the nature of your thoughts? Did this practice help you feel more in control of your emotional responses?

Integration: Incorporate the habit of challenging negative thoughts into your daily routine. Over time, as you question the accuracy of negative thoughts and consider alternative perspectives, you'll likely find that your overall outlook becomes more positive and realistic. This ongoing practice is a powerful tool in your overcoming depression tool kit.

Week 2 Day 4

Objective: Today, we will focus on behavioral activation, a strategy designed to help you overcome the inertia that often accompanies depression. By engaging in planned, rewarding activities, you can start to break the cycle of depression, improving your mood and energy levels.

Information: Behavioral activation is based on the idea that depression can lead to a decrease in enjoyable activities, which in turn leads to a further decrease in mood. By actively engaging in positive activities, even when you don't initially feel like it, you can create a positive feedback loop that lifts your mood and increases your motivation.

Instructions:

1. **Morning Planning: Selecting an Activity**
   - **Purpose:** To set a positive intention for the day by planning an enjoyable or rewarding activity.
   - **Activity:** Think of an activity you enjoy or have wanted to try. It should be something specific and achievable today. This could be as simple as walking in a park, reading a book, or trying a new hobby.
   - **Recording:** Write down your planned activity in your journal, including when and where you will do it. Plan it out so it fits comfortably into your day.
2. **Activity: Engaging in the Planned Activity**
   - **Purpose:** To experience the mood-enhancing effects of participating in something enjoyable or rewarding.
   - **Activity:** Carry out the activity you planned in the morning. While engaging in this activity, pay close attention

to how it affects your mood and thoughts. Try to immerse yourself fully in the experience, allowing yourself to enjoy it.

- ○ **Tips for Success:** If you find yourself resistant or your mood is low, remind yourself of the purpose behind this activity. The goal is to break the cycle, even if it initially feels challenging.

3. **Evening Journal: Reflecting on Your Experience**

- ○ **Purpose:** To reflect on how the activity impacted your mood and thought patterns.
- ○ **Activity:** Spend some time writing about your experience in your journal. Did you notice any shift in your mood or thoughts before, during, or after the activity? Did engaging in the activity challenge any negative thoughts or feelings you've been having?
- ○ **Recording:** Document any changes in your mood, any surprises you encountered, and how you felt about the activity overall.

Reflection: Reflect on the process of planning and engaging in a rewarding activity. Consider how this single action influenced your day. Were there any barriers to enjoyment that you were able to overcome? How can you apply this experience to other days and activities?

Integration: Incorporate behavioral activation into your routine. Plan at least one enjoyable activity each day, no matter how small. Over time, these positive experiences can accumulate, gradually lifting your mood and improving your outlook. This strategy is a powerful tool in your arsenal against depression, helping to bring back pleasure and satisfaction in daily living.

Week 2 Day 5

Objective: The goal for today is to gently push the boundaries of your comfort zone by experimenting with a new behavior that you typically avoid due to negative thoughts or feelings. This exercise is designed to challenge these thoughts and to provide you with direct experience that can help reshape your beliefs and attitudes.

Information: Avoidance behaviors can reinforce depression by preventing exposure to situations that might disprove our negative beliefs. By facing these situations, even in small, controlled ways, you can gather evidence against distorted negative thinking and gradually reduce avoidance.

Instructions:

1. **Morning Reflection: Identifying Avoidance Behavior**
   - **Purpose:** Choose a behavior you usually avoid due to negative thoughts or fears.
   - **Activity:** Reflect on your typical daily activities and identify one behavior you avoid. Consider why you avoid it—is it due to fear of judgment, failure, or something else?
   - **Recording:** Write down the behavior you've identified and your reasons for avoiding it. Be honest and specific in your exploration.

2. **Activity: Design and Conduct a Safe Experiment**
   - **Purpose:** To test a new behavior in a low-risk, controlled environment.
   - **Activity:** Based on your identified behavior, design a small, manageable experiment that challenges this avoidance.

For example, if you avoid social interactions due to fear of judgment, plan to initiate a brief conversation with a colleague or a neighbor.

- ○ **Tips for Success:** Keep the experiment simple and achievable. The goal is not to overwhelm yourself but to take a small step outside your comfort zone.

3. **Evening Review: Reflecting on the Experiment**

- ○ **Purpose:** To assess the outcome of your experiment and evaluate your pessimistic predictions.
- ○ **Activity:** Reflect on your experiment, focusing on the actual outcome versus your feared outcome. Were your negative predictions accurate? How did it feel to engage in the behavior?
- ○ **Recording:** Document your reflections, noting discrepancies between your expectations and reality. Consider how this experience might inform your future actions and beliefs about yourself.

Reflection: Spend time reflecting on the process and outcomes of your experiment. Did engaging in the behavior provide insights or relief from your negative thoughts? How might this experience influence your willingness to engage in similar behaviors in the future?

Integration: Use the insights gained from today's experiment to challenge other avoidance behaviors. Recognize that stepping outside your comfort zone, even in small ways, can lead to significant positive changes in your thoughts, feelings, and behaviors. Continuously seek opportunities to experiment with new behaviors as part of your journey toward overcoming depression.

Week 2 Day 6

Objective: Today aims to cultivate gratitude and positivity, enriching your emotional landscape and counteracting the tendency of negative thinking. Focusing on gratitude and your strengths can shift your perspective and enhance your overall well-being.

Information: Gratitude practice has been shown to have significant psychological benefits, including increased happiness, reduced depression, and improved resilience. Similarly, recognizing and affirming your strengths and accomplishments can bolster self-esteem and encourage a positive outlook.

Instructions:

1. **Morning Exercise: Acknowledging Gratitude**
   - **Purpose:** Start your day with a positive frame of mind by recognizing the good in your life.
   - **Activity:** Write down three things you are grateful for today. These can be as simple as a sunny day, a comfortable home, or a supportive friend. For each, explain why you are grateful.
   - **Recording:** Keep a gratitude journal or a designated section in your daily journal for this activity. Reflecting on why you are grateful for these things deepens the practice.

2. **Throughout the Day: Practicing Mindfulness**
   - **Purpose:** To enhance present-moment awareness and reduce judgmental thinking.
   - **Activity:** During the day, gently focus on the present moment. Observe your thoughts, feelings, and sensations

without criticism or judgment. When you find your mind wandering to the past or future, kindly guide it back to the here and now.

- ○ **Tips for Success:** Use reminders or set alarms at intervals as prompts to return to mindfulness throughout the day.

3. **Evening Activity: Self-Affirmation Letter**

- ○ **Purpose:** To reinforce self-esteem and acknowledge your personal growth and achievements.

- ○ **Activity:** Write a letter to yourself, highlighting your strengths and any recent accomplishments, no matter how small they may seem. Address the letter as if you were speaking to a dear friend with kindness and compassion.

- ○ **Recording:** Keep this letter in your journal or somewhere you can return to it. It can be a powerful reminder of your positive qualities and achievements, especially on more challenging days.

Reflection: Reflect on how the day's activities made you feel. Did practicing gratitude and mindfulness affect your mood or outlook? How did it feel to write a letter acknowledging your strengths and accomplishments?

Integration: Incorporate gratitude, mindfulness, and self-affirmation into your daily routine. Regular practice can gradually shift your focus from negative preoccupations to a more balanced and positive perspective, providing a strong foundation for emotional well-being.

Week 2 Day 7

Objective: Today is about reflection and forward planning. You'll review the insights and skills gained over the past week, identifying the most impactful for you. This day also focuses on setting intentions and outlining concrete steps to continue applying Cognitive Behavioral Therapy (CBT) principles in your life.

Information: Reflection is a critical part of the learning process, allowing us to consolidate what we've learned and recognize our growth. Planning forward involves using these insights to create a roadmap for continued personal development and application of CBT techniques, ensuring that the progress made becomes a sustained part of your daily routine.

Instructions:

1. **Morning Reflection: Reviewing the Week**
   - **Purpose:** To assess the past week's experiences, focusing on growth, challenges, and rewarding moments.
   - **Activity:** Reflect on the past week. Which exercises did you find most challenging? Which were most rewarding? What insights have you gained about yourself and your thought patterns?
   - **Recording:** Write down your reflections, highlighting any breakthrough moments or areas where you continue to struggle. Acknowledge your progress and any shifts in your thinking or behavior.
2. **Throughout the Day: Incorporating CBT Techniques**

- **Purpose:** To think about how the CBT techniques you've practiced can be woven into the fabric of your daily life.
- **Activity:** As you go about your day, consider the CBT exercises from the past week. How can these practices help you in everyday situations? When might you use thought-challenging or behavior experiments in the future?
- **Tips for Success:** Keep a notepad or digital note app handy to jot down ideas as they come to you. These notes can remind you of the tools you have at your disposal.

3. **Evening Planning: Setting Goals for Continuation**
   - **Purpose:** To outline a plan to continue applying CBT principles.
   - **Activity:** Based on your reflections and the insights gathered throughout the day, set specific, achievable goals for continuing to use CBT techniques. What steps can you take to maintain and build upon your progress? Are there new techniques you want to try or existing ones to deepen your practice?
   - **Recording:** Document your goals and the steps you plan to take. Be as specific as possible, breaking down larger goals into manageable actions. This plan will serve as your roadmap for continuing the journey of self-improvement and mental health management.

Reflection: Reflect on the process of reviewing your week and planning for the future. How does it feel to see the progress you've made? What emotions or thoughts arise as you consider continuing this journey?

Integration: Moving forward, regularly revisit your goals and the plan you've outlined today. Adjust as necessary based on your experiences and any new insights. Continual reflection and adaptation are key to making CBT principles a lasting part of your mental health toolkit.

Bridge Week 2

As you conclude this week, take a moment to connect with your journey across the bridge. Reflect on the experiences, emotions, and insights you've gathered. Here's a gentle reminder to track your progress on the bridge, an essential practice that will accompany you through each week of this transformative journey.

- **Visualize the Bridge**: Recall the image of the bridge that represents your path from the current challenges towards a brighter, depression-free horizon. Each section of the bridge symbolizes a part of your journey, with the far side representing your goals and aspirations for healing and happiness.
- **Reflect Intuitively**: Ask yourself where you "think" and "feel" you are on the bridge right now. This isn't about precision but about your inner sense of progression and change. How has this week influenced your position on the bridge?
- **Mark Your Spot**: On your visual representation of the bridge (whether it's a drawing, a printed image, or a journal entry), mark where you feel you currently stand. Use a symbol, color, or word that captures your state at this moment. This act of marking your progress is a powerful affirmation of your journey and growth.
- **Embrace Your Feelings**: Remember, there's no 'right' place to be on the bridge. Whether you've moved forward, stayed in the same spot, or even taken a few steps back, each position tells a part of your story. Embrace where you are as a valid and valuable part of your journey towards healing.
- **Look Ahead with Hope**: As you mark your place on the bridge, take a moment to look forward across it. Allow yourself to feel

hope for the journey ahead. Each week brings new opportunities for progress and insight.

8

Acceptance and Commitment Therapy

On this depression-free journey, it's essential to explore various therapeutic approaches that can empower us to manage our thoughts, feelings, and behaviors more effectively. Amidst the myriad of options available, one approach stands out for its unique ability to foster resilience, adaptability, and personal growth. This week, we delve into Acceptance and Commitment Therapy (ACT), a dynamic psychotherapy technique that stands at the intersection of acceptance and change.

Acceptance and Commitment Therapy (ACT) is a proven method of coping and a powerful pathway to transformation. It teaches us that by accepting what is out of our personal control, we can free ourselves from the futile struggle against unwanted thoughts and feelings. This acceptance, however, is not passive resignation but a conscious choice to embrace the full spectrum of human experience. From this place of acceptance, ACT invites us to commit to actions that align with our deepest values, thereby infusing our lives with meaning, purpose, and vitality.

In this week's exploration of ACT, will we will explore the theoretical underpinnings of ACT. These underpinnings state that psychological suffering is often the result of our attempts to avoid pain and discomfort. ACT posits that a more fulfilling life can be achieved not by avoiding pain but by embracing life fully, with all its complexities and challenges.

We will also introduce the six core processes of ACT, which are designed to develop psychological flexibility. This flexibility is needed for adapting to life's inevitable changes and challenges, allowing us to move in the direction of our chosen values despite the presence of difficult thoughts and feelings.

Furthermore, this chapter will offer practical exercises and strategies to integrate ACT into your daily life. These tools are designed to help you practice acceptance, mindfulness, and committed action in a way that are manageable and meaningful. Whether you are new to ACT or familiar with its concepts, this week's content is structured to provide valuable insights and practical steps that can be applied immediately.

As we embark on this week's journey, remember that the goal of ACT is not to eliminate discomfort or solve all of life's problems. Instead, ACT aims to help us live a rich, full, and meaningful life, even in the face of pain and suffering. It teaches us that our thoughts and feelings do not have to dictate our actions. We can choose to live according to our values, regardless of the challenges we face.

By the end of this week, you will have a deeper understanding of ACT and how its principles can be applied to combat depression and enhance your overall well-being. You will learn to view your thoughts and feelings from a new perspective, one that encourages acceptance, compassion, and action.

Understanding ACT: A Foundation for Healing

Acceptance and Commitment Therapy (ACT) is built upon a sophisticated and empirically supported theoretical framework that offers a unique perspective on human suffering, mental health, and behavior change. At the heart of ACT's foundation is the understanding that much of human suffering is rooted in the nature of language and cognition. This understanding is deeply informed by Relational Frame

Theory (RFT), a comprehensive theory of language and cognition that is critical to grasping the mechanisms behind ACT.

Acceptance and Commitment Therapy (ACT) posits that the struggle with unwanted thoughts, feelings, and sensations can lead to a wide range of psychological difficulties, including depression. This struggle often stems from our innate evolutionarily developed tendency to avoid pain and discomfort. However, while avoidance might protect us from physical harm, it can trap us in cycles of psychological suffering when applied to internal experiences. Acceptance and Commitment Therapy (ACT) teaches that by accepting these internal experiences while committing to action that aligns with our values, we can lead a more fulfilling life.

Relational Frame Theory (RFT) is central to understanding the ACT model. Relational Frame Theory (RFT) suggests that the human ability to relate events arbitrarily through language and cognition is a source of tremendous advantage but also profound suffering. According to RFT, it is our capacity to form complex networks of associations between stimuli (e.g., words, events, emotions) that enables us to think abstractly, plan for the future, and learn from the past. However, this same ability also allows us to mentally construct scenarios that cause us pain, to dwell on past regrets, or to live in fear of future possibilities.

One of the core principles of RFT is the concept of *relational frames.* These are essentially patterns of relating one thing to another, such as in terms of similarity, difference, cause and effect, or time. Through relational frames, we can understand complex concepts like *more than, less than,* or *opposite of.* This ability is foundational to human language and cognition, allowing us to navigate and make sense of the world.

In the context of ACT, RFT helps explain why we get entangled in our thoughts and feelings. For example, if someone has the thought "I am worthless," through relational framing, this thought can become linked with past failures, feared future outcomes, and even physical sensations of discomfort or anxiety. This network of associations can trap individuals in negative thought cycles that contribute to depression.

Understanding the role of relational frames helps us to develop strategies for changing the relationship with and between negative thoughts and feelings. Techniques such as *cognitive defusion* involve learning to see thoughts as just words or images, rather than truths or commands that must be acted upon or avoided. This is possible because RFT provides a framework for understanding how thoughts can be observed and altered based on their relational properties, rather than their content.

Furthermore, RFT elucidates why efforts to directly change or suppress thoughts often lead to paradoxical effects, wherein the more one tries not to think about something, the more one ends up thinking about it. Through understanding and applying RFT principles, ACT encourages a shift from a content-focused approach to mental health to one that emphasizes context and function. This shift is critical for fostering psychological flexibility, the hallmark of ACT, which enables individuals to pursue a values-driven life despite the presence of difficult internal experiences.

To sum this us, the theoretical underpinnings of ACT, grounded in Relational Frame Theory, offer insights into the nature of human suffering and the path to healing. By embracing our capacity for complex language and cognition, not as flaws but as features to be understood and navigated, ACT provides a robust framework for developing resilience, acceptance, and commitment to action that enriches our lives.

The Core Processes of ACT

In Acceptance and Commitment Therapy (ACT), we navigate through a series of steps that altogether aim to enhance our ability to adapt, choose wisely, and follow paths that gives life meaning. This approach is practical, focused on here-and-now actions, and rooted in understanding how our minds work.

Cognitive defusion is essentially about changing how we interact with our thoughts. It's recognizing that thoughts are just thoughts they're not commands, and they're certainly not always truths about who we are or our worth. For example, if you often find yourself thinking, "I'm not capable," cognitive defusion teaches you to see this as just words passing through your mind, not a fact about your abilities.

Then, there's the concept of acceptance. This is about allowing ourselves to feel whatever we're feeling without immediately trying to push the feelings away or judge ourselves for having them. It's okay to feel sad, anxious, or angry; these are natural responses to life's challenges. Acceptance means letting these feelings be, without adding extra layers of criticism or avoidance.

Present moment awareness, or what many call mindfulness, encourages us to live more in the moment rather than getting lost in regrets about the past or worries for the future. It's about fully engaging with the here and now, whether that's noticing the sensations of breathing, the sounds around us, or the details in our immediate environment.

Acceptance and Commitment Therapy (ACT) also talks about self-as-context, which is a bit like understanding that we are the stage on which our thoughts and feelings play out. It means seeing ourselves as more than just our thoughts or the roles we play in life. You're not just a student, a parent, or a worker; you're a complex individual with your own experiences and perspectives.

Values clarification is next. Values clarification is about figuring out what really matters to us, not what we think should matter based on society's expectations or what others want for us. What do you truly care about? What makes you feel fulfilled? Identifying these values can guide our decisions and actions, making life more meaningful.

Lastly, committed action ties it all together. It's about making real changes based on our values, even when it's tough. This could mean setting small, achievable goals, like reaching out to a friend if connecting with others is important to you, or dedicating time each week to a hobby that brings you joy.

By moving through these steps, ACT helps us build a life that's not just about avoiding discomfort but about actively doing what makes life rich and fulfilling. It's a practical, action-oriented approach that acknowledges the complexity of human emotions and behaviors, offering a way to navigate them with intention and purpose.

In Acceptance and Commitment Therapy (ACT), putting what we've learned into action is key to making real, impactful changes in our lives. Here's a straightforward look at how we can practice ACT techniques and exercises in our daily routines.

Starting with defusion techniques, the idea is pretty simple but powerful. When you catch yourself stuck in a loop of negative thoughts, change how you relate to these thoughts. You might, for instance, repeat a negative thought in a funny voice or imagine it written on a movie screen and then visualize it drifting away. This can make the thought seem less intimidating and more manageable.

Mindfulness practices are another core part of ACT. The goal is to become more aware of the present moment without judgment. You can practice mindfulness in everyday activities like eating, where you focus fully on the taste, texture, and experience of the food, or walking, where you pay attention to the sensation of each step and the environment around you. These practices help you become more attuned to the present, reducing the impact of distressing thoughts and feelings.

Values clarification involves taking some time to really think about what's most important to you across different aspects of your life, such as your family, career, and personal development. It's about figuring out what you truly value, not what you're supposed to value based on others' expectations. You can do this by writing down your values and reflecting on how your current actions align or don't align with these values. This exercise can provide clarity on what changes you might want to make to live more authentically according to your values.

Finally, committed action is about setting and pursuing goals that reflect your values. Start with small, achievable goals that are in line with your values. Breaking these goals down into smaller steps can make them more manageable, and tracking your progress helps maintain motivation and focus. For example, if connecting with others is important to you, a goal could be to reach out to a friend or family member each week.

These ACT practices will help you live a more engaged, meaningful life. By incorporating them into your daily routine, you can start to see shifts in how you relate to your thoughts and feelings and how you act in the world.

Integrating ACT into Your Life

Integrating Acceptance and Commitment Therapy (ACT) into your life is a practice of exploration, commitment, and a bit of patience. The essence of ACT is not a quick fix for life's challenges. It is about embedding its principles into the fabric of your daily life, making meaningful changes that align with your deepest values and aspirations.

This integration means consciously applying ACT techniques to various aspects of your life, from how you handle stress at work to how you interact with family and friends, and even how you approach your personal goals and hobbies. It's about recognizing when you're caught up in unhelpful thought patterns and using defusion techniques to create distance from these thoughts. It's about choosing to engage with the present moment, whether that's savoring a meal, fully listening to a loved one, or simply noticing the sensations of breathing.

Incorporating mindfulness into your daily routine is a foundational aspect of living an ACT-aligned life. This could be as simple as spending a few minutes each morning sitting quietly, focusing on your breath, or as integrated as bringing a mindful awareness to every task you undertake, acknowledging and letting go of judgments that arise.

Values clarification is another critical piece of the puzzle. This involves regularly reflecting on and refining your understanding of what truly matters to you. Life is dynamic, and your values might evolve over time. Regularly checking in with yourself to ensure your actions reflect your current values is key to living authentically. This might mean setting aside time each week to reflect on your experiences, how they align with your values, and adjusting your course as necessary.

Committed action, then, is about taking steps, big or small, to attain your values-driven goals. This could involve setting specific, achievable objectives, like improving a skill, deepening relationships, or contributing to your community in some way. The emphasis here is on action that is consistent with your values, even when it's challenging or when you face setbacks. It's about recognizing that progress is often incremental and celebrating the small victories along the way.

Integrating ACT into your life also means embracing its ethos of compassion and self-kindness. It's normal to encounter resistance or to fall back into old patterns of behavior. When this happens, treating yourself with kindness and understanding, rather than harsh judgment, can make a significant difference in your ability to persist and grow.

Ultimately, living an ACT-aligned life is about making a deliberate choice to live fully and meaningfully, even in the face of life's inevitable pains and challenges. It's about building a life that reflects your unique values and aspirations, one small step at a time. This journey is deeply personal and uniquely yours, enriched by each act of acceptance, each moment of presence, and every step taken in alignment with your values.

Challenges and Reflections

Embarking on the journey of Acceptance and Commitment Therapy (ACT) involves stepping into a process of deep self-exploration and change, which, while ultimately rewarding, can present its own set of challenges and discomforts. This week, as you dive into the exercises designed to bring you closer to a life aligned with your values, it's important to acknowledge and prepare for the resistance you might encounter along the way.

The act of confronting our thoughts, feelings, and behaviors head-on can be daunting. You might find yourself resisting certain exercises, feeling uncomfortable with the level of self-disclosure they require, or struggling to accept certain aspects of your experience. These responses are entirely natural and are a sign that you're engaging with the process in a meaningful way.

Journaling can be an invaluable tool during this phase of your journey. It offers a safe space to document your experiences, thoughts, and feelings as you work through the ACT exercises. More than just a record of your journey, your journal can serve as a reflective tool, helping you to process your experiences, identify patterns in your thoughts and behaviors, and track your progress over time.

As you navigate this week's exercises, encourage yourself to approach each challenge with curiosity and openness. When resistance or discomfort arises, instead of turning away, lean into these feelings. Ask yourself what they might be teaching you about your values, your fears, and the barriers that have been holding you back from living the life you want to lead.

In your journal, make a note of any resistance you encounter, along with the thoughts and feelings that accompany it. Reflect on why a particular exercise might be challenging for you and what that challenge might reveal about your inner world. Are there certain thoughts you're avoiding? Are there feelings you're finding difficult to accept? What does your reaction to the exercise tell you about your values and the gaps between your current life and the life you aspire to?

Also, document any shifts in perspective or insights you gain through this process. These moments of clarity can be incredibly empowering, illuminating the path forward and motivating you to continue with your journey. Even small shifts can represent significant progress, helping to gradually align your life more closely with your values.

Remember, the goal of this week is not to achieve perfection or to eliminate discomfort entirely but to deepen your understanding of yourself and your values. By engaging with the exercises, even when they're challenging, you're becoming more authentic and resilient. This process of reflection and growth is ongoing, and each step, no matter how small, is a vital part of your values-driven life journey.

As we wrap up this week's deep dive into Acceptance and Commitment Therapy (ACT), it's important to recognize the significant strides you've made that are values-aligned. The journey through ACT is rich with challenges, but equally, it's filled with opportunities for growth, self-discovery, and meaningful change. Embracing your experiences and committing to actions that reflect your true values are cornerstone principles that set the foundation for a life marked not just by the absence of depression but by the presence of genuine fulfillment and joy.

Remember, integrating ACT into your life is an ongoing process, one that unfolds day by day. The steps you've taken this week are just the beginning. There's much more to explore and many more insights to gain as you continue to apply these practices in your daily life.

Looking ahead, we're poised to delve even deeper into this transformative journey. The upcoming week promises to build upon the foundation we've laid, introducing new strategies and exercises designed to further strengthen your ability to live in alignment with your values. This continuous building of skills and insights is crucial for navigating the complexities of life with resilience, grace, and purpose.

To support your ongoing journey, the following 7-day homework guide is crafted to help you solidify the principles and practices of ACT in your daily routine. Each day's assignment is designed to encourage reflection, practice, and exploration, ensuring that the lessons learned this week are not just theoretical concepts but active, living parts of your everyday experience.

Stay committed to this path, remain curious about what you can discover about yourself, and, perhaps most importantly, practice self-compassion. The journey of personal growth is not a linear one; it's filled with ups and downs, successes and setbacks. Your willingness to stay engaged, even when it's difficult, speaks volumes about your resilience and determination.

As we transition into the next phase of our journey together, remember that every step forward, no matter how small, is a step nearer to a life that truly reflects who you are and what matters most to you. Let's continue to explore, grow, and thrive together, armed with the tools and insights that ACT provides.

Week 3 Self-Help Guide

Continuing your journaling practice from the previous weeks into Week 2 is vital for deepening your understanding and reinforcing the positive changes in your life. Reflecting on insights from the previous week and connecting them with your current experiences enriches your journey through depression. This ongoing record not only tracks your progress but also highlights patterns and growth areas, offering a clearer perspective on your path forward. The "positivity log" remains a cornerstone of this practice, emphasizing the importance of acknowledging daily wins and cultivating gratitude. This helps solidify a more positive outlook and a depression-free life.

Week 3 Day 1

Objective: Today's exercise invites you to ground yourself in the present moment by engaging your senses in a simple yet profound way. This practice is designed to help you cultivate mindfulness, a state of active, open attention to the present. Mindfulness can help reduce stress and anxiety, improve focus, and contribute to a range of positive mental health outcomes.

Instructions for Today's Practice:

1. **Find a Quiet Space:** Begin by finding a comfortable and quiet space where you can sit or stand without interruptions for a few minutes.
2. **Engage Your Senses:**
   - **Hearing:** Close your eyes and focus on your hearing. Identify three different sounds you can hear. These might be the distant sound of traffic, the hum of a refrigerator, or the faint rustling of leaves. Spend a moment to acknowledge each sound, letting them come and go without judgment.
   - **Smell:** Next, shift your attention to your sense of smell. Identify two scents in your environment. Maybe you can smell the faint scent of your own laundry detergent, or perhaps there's a freshness in the air that you hadn't noticed before. If you're indoors and scents aren't readily apparent, you might want to briefly open a window or smell a nearby plant or cup of coffee.
   - **Taste:** Finally, focus on one thing you can taste. This might require taking a sip of a drink or simply noticing

the residual taste in your mouth from a recent meal. Pay attention to the taste as if experiencing it for the first time.

3. **Reflect:** After completing this exercise, take a few deep breaths and gently open your eyes. Reflect on the experience in your journal or simply take a moment to appreciate the state of presence you've cultivated. How do the sensations you've observed contribute to your current state of being? How does grounding yourself in the present moment with mindfulness alter your perspective or mood?

4. **Carry Mindfulness with You:** As you move through your day, try to recall this mindful state during moments of stress or distraction. Remembering the sensations you've observed can serve as a quick anchor, bringing you back to the present and helping you stay grounded and focused.

This mindfulness practice is more than an exercise; it's a tool that you can use anytime, anywhere to reconnect with the present moment. By starting with this simple sensory engagement, you're incorporating mindfulness into your daily life, enhancing your overall well-being and mental clarity.

Week 3 Day 2

Objective: Cognitive defusion is a core process in Acceptance and Commitment Therapy (ACT) aimed at changing how we interact with our thoughts, particularly those that are negative or self-critical. By practicing cognitive defusion, you learn to observe your thoughts without getting caught up in them, which decreases their impact and influence over your feelings and actions.

Instructions for Today's Practice:

1. **Identify a Negative Thought:** Begin by bringing to mind a specific negative self-criticism you often find yourself believing, such as "I'm not good enough," "I'm a failure," or "I can't do anything right." It's important to choose a thought that you notice frequently influences your mood or behavior.

2. **Acknowledge the Thought:** Once you have your thought in mind, simply acknowledge its presence. This step is about recognizing that the thought is occurring without trying to change it or judge yourself for having it.

3. **Defusion Technique:**
   - **Step 1:** Start by mentally stating the thought as you normally would, for example, "I'm not good enough."
   - **Step 2:** Then, rephrase the thought by adding "I'm having the thought that..." in front of it. This changes the statement to "I'm having the thought that I'm not good enough." This step creates a small distance between you and the thought, highlighting that it's just a thought, not a fact.

- **Step 3:** Go one step further by adding, "I notice I'm having the thought that..." to the beginning. Now, the statement will be "I notice I'm having the thought that I'm not good enough." This further distances you from the thought, allowing you to observe it as an outside witness might.

4. **Reflect on the Experience:** After you've gone through these steps, take a moment to reflect on any changes in how connected you feel to the original thought. Do you notice a shift in how believable or significant the thought seems? How does the process of defusion alter your emotional response to the thought?

5. **Journaling:** Consider writing down your experiences with this exercise in a journal. Note the thought you worked with, the steps you took to defuse from it, and any changes you observed in your relationship with the thought. This can be a valuable way to track your progress and insights over time.

6. **Practice Regularly:** Cognitive defusion is a skill that gets easier and more effective with practice. Throughout your day, whenever you notice a negative or self-critical thought arising, apply this defusion technique. Over time, you'll likely find that these thoughts have less power over your emotions and behaviors.

Incorporating cognitive defusion into your daily routine, will reduce the influence of negative self-criticism and enhance psychological flexibility. This technique can be a powerful tool in the broader context of living a more mindful and values-driven life.

Week 3 Day 3

Developing an understanding of the Observer Self is a transformative aspect of Acceptance and Commitment Therapy (ACT). This concept invites you to explore the part of yourself that remains constant and unchanging despite the various roles you assume and the thoughts, feelings, and experiences that come and go. By engaging in the Observer meditation, you cultivate the ability to watch your internal experiences from a place of detachment and non-judgment.

Instructions for Today's Practice:

1. **Find a Comfortable Space:** Choose a quiet and comfortable place where you won't be disturbed. Sit in a relaxed position, either on a chair with your feet flat on the ground or on a cushion in a cross-legged position.

2. **Begin with a Few Deep Breaths:** Close your eyes and take a few deep breaths to center yourself. Notice the sensation of the air entering and leaving your body, and allow any tension to melt away with each exhale.

3. **Reflect on Your Roles:** Think about the various roles you play in life—perhaps you're a parent, a friend, an employee, a student, or a partner. Acknowledge how these roles influence your thoughts, feelings, and actions. Recognize that while these roles are part of your life, they do not define the essence of who you are.

4. **Shift to the Observer Perspective:** Imagine stepping back within your own mind to a place of observation. From this vantage point, you can see your thoughts, feelings, and physical sensations as if they are happening to someone else. Notice

how they appear, change, and eventually fade away, yet you, the observer, remain constant.

5. **Practice Detached Observation:** Spend a few minutes in this state of detached observation. If you find yourself getting caught up in a particular thought or emotion, gently remind yourself that you are the observer. You are not these transient experiences. They are simply phenomena passing through your field of awareness.

6. **Gently Return:** After spending some time in this state of observation, gently bring your awareness back to your physical surroundings. Take a few deep breaths, and when you feel ready, open your eyes.

7. **Reflect on Your Experience:** Take a moment to reflect on what it was like to adopt the perspective of the Observer Self. Did you notice a shift in how you relate to your thoughts and feelings? How does recognizing the part of you that remains unchanged by external roles or internal experiences affect your sense of self?

8. **Journal Your Insights:** It can be helpful to journal about your experience with the Observer meditation. Writing down your reflections can deepen your understanding of the Observer Self and how this perspective can be a resource for navigating life's challenges with greater equanimity.

This practice of engaging with the Observer Self can be a powerful way to develop mindfulness, reduce identification with passing thoughts and emotions, and cultivate a deeper sense of inner peace and stability. Remember becoming adept at observing your internal experiences without attachment takes practice. Integrating this exercise into your daily routine can significantly enhance your ability to remain centered amid life's ever-changing landscape.

Week 3 Day 4: Values Clarification

Values clarification is a vital step in Acceptance and Commitment Therapy (ACT) that helps you identify what is truly important in your life—your core values—and understand how your current behaviors, emotions, and goals align or misalign with these values. This process is about uncovering what motivates you, what you want your life to stand for, and the kind of person you wish to be.

Instructions for Today's Practice:

1. **Prepare Your Space and Mind:** Find a quiet, comfortable place where you can reflect without interruptions. Keep a journal or piece of paper and a pen handy for this exercise.

2. **Reflect on Problem Emotions and Behaviors:** Start by thinking about the emotions and behaviors that trouble you. These could be recurring feelings of anxiety, patterns of avoidance, procrastination, or any actions that seem to pull you away from the life you want to lead. Write these down.

3. **Identify Your Core Values:** Shift your focus to identifying your core values. Values are chosen qualities of purposive action that you can do on an ongoing basis. They are different from goals in that they are ongoing and never fully achieved; rather, they guide your way of being and acting in the world. Consider areas such as relationships, career, personal growth, health, and leisure. What matters most to you in these areas? Write down the values that resonate with you deeply.

4. **Goals/Actions Alignment:** Now, think about your current goals and actions. How do they align with the values you've identified? Are there goals you're pursuing that don't actually reflect your core values? Or perhaps there are values you hold dear for which you haven't set any goals. Make a list of your goals and next to each, note the value(s) they align with.

5. **Realign Your Actions:** Based on the alignment (or lack thereof) you've identified, consider what steps you can take to bring your actions more in line with your values. This might mean setting

new goals, modifying your current goals, or even dropping goals that don't serve your core values. Write down at least one action step for each value you want to focus on.

6. **Commit to Small Changes:** Start with small, achievable changes that can gradually bring your life into closer alignment with your values. Commit to these changes by writing them down and considering how you will implement them in your daily life.

7. **Reflect and Adjust Regularly:** Values clarification is not a one-time activity. As you grow and change, your values might shift. Make it a regular practice to revisit your values, goals, and actions, adjusting them as necessary to ensure they remain aligned.

This exercise is about creating a life that reflects what's truly important to you. By regularly engaging in values clarification, you can ensure that your path is always moving you closer to the fulfilling and meaningful life you envision.

Week 3 Day 5

Objective: This exercise involves ranking your values to understand where your life might not align with what's truly important to you.

Instructions:

1. **List Life Domains**: Start by writing down various life domains that matter to you, such as relationships, career, health, spirituality, and personal growth.
2. **Rate Importance**: Next, rate each domain on its importance to you on a scale of 1-10.
3. **Assess Fulfillment**: Then, rate how fulfilled you currently feel in each domain on a scale of 1-10.
4. **Calculate Deviation**: Subtract the fulfillment score from the importance score for each domain to find your "life deviation score."
5. **Identify Focus Areas**: Higher deviation scores indicate domains where your life may not align with your values, signaling areas for potential growth and development.

After completing the Day 5 exercise of ranking your values and calculating your life deviation scores, take some time to journal about the experience. Reflecting on and writing down your thoughts can deepen your understanding of where your life aligns or diverges from your core values. Consider how the exercise made you feel, which areas of your life need more attention, and why these particular domains are important to you.

Week 3 Day 6

On Day 6, after identifying which areas of your life significantly diverge from your values, focus on establishing specific, actionable goals for the top three areas that need improvement. Begin by defining long-term goals that illustrate what living according to your values would look like in the future. Then, break these down into short-term, achievable objectives that can help you move from your current situation closer to your desired state. For each goal, specify the exact steps needed, ensuring they are realistic and within your ability to implement. This approach not only makes your goals clearer but also divides larger ambitions into smaller, manageable tasks.

Incorporate the SMART criteria into your goal-setting for the three life areas where there's the greatest discrepancy between your current situation and your values. Remember, SMART goals are Specific, Measurable, Achievable, Relevant, and Time-bound. This framework ensures that each goal is clearly defined and trackable, with concrete steps and a realistic timeframe. By applying the SMART principles, you create a structured path for tangible progress, making it easier to monitor how each action helps narrow the gap between your present and your ideal future aligned with your values.

Week 3 Day 7

As part of our journey through Acceptance and Commitment Therapy (ACT), today we focus on the skills and processes for living in alignment with our core values. This process is about integrating what matters most to us into our daily lives, moving beyond the identification of values to the active phase of planning and execution.

1. Start by selecting a single value that you feel particularly drawn to right now. This might be something you've noticed is lacking in your life or an area where you desire more fulfillment. Examples of values include connection, health, learning, creativity, or service.

2. Next, define a specific, achievable goal that reflects this value. Your goal should be clear and meaningful, something that, when you think about achieving it, brings a sense of purpose and excitement. For instance, if your value is health, your goal might be to incorporate more physical activity into your week.

3. With your value and goal in mind, list specific actions you can take to move closer to your goal. These actions should be small, manageable steps that, when combined, will be in alignment with your chosen value.

4. For example, if your goal is to be more physically active, your actions might include scheduling three 30-minute walks each week, joining a dance class, or researching a local hiking group to join.

5. After planning your actions, spend some time reflecting on potential obstacles you might encounter. These could be internal, such as feelings of doubt, physical sensations of tiredness, or unproductive thoughts like "I'm not the kind of person who

can stick to a plan." They could also be external, such as time constraints or lack of access to resources.

6. For each obstacle identified, develop a strategy to overcome it. This might involve revisiting your thoughts and feelings through the lens of ACT, reminding yourself of the importance of your values and the willingness to experience discomfort for the sake of what matters to you. It may also involve practical solutions, such as adjusting your schedule or seeking support from others.

7. Finally, commit to taking the first step. Determine which action you will take first, set a time and date by when you will do it, and consider telling someone about your plan to help hold yourself accountable.

Remember, the goal here is not perfection but progress. It's about moving closer to living a life that reflects your values, even in the face of obstacles. By taking values-driven actions, you actively construct a life that feels meaningful and fulfilling.

Bridge Week 3

It's time to chart your journey across the bridge.

- **Visualize the Bridge**: Recall the image of the bridge that represents your path from the current challenges towards a brighter, depression-free horizon. Each section of the bridge symbolizes a part of your journey, with the far side representing your goals and aspirations for healing and happiness.
- **Reflect Intuitively**: Ask yourself where you "think" and "feel" you are on the bridge right now. This isn't about precision but about your inner sense of progression and change. How has this week influenced your position on the bridge?
- **Mark Your Spot**: On your visual representation of the bridge (whether it's a drawing, a printed image, or a journal entry), mark where you feel you currently stand. Use a symbol, color, or word that captures your state at this moment. This act of marking your progress is a powerful affirmation of your journey and growth.
- **Embrace Your Feelings**: Remember, there's no 'right' place to be on the bridge. Whether you've moved forward, stayed in the same spot, or even taken a few steps back, each position tells a part of your story. Embrace where you are as a valid and valuable part of your journey towards healing.
- **Look Ahead with Hope**: As you mark your place on the bridge, take a moment to look forward across it. Allow yourself to feel hope for the journey ahead. Each week brings new opportunities for progress and insight.

9

CBT and ACT

This week we will explore the synergy between Cognitive Behavioral Therapy (CBT) and Acceptance and Commitment Therapy (ACT). We will showcase how these evidence-based approaches can intertwine to support your path to wellness. Our focus shifts as we build on the foundations laid in previous weeks. The emphasis is on deepening your self-awareness, a critical step in navigating the complexities of depression.

Self-awareness is the cornerstone of mental health management. It involves understanding your thoughts, feelings, and behaviors in a way that enlightens your path to recovery. This week, we introduce journaling as a practice and an exploration of the self. Through reflective writing, you'll uncover patterns in your thoughts and feelings, providing clarity and insight into your emotional well-being.

Moreover, we're introducing mood tracking as an essential tool for this journey. Mood tracking offers a concrete, data-driven approach to observing your emotional fluctuations over time. It's about noting the ebb and flow of your feelings in relation to your daily activities, thoughts, and experiences. This practice empowers you to make informed decisions about your mental health, identify triggers, and understand the impact of various aspects of your life on your mood.

Integrating CBT and ACT into your daily life means adopting a new perspective on how you relate to your thoughts and feelings. Cognitive Behavioral Therapy provides the tools to question and challenge negative thought patterns, fostering a mindset that encourages positive change. Synergistically, Acceptance and Commitment Therapy invites you to accept those thoughts and feelings without judgment, committing to actions that align with your values and contribute to a meaningful life. Together, these therapies offer a balanced approach to mental health, emphasizing change and acceptance in equal measure.

As we delve into journaling and mood tracking this week, we encourage you to approach these practices with curiosity and openness. It's an opportunity to observe your inner world, learn from it, and use that knowledge to guide your actions and choices. By integrating the principles of CBT and ACT into these practices, you'll discover powerful ways to manage depression, enhance your well-being, and move closer to a life that reflects valid values and aspirations.

The Synergy Between CBT and ACT

Cognitive Behavioral Therapy (CBT) and Acceptance and Commitment Therapy (ACT) are two powerful, evidence-based approaches that, despite their distinct methodologies, converge on a shared objective: guiding you on a healthier, more fulfilling path through the management of your thoughts, feelings, and behaviors. Understanding how these therapies complement each other can significantly enhance your ability to cope with depression, offering a dual pathway to mental wellness that leverages the strengths of both.

As a review, CBT is grounded in the principle that our thoughts, feelings, and behaviors are interconnected and that changing negative thought patterns can lead to changes in feelings and behaviors. It employs strategies such as cognitive restructuring to challenge and alter unhelpful beliefs and behavioral activation to encourage engagement in activities that can improve mood and well-being. CBT is particularly effective in identifying and dismantling cognitive distortions—

misguided beliefs or thought patterns that distort reality and contribute to depressive symptoms.

Acceptance and Commitment Therapy (ACT), on the other hand, emphasizes the importance of accepting your thoughts and feelings rather than fighting against them. It introduces the concept of psychological flexibility, which encourages you to recognize and embrace your thoughts and emotions as they are. ACT focuses on values and committed action, guiding you to live a life aligned with your deepest values, even in pain and struggle. This approach helps detach from negative thoughts and makes room for actions contributing to a rich, full, and meaningful life.

The Integrative Power of CBT and ACT

When Cognitive Behavioral Therapy (CBT) and Acceptance and Commitment Therapy (ACT) integrate, they form a comprehensive approach to mental health that masterfully combines the principles of change with acceptance. This fusion creates a dynamic framework for understanding and navigating emotional experiences with greater flexibility and resilience.

The essence of this integration lies in how CBT's change-oriented strategies are seamlessly woven with ACT's acceptance-based approach, creating a holistic path to mental wellness. Imagine someone struggling with persistent negative self-talk—a common issue in depression. Cognitive Behavioral Therapy provide tools to identify, challenge, and replace these negative thoughts with more balanced and realistic ones. For instance, the thought "I'm worthless because I made a mistake" could be challenged and reframed to "Making a mistake does not define my worth as a person." This process of cognitive restructuring is at the heart of CBT, aiming to alter the underlying beliefs that contribute to depressive symptoms.

Simultaneously, ACT introduces a complementary perspective by encouraging acceptance of thoughts and feelings without judgment. This doesn't mean resigning to negative thoughts but rather acknowledging their presence without allowing them to dictate your actions. Using the earlier example, ACT would guide the individual to notice the thought "I'm worthless because I made a mistake," acknowledge it as a passing mental event and then focus on actions that align with their values, such as learning from the mistake and moving forward. This acceptance-based approach helps individuals engage with life more fully, even if experiencing complex thoughts and feelings.

The concept of psychological flexibility, central to ACT, further enhances the therapeutic process by fostering an ability to adapt to changing circumstances with a balanced mindset. This flexibility is vital for managing depression as it equips individuals with a range of strategies to face life's challenges. Instead of being trapped in a cycle of unhelpful thinking patterns, psychological flexibility allows for a more adaptive response. It enables individuals to choose their actions based on what is most meaningful and valuable to them rather than being led by transient thoughts and feelings.

Moreover, integrating CBT and ACT enriches the behavioral component of therapy by aligning actions with personal values. This alignment is crucial for fostering a sense of purpose and direction in life. For example, if people value connection with others, they might aim to strengthen their relationships. CBT strategies can support this goal by helping to overcome barriers such as social anxiety or withdrawal, often associated with depression. In doing so, you are changing unhelpful behaviors while committing to actions that bring a deeper sense of fulfillment and meaning to their lives.

This synergistic approach does not merely offer tools for immediate relief from depressive symptoms but also lays the groundwork for long-term wellness. By embracing change and acceptance, individuals learn to navigate their mental health journey with a balanced perspective, enabling them to face life's ups and downs with resilience and grace. This comprehensive framework supports cultivating a fulfilling life, underscored by a profound understanding that while we may not have control over every thought or feeling, we can choose how we respond to them, guided by our deepest values and commitments.

Journaling: A Tool for Reflection and Growth

Journaling is a cornerstone in the architecture this self-help guide and the therapeutic practices within. Writing offers a unique and profound way to engage with your inner world. This method of self-reflection is a way to document your daily experiences. Journaling also acts as a reflective surface, revealing the depths of your thoughts, emotions, and the patterns that weave through your life's tapestry. As we venture into this week of your journey, we extend an invitation to deepen your engagement with journaling, transforming it from a routine exercise into a meaningful exploration of self.

This exploration goes beyond the surface-level recounting of events or the mere acknowledgment of feelings. It's an invitation to delve into the 'whys' behind your emotions and thoughts, uncover your feelings' root causes, and understand the complex interplay between your internal and external worlds. By doing so, you embark on a journey of self-discovery, where each entry becomes a step closer to understanding and managing your depression more effectively.

Consider, for instance, a recurring feeling of sadness or anxiety. Instead of simply noting these feelings, ask yourself what thoughts or events trigger these emotions. Is there a pattern you recognize? Perhaps you notice that your mood dips significantly on days when you're reminded of past failures or when you anticipate future challenges. This observation can be pivotal, offering insights into how your thought processes influence your emotional state.

Once these patterns and triggers are identified, you can apply the principles of Cognitive Behavioral Therapy (CBT) and Acceptance and Commitment Therapy (ACT) to address them. From a CBT perspective, you might challenge the validity of the thoughts that lead to sadness, questioning their accuracy and reframing them into more balanced and constructive alternatives. For example, the thought "I will never be good enough" can be challenged and replaced with "I am capable of growth and improvement."

Through the lens of ACT, you might focus on accepting these thoughts and feelings without judgment, recognizing them as part of your experience but not defining your actions. This acceptance paves the way for committed action based on your values rather than your momentary feelings. You might decide to engage in activities that align with your values, such as kindness, creativity, or learning, even when faced with challenging thoughts and emotions.

Furthermore, journaling can serve as a therapeutic dialogue with yourself, fostering a compassionate and understanding relationship with your inner world. It can be a space where you practice self-compassion, acknowledge your struggles, and celebrate your progress, no matter how small. Through regular journaling, you build a repository of personal insights, achievements, and reflections that can serve as a source of motivation and encouragement throughout your journey.

As you continue to journal, remember that this practice is not about striving for perfection. It is about embracing the process of exploration and discovery with willingness and curiosity. Each entry unlocks greater self-awareness, offering a clearer understanding of how to navigate your thoughts and emotions effectively. By integrating journaling into your daily routine, you cultivate a powerful tool for reflection and growth. This supports building a more fulfilling and depression-free life.

Introducing Mood Tracking

Mood tracking is a tool for emotional clarity and self-awareness. This practice, simple in its execution, offers insights into the fluctuations of your emotional state, serving as a compass to navigate the often complex terrain of your feelings. By dedicating yourself to the regular recording of your mood, you embark on a journey of discovery, unearthing patterns, triggers, and previously obscured insights.

Mood tracking transcends mere observation; it is an exercise in mindfulness and self-connection. As you note down your emotional states, you may begin to observe how certain events, interactions, or even times of day influence your mood. This heightened awareness is instrumental in applying the principles of Cognitive Behavioral Therapy (CBT) and Acceptance and Commitment Therapy (ACT) with precision and intention. For instance, you might notice a recurring dip in mood every Sunday evening, prompting feelings of anxiety and dread about the upcoming week. With this insight, you can employ CBT techniques to challenge and reframe negative anticipatory thoughts or use ACT strategies to accept these feelings without allowing them to dominate your actions.

The beauty of mood tracking lies in its flexibility and adaptability; there are myriad ways to engage with this practice, each adaptable to your personal preferences and lifestyle. For those who appreciate the tactile and reflective nature of writing, a traditional pen-and-paper approach allows for a meditative and unplugged method of mood recording. Here, you can create a mood chart or simply jot down notes about your emotional state, using symbols, colors, or words to represent different moods.

Alternatively, the digital age offers a plethora of mood-tracking apps designed with user-friendliness and interactivity in mind. These apps often come with features such as mood graphs, trend analysis, and reminders, making it easier to maintain consistency and gain actionable insights. Some apps even offer the option to record triggers, thoughts, and actions alongside your mood, providing a comprehensive view of your emotional landscape.

Regardless of the method chosen, the crux of mood tracking is consistency. The actual value of this practice unfolds over time, with each entry contributing to a richer, more nuanced understanding of your emotional patterns. As you collect data on your moods, you'll see a clearer picture of your emotional trends, informing your healing and growth.

Moreover, mood tracking can foster a sense of empowerment and control over your mental health journey. It provides tangible evidence of your emotional cycles and progress, reminding you that your feelings are valid and informative. This practice encourages a proactive stance regarding managing your emotions, guiding you to recognize when and how to apply therapeutic techniques, seek support, or engage in self-care.

As you integrate mood tracking into your daily routine, approach it with an open heart and a curious mind. This is not just a task but an invitation to connect with yourself on a deeper level, to honor your emotions, and to navigate your journey with insight and compassion. By attuning to your emotional landscape through mood tracking, you lay the groundwork for a more mindful, responsive, and fulfilling approach to managing depression.

How to Effectively Use Mood Tracking and Journaling

Integrating mood tracking with journaling creates a powerful duo for deepening your understanding of your mental health. To effectively harness the strengths of these tools, embedding them into your daily life as consistent practices is crucial. Consistency not only aids in identifying emotional patterns but also paves the way for meaningful transformations in how you perceive and manage your emotions.

Making mood tracking and journaling a part of your daily routine is akin to setting up a personal check-in system, where you pause, reflect, and record your emotional and mental states. This ritual becomes a dedicated time for self-reflection, offering a moment of pause in your day to connect with yourself on a deeper level. Regularly noting down your feelings and the nuances of your mood instills a discipline essential for uncovering the rhythms and cycles of your emotional life.

Approaching your entries with honesty and a non-judgmental attitude is foundational to the process. This practice is your sanctuary for raw expression, a space where you can lay bare your thoughts and feelings without fear of critique. Embracing this mindset encourages a compassionate dialogue with yourself, fostering an environment where understanding flourishes over self-criticism. In this space, you can freely explore the depths of your emotions, acknowledging your experiences without reservation or censorship.

As you continue to track your mood and journal, a narrative unfolds—one that reveals the intricate links between your daily activities, thought processes, and emotional states. This narrative is rich with insights, offering clues and patterns that might have remained obscured without this reflective practice. For example, you may notice how specific interactions or activities consistently impact your mood, illuminating potential triggers or sources of joy. This awareness is instrumental in crafting a more mindful approach to daily activities and interactions.

The fundamental transformation occurs when you begin to apply the insights gained from mood tracking and journaling to your journey of emotional growth. The patterns and correlations you uncover provide a roadmap for applying Cognitive Behavioral Therapy (CBT) and Acceptance and Commitment Therapy (ACT) techniques more precisely. For instance, identifying a pattern of negative thinking that precedes a mood dip can lead you to engage in CBT exercises that challenge and reframe these thoughts. Similarly, recognizing moments of resistance or avoidance in your journal can help you embrace these experiences with the acceptance and mindfulness practices central to ACT.

By intertwining mood tracking and journaling with the principles of CBT and ACT, you equip yourself with a dynamic toolkit for navigating the complexities of your mental health. This integrated approach enhances self-awareness and emotional well-being. Through the disciplined practice of regular entries, the cultivation of an honest and non-judgmental attitude, and the thoughtful application of therapeutic insights, mood tracking, and journaling evolve into transformative practices that support a deeper understanding and management of your emotional world.

This week is about deepening your understanding of yourself through the integrated use of CBT and ACT, journaling, and mood tracking. Each tool offers a unique lens through which to view your experiences, and together, they can provide a comprehensive picture of your emotional health. By continuing to engage with these practices, you are building a solid foundation for managing depression and creating a life that reflects your values and aspirations.

Remember, this journey is uniquely yours. While the tools and techniques we discuss are universal, how you apply them is very personal. Be patient with yourself and recognize your progress, even in the smallest of steps.

Week 4 Self-Help Guide

Week 4 Day 1

Today, your task is to dive into the practices of Cognitive Behavioral Therapy (CBT) and Acceptance and Commitment Therapy (ACT) through reflective journaling. This exercise is designed to help you understand the complementary nature of these therapies by applying their principles to a real-life situation where negative thoughts have influenced your mood.

1. **Select a Recent Event:** Think of a recent event or situation that led to negative thoughts and noticeably affected your mood. This could be an interaction with someone, a personal setback, or any scenario that left you feeling down or anxious.

2. **Describe the Situation and Your Initial Thoughts:** Begin your journal entry by describing the chosen event in detail. What happened? When and where did it occur? What were the immediate thoughts that came to your mind? How did these thoughts impact your mood? Be as specific as possible to set the stage for your analysis.

3. **Apply ACT - Acceptance of Thoughts:** Reflect on the concept of acceptance central to ACT. Instead of trying to push away or fight your negative thoughts, explore what it means to acknowledge and accept them as they are. Write about how accepting these thoughts without judgment could shift your perspective. Consider questions like: Can I make room for these thoughts? How does accepting these thoughts feel compared to resisting them?

4. **Apply CBT - Challenging Negative Thoughts:** Now turn to the CBT approach, which involves challenging and reframing negative thoughts. Identify the specific negative thoughts you

had about the event. Use CBT techniques to question the accuracy and helpfulness of these thoughts. Could these thoughts be based on cognitive distortions (e.g., overgeneralization, catastrophizing, black-and-white thinking)? How can you reframe these thoughts to be more balanced and realistic? Write down alternative thoughts that could lead to more positive feelings.

5. **Reflect on the Integration of CBT and ACT:** After applying both ACT and CBT principles, reflect on the experience of integrating these approaches. How did accepting your thoughts affect your ability to challenge and reframe them? Did you notice a shift in your mood or perspective by combining acceptance with cognitive restructuring?

6. **Concluding Thoughts:** Conclude your journal entry with some final thoughts on how integrating CBT and ACT might help you manage similar situations in the future. Consider the value of accepting thoughts and emotions as they are while being proactive in challenging unhelpful thought patterns.

This exercise aims to provide a practical understanding of how CBT and ACT can work together to offer a more nuanced approach to managing negative thoughts and improving your mood. Reflecting on and writing about your experiences reinforces integrating these therapeutic practices into your daily life, fostering greater emotional resilience and flexibility.

Week 4 Day 2

Today, you'll delve deeper into understanding cognitive distortions, which are essentially the biased perspectives we sometimes adopt about ourselves and the world around us. These distortions often play a significant role in the development and maintenance of depression and anxiety. Today's activity aims to enhance your awareness of these thought patterns in your daily life and practice applying Cognitive Behavioral Therapy (CBT) techniques to challenge and reframe at least one of these thoughts.

1. **Reflect on Your Day:** Begin by reflecting on the events of your day. Consider interactions, tasks, challenges, or even moments of downtime. Try to recall specific thoughts that arose in response to these situations. Don't filter these thoughts; the goal is to capture a wide range of internal dialogues, including those that might seem minor or inconsequential.

2. **Write Down Your Thoughts:** In your journal, list the thoughts you've identified. Write them down as they came to you, without editing or judging them. This process is about observation and recognition, not yet about evaluation.

3. **Identify Cognitive Distortions:** Review the thoughts you've listed and identify any that may be influenced by cognitive distortions. Common distortions include all-or-nothing thinking, overgeneralization, mental filtering, disqualifying the positive, jumping to conclusions, magnification or minimization, emotional reasoning, should statements, labeling and mislabeling, and personalization. Briefly note next to each thought what type of distortion it may represent. If you're unsure, make your best

guess; this exercise is as much about learning to recognize patterns as it is about accurate classification.

4. **Choose One Thought to Reframe:** Select one thought from your list that stands out or has a significant emotional charge. This will be the thought you work on reframing.

5. **Analyze the Chosen Thought:** Before you attempt to reframe the thought, spend a moment analyzing it:

   - Why did this thought arise?
   - What evidence supports this thought?
   - What evidence contradicts it?
   - Is this thought based on facts or feelings?
   - What might be a more balanced or rational way of looking at the situation?

6. **Practice Reframing:** Using your analysis, attempt to reframe the chosen thought. Reframing involves looking at the situation in a new, more balanced way. It's not about dismissing your feelings but rather about challenging the accuracy of the thought and considering alternative perspectives. Write down the reframed thought in your journal.

7. **Reflect on the Process:** Finally, reflect on this exercise. How did it feel to identify cognitive distortions in your thoughts? Was reframing the thought challenging? How does the reframed thought compare to the original in terms of how it makes you feel? Do you think you could believe and act on this reframed thought in similar future situations?

This activity is designed to enhance your skill in recognizing and modifying unhelpful thought patterns through CBT techniques. By practicing these steps regularly, you can begin to automatically identify and adjust cognitive distortions in your daily life, paving the way for more positive mental health outcomes.

Week 4 Day 3

Today, you're invited to engage in a practice of emotional acceptance, an essential component of Acceptance and Commitment Therapy (ACT). The objective is to cultivate a stance of openness and non-judgment toward your emotions, regardless of their nature. By tracking your mood throughout the day and reflecting on these emotional states, you'll practice acknowledging your feelings without the impulse to alter or judge them.

1. Set Mood Tracking Times: Choose three times throughout your day for mood tracking. Aim for a spread that captures different parts of your day, such as morning, midday, and evening. Setting reminders can be helpful to ensure you follow through at these times.

2. Track Your Mood: At each of the predetermined times, take a moment to check in with yourself and identify your current mood. You can use a simple descriptor (e.g., happy, anxious, calm), a scale (e.g., 1-10 on a happiness or stress scale), or even a color or image that you feel represents your mood. Record this in your journal without adding any further detail at this time.

3. Reflect Without Judgment: After tracking your mood for the third and final time, set aside a quiet moment for reflection. Review the moods you've recorded throughout the day. For each mood, reflect on what you were feeling and write about the experience of simply accepting these emotions as they were:

- Describe the context of each mood briefly. What was happening around you, or what were you doing at the time?

- Explore the sensations associated with each emotion. Where did you feel it in your body? What physical sensations accompanied the emotion?
- Write about the experience of allowing these emotions to be present without trying to change them. Was it difficult not to judge or attempt to alter your mood? What thoughts came up during this process?

4. Practice Acceptance: For each mood you've tracked, practice a brief exercise of acceptance. This might involve saying to yourself, "In this moment, I accept my feelings of [emotion]. I allow myself to feel this without judgment." Note any shifts in your perspective or emotional state as you consciously accept each emotion.

5. Reflect on the Process: Conclude your journaling by reflecting on the overall experience of mood tracking and emotional acceptance. Consider questions like:

- How did this practice of acceptance compare to your usual response to emotions?
- Did accepting your emotions change the intensity or duration of these feelings?
- How do you feel about continuing to practice emotional acceptance in your daily life?

Today's activity is designed to deepen your understanding and practice of emotional acceptance, an essential skill for emotional resilience and well-being. By learning to accept your emotions as they are, you're likely to find that they have less power over you, and you may begin to experience a greater sense of peace and balance in your emotional life.

Week 4 Day 4

For Day 4, the emphasis shifts to clarifying and understanding your core values, which are fundamental beliefs that guide your decisions and actions in life. Values clarification is a pivotal aspect of Acceptance and Commitment Therapy (ACT), as it helps you to live a more focused, meaningful life aligned with what truly matters to you. Today, you'll explore your top values and examine how your daily actions reflect these principles.

1. Reflect on Your Values: Begin by reflecting on what values are most important to you. Values encompass relationships, personal growth, health, career, creativity, and community. Think about what truly brings you fulfillment, joy, and a sense of purpose.

2. List Your Top Five Values: After some reflection, narrow down your values to the top five that feel most essential to your sense of self and well-being. Write these down in your journal. If you find this step challenging, consider situations that have made you feel most proud, happy, or fulfilled as clues to your values.

3. Assess Alignment with Daily Actions: For each of the five values, write a brief reflection on how your current daily actions align or do not align with these values. Be honest with yourself. For example, if one of your values is health, consider how your daily habits support or detract from this value.

4. Identify Discrepancies: You may notice discrepancies between your values and actions as you reflect. This is normal and provides valuable insights into areas of your life where changes could lead to greater fulfillment and alignment with your values.

5. Explore the Role of CBT and ACT: Consider how Cognitive Behavioral Therapy (CBT) and Acceptance and Commitment Therapy (ACT) can support living according to your values. For instance, CBT can help by addressing negative thoughts or beliefs that hinder your ability to act on your values. ACT, with its focus on committed action in the service of values, can guide you in making choices that bring you closer to the life you want to live. Reflect on specific ways these therapies could help you bridge the gap between your values and actions.

6. Set Small, Actionable Goals: Based on your reflections, set one small, actionable goal for each value to make your daily actions more aligned with your values. These goals should be specific, measurable, and achievable. For example, if one of your values is connection with family, your goal could be to dedicate uninterrupted time each day to spend with a family member.

7. Reflect on the Process: Conclude by reflecting on this values clarification exercise. How did it feel to explicitly identify your values and assess the alignment of your actions with these values? What insights have you gained, and how do you think about the goals you've set?

This activity aims to deepen your understanding of your values and how they manifest in your daily life, providing a clear direction for making choices congruent with what you hold most dear. By aligning your actions with your values, you can create a more meaningful and satisfying life supported by the principles of CBT and ACT.

Week 4 Day 5

The journey now takes you into the heart of mindfulness, a practice central to fostering present-moment awareness and a key component of Acceptance and Commitment Therapy (ACT). Mindfulness meditation offers a pathway to observe your thoughts and emotions without judgment, grounding you in the here and now. This activity is designed to enhance your mindfulness skills and deepen your connection to the present moment.

1. Prepare for Meditation: Choose a quiet and comfortable space where you can sit undisturbed for 10 minutes. You can sit on a chair with your feet flat on the ground, on a cushion on the floor, or anywhere you feel comfortable. The key is to maintain a posture that is alert yet relaxed. Turn off or silence any potential distractions like your phone or other devices.

2. Start Your Meditation: Close your eyes gently and bring your attention to your breath. Notice the sensation of the air flowing in and out of your nostrils or the rise and fall of your chest or abdomen as you breathe. You don't need to change your breathing pattern; simply observe it.

3. Observe Your Experience: As you meditate, you'll likely notice thoughts, emotions, or physical sensations arising. This is normal and to be expected. When you become aware of these experiences, acknowledge them without judgment and gently redirect your focus to your breath. The goal is not to be free of thoughts or feelings but to observe them as they come and go without getting caught up in them.

4. Use a Mindfulness Prompt If Needed: If you find it challenging to maintain focus on your breath, you can use a simple prompt to help. Each time you notice your mind wandering, silently say to yourself "thinking" or "feeling" as a gentle reminder to return your attention to the breath. This labeling can help to acknowledge and let go of distractions.

5. Conclude Your Meditation: After 10 minutes, slowly bring your awareness back to the room. Open your eyes gently, take a moment to notice how your body feels, and observe any changes in your mental or emotional state.

6. Journal About Your Experience: Write about your mindfulness meditation experience in your journal. Note any thoughts or emotions that arose during the practice. How did you engage with these experiences? Were you able to observe them without judgment and return your focus to your breath? How did your body feel during and after the meditation? Reflect on the ease or difficulty of staying present and any insights you gained from this practice.

7. Reflect on Present-Moment Awareness: Reflect on how mindfulness and present-moment awareness can be applied in your daily life. Consider situations where being more present could change your experience or response. How might incorporating mindfulness into your daily routine impact your overall well-being?

This activity aims to cultivate a deeper sense of mindfulness and connection to the present moment, enhancing your ability to observe thoughts and emotions non-judgmentally. As you develop your mindfulness practice, you may find it becomes easier to navigate daily stresses and challenges with greater calm and clarity.

Week 4 Day 6

For Day 6, you're invited to actively engage in an exercise that brings together Behavioral Activation, a core aspect of Cognitive Behavioral Therapy (CBT), and Committed Action, a fundamental component of Acceptance and Commitment Therapy (ACT). This day is about putting into practice the concept of taking actions aligned with your values, even when faced with emotional challenges, to improve your mood and enhance your life quality.

1. Reflect on Your Values: Begin by revisiting the values you identified on Day 4. Reflect on these values deeply, considering which one you feel particularly drawn to or disconnected from. The aim is to select a value you wish to integrate more fully into your daily life through action.

2. Choose a Value-Aligned Activity: Based on the value you've chosen to focus on, identify an activity that embodies this value and has the potential to influence your mood positively. For instance, if your selected value is "connection," your activity could be reaching out to a friend or family member for a meaningful conversation. If it's "health," you might plan a nutritious meal or physical exercise session.

3. Plan the Activity: Once you've chosen your activity, plan it in detail. What steps do you need to take to make this activity happen? When and where will it take place? What materials or preparations are required? Setting a specific time and place increases the likelihood of following through.

4. Engage in the Activity: Carry out the planned activity, keeping your chosen value at the forefront of your mind. As you engage in this activity, try to stay fully present, noticing how it feels to act in a way that is congruent with your values. Be mindful of any thoughts or emotions that arise, observing them with curiosity rather than judgment.

5. Journal About the Experience: After completing the activity, take some time to journal about the experience. Write about how it felt to engage in an activity that aligns with your values. Did you notice any shifts in your mood or overall sense of well-being? Were there any barriers or challenges you encountered, and how did you address them? Reflect on any insights gained from this experience, particularly in relation to how CBT and ACT principles supported you in taking committed action.

6. Reflect on Behavioral Activation and Committed Action: Finally, reflect on the concepts of Behavioral Activation and Committed Action. How does taking value-aligned action, even when challenging, contribute to your mental health and emotional resilience? Consider how this practice might be applied to areas where you seek improvement or fulfillment.

This activity is designed to empower you by demonstrating the positive impact of living in accordance with your values, supported by the therapeutic frameworks of CBT and ACT. Through planning, executing, and reflecting on a value-aligned activity, you not only enhance your mood but also strengthen your commitment to a life that reflects your deepest values and aspirations.

Week 4 Day 7

Today you are at a pivotal moment of integration and reflection, a day dedicated to synthesizing the insights and growth experienced throughout the week. This day is about looking back at your journey, recognizing the patterns and shifts in your thoughts, emotions, and behaviors, and envisioning how you can continue to apply the principles of Cognitive Behavioral Therapy (CBT) and Acceptance and Commitment Therapy (ACT) moving forward.

Detailed Activity Instructions for Day 7

1. Compile Your Journal Entries: Gather your journal entries from the previous six days. Ensure you have a comfortable, quiet space to read and reflect without interruptions. This preparation sets the stage for a meaningful review of your insights and growth over the week.

2. Review and Note Patterns: Carefully read through each entry, paying attention to recurring themes, patterns in your thoughts or emotions, and notable shifts in your perspective. Use highlighters or note markers to underline or mark segments that stand out to you, whether they're insights about yourself, changes in how you relate to your thoughts and feelings, or actions that align with your values.

3. Identify Key Insights: After reviewing your entries, jot down the key insights or lessons learned from each day's focus. This might include newfound awareness of cognitive distortions, the power to accept emotions without judgment, the clarity gained from aligning actions with values, or the peace in present-moment awareness.

4. Reflect on the Integration of CBT and ACT: Write a reflective summary about how integrating CBT and ACT techniques throughout the week has influenced your understanding and management of your thoughts, emotions, and behaviors. Consider how each practice contributed to a more nuanced approach to mental health and personal growth. How did the blend of challenging negative thoughts (CBT) and accepting emotional experiences (ACT) impact your overall well-being?

5. Plan for Future Application: Based on your reflections and insights, outline a plan for how you can continue to apply these CBT and ACT principles in your daily life. This plan might include specific strategies you found particularly beneficial, habits you want to develop further, or areas where these practices make a significant difference. Set realistic goals for incorporating these techniques into your routine, keeping in mind the importance of flexibility and self-compassion as you progress.

6. Closing Reflection: Finally, take a moment to acknowledge the work you've done over the past week. Reflect on any changes in your attitude regarding yourself and your mental health journey. What aspects of this week's practices do you feel most drawn to continue exploring? How do you envision these practices supporting a more balanced and fulfilling life?

This activity serves as a cornerstone for the week, allowing you to consolidate your learning, appreciate your progress, and set intentions for your continued journey. By taking the time to integrate and reflect on your experiences, you solidify the foundation for ongoing growth and well-being.

Bridge Week 4

As you conclude another week on your journey, pause for a brief moment to reconnect with your path across the bridge. Remember to visualize where you stand today, reflect on your recent experiences, embrace all feelings that arise, and look ahead with hope. Please mark your current spot on the bridge, capturing this week's progress and emotions.

10

Internal Family Systems (IFS)

This week our focus shifts to the Internal Family Systems (IFS) model. This approach sees our mind as a complex system of interrelated parts akin to a family within us. Each part has its unique role, perspective, and way of interacting. They each affect how we think, feel, and behave. At the core of IFS is the understanding that multiplicity within our psyche is natural and that each of us has a *Self*, embodying qualities like compassion, clarity, and curiosity, capable of leading and healing our internal family.

The IFS model suggests that every part within us, even those that seem problematic, has positive intentions and that healing comes not from eliminating parts but from helping them find their non-extreme roles. It suggests that our complex internal system can change rapidly when reorganized, impacting our external life. According to IFS, the therapeutic journey aims for balance and harmony, elevating the Self to lead and ensuring that all parts can contribute positively to our well-being.

This chapter will go deeper into understanding these parts and the Self. We will illustrate how a compassionate, curious, and calm Self can facilitate internal harmony. This process is about symptom relief and fostering a deeper self-understanding and healing. Through IFS, we learn to navigate our internal world with empathy, leading to changes in how we experience ourselves and interact with the world around us.

In expanding our exploration of the Internal Family Systems (IFS) model, we delve into the roles of our inner Managers, Firefighters, and Exiles, each representing distinct functions within our internal system.

Managers. In the Internal Family Systems (IFS) model, Managers play a multifaceted role in our psychological makeup. Managers embody the aspects of our psyche dedicated to preemptively protecting us from harm. These parts are like the overseers of our internal world. They vigilantly work to prevent the emergence of pain and trauma into our conscious awareness. They employ various strategies to maintain safety and order, acting out of a deep-seated desire to shield us from potential failure, criticism, and emotional distress.

Managers are characterized by their proactive approach. They meticulously plan, evaluate, and control our thoughts, behaviors, and interactions with the world to minimize risk and ensure a sense of security. Their methods, though varied, share a common goal: to keep vulnerability and pain at bay. For instance, a Manager requires perfectionism, compelling us to meet exceedingly high standards in everything we do. This drive stems from a fear of criticism or failure, with the Manager believing that perfection is the only way to avoid such outcomes.

However, the actions of Managers, while protective in intent, can sometimes lead to stress, anxiety, and a sense of being overwhelmed. This is because the strategies Managers employ, such as over-planning or self-criticism, can be rigid and unforgiving. This leaves little room for the messiness of human experience. It's as if they are constantly on guard, scanning for threats and often seeing them even where they don't exist.

The narrative of inner Managers illustrates the complex, often paradoxical nature of their protective efforts. For example, consider the person who stays late at work every night, obsessing over every detail of a project. Here, the Manager is at play, driven by an underlying fear of not being good enough. Or think of the individual who avoids intimate relationships, guided by a Manager who equates vulnerability with danger, thus keeping potential hurt at arm's length.

Understanding the role of and recognizing that their protective strategies stem from a place of care, albeit sometimes misguided, allows us to approach them with empathy and curiosity. This shift in perspective is the first step in transforming our relationship with these parts, enabling us to find more balanced and less extreme ways of meeting our needs for safety and self-protection.

In essence, Managers in our internal family system, with their complex web of strategies and intentions, embody our innate drive for self-preservation. Managers are part of the multifaceted nature of our inner lives, highlighting the importance of self-awareness and compassion.

Firefighters emerge in moments of acute emotional distress. Unlike Managers, who work preemptively to shield us from pain, Firefighters react instantly when intense emotions threaten to surface. Their strategies, while varied, are united by a singular aim: to quench the flames of our discomfort, often through quick, sometimes drastic, measures.

Firefighters often resort to substance abuse, binge eating, or mindless scrolling through digital content—anything that can momentarily distract or numb us from our pain. Though seemingly destructive, these behaviors are rooted in an unconscious desire to protect. They are the emergency responders of our internal system, acting out of an urgent need to keep unbearable feelings or traumatic memories at bay.

This part of our psyche is not concerned with the long-term consequences of its actions; its focus is solely on immediate relief. The impulsive decisions made by Firefighters can lead to cycles of behavior that, while providing short-term escape, may exacerbate feelings of shame, guilt, or worthlessness in the aftermath. Recognizing the protective intent behind these actions allows us to approach our Firefighters with compassion and curiosity, paving the way for healing and integration.

Understanding the dynamic interplay between Managers, Firefighters, and Exiles enriches our comprehension of the IFS model. It reveals the depth of our inner complexity and the lengths to which parts of us go to protect our overall well-being. By acknowledging and appreciating the role of Firefighters, we can begin to explore healthier strategies for managing emotional pain, fostering a sense of balance and peace within our internal family system.

Exiles hold a poignant place in the internal family, embodying the deep emotional scars that result from our past traumas, fears, and unresolved pain. These parts, often formed in childhood or during moments of significant emotional distress, are burdened with feelings that were too overwhelming to process when they occurred. As a result, they are exiled from our conscious awareness, relegated to the shadows of our psyche, in a well-intentioned but ultimately harmful attempt to protect us from their pain.

The life of an Exile is one of longing for recognition, healing, and the chance to be integrated into our internal system in a healthy and productive way. Yet, they find themselves trapped, held back by Managers and Firefighters who fear the chaos and disruption that might ensue if these painful emotions were to be acknowledged and felt. This creates a dynamic where the Exiles' needs for care and healing are continually unmet as the more active parts of our system work tirelessly to keep them out of sight and out of mind.

Consider, for example, the memory of a young child who felt deeply rejected after being criticized in front of their classmates. This memory, and the intense feelings of shame and unworthiness it evokes, becomes an Exile. As this child grows, any situation vaguely reminiscent of this initial trauma might trigger an intense emotional response. Managers step in to avoid such situations at all costs, while Firefighters might engage in distracting behaviors whenever those feelings start to surface. The Exile remains hidden, its pain unaddressed, and the cycle continues.

The healing journey involves acknowledging the presence of these Exiles, understanding their pain, and welcoming them back into the fold with compassion and care. This process is delicate, requiring the guidance of the Self to ensure that reconnection does not overwhelm but rather enriches and harmonizes the internal system. Through this reintegration, we not only heal the Exiles but also transform our relationship with ourselves, fostering a deeper sense of inner peace and wholeness.

In the world of the Internal Family Systems (IFS) model, our exploration reveals the complexity of our internal landscape and the profound capacity for healing within it. The IFS framework offers a compassionate lens through which to view the various parts of ourselves—Managers, Firefighters, and Exiles—each playing a distinct role in our psychological ecosystem to safeguard our well-being. In their efforts to protect, these parts can sometimes act in ways that paradoxically contribute to our struggles. However, we embark on a transformative journey by engaging with these parts from a place of curiosity and compassion, led by the grounded presence of the Self. This inner dialogue and understanding process fosters a movement from internal conflict and pain.

This deep engagement with our inner parts illuminates the pathways through which depression and emotional suffering are maintained. It provides a roadmap for addressing these issues at their roots, offering hope for profound change. As we learn to navigate the complexities of our inner world, we gain the tools to heal from within, fostering resilience and a greater sense of self-understanding. This journey, rich with self-discovery, empowers us to reconstruct our internal narrative, shaping a future where emotional well-being and inner peace are within reach. Through the practice of IFS, we are managing symptoms and actively participating in reconfiguring our internal dynamics, paving the way for lasting transformation and a life marked by emotional health and fulfillment.

A fundamental goal of IFS therapy is to foster a relationship where the Self assumes a leadership role, calling for healthier interactions and roles. By doing so, we aim to achieve a balanced and harmonious internal system. This transformation is about alleviating symptoms, fostering a deeper understanding of ourselves, and promoting lasting healing.

Consider the story of Alex, who is grappling with depression. Alex's Manager part works tirelessly to maintain perfection in all tasks, driven by a fear of criticism and failure. When this pressure becomes overwhelming, Alex's Firefighter part turns to binge-watching series, a temporary escape from feelings of inadequacy. Beneath these protective strategies lie Exiles, parts frozen in past moments of embarrassment and criticism, whose unaddressed pain fuels Alex's depression.

Through IFS therapy, Alex learns to approach these parts with curiosity and compassion. Alex addresses the Exiles' needs directly by recognizing the protective intentions behind the Manager's perfection-ism and the Firefighter's escapism. Guided by the Self, Alex offers these vulnerable parts the care and validation they've longed for, easing their burdens and transforming their roles within the internal system.

As you turn your gaze inward this week, examine the parts within you that serve as guardians against emotional distress. In their unique ways, these protectors strive to shield you from the complexities of pain, often through mechanisms developed over the years.

Through reflective exercises and guided introspections, we'll engage with these parts, aiming to understand their intentions and appreciate their efforts to safeguard your well-being. This exploration is about acknowledgment and forging a connection, inviting the wisdom and guidance of the Self to lead this internal assembly. This engagement marks a pivotal stride, offering a pathway out of depression and a rejuvenated sense of self.

Embracing the principles of IFS, we embark on a transformative journey that promises a richer understanding of our inner work-ings, fostering an environment where compassion and resilience can flourish. This journey lays the groundwork for a life not just survived but lived fully, with an enriched sense of personal understanding and emotional harmony.

Week 5 Self-Help Guide

As you transition into the Week 5 self-help guide, it's crucial to maintain the momentum of your journaling practice established in the earlier weeks. This continuous engagement with your thoughts and experiences is key to deepening your self-awareness and fostering the transformative shifts you're making. Journaling serves as a reflective mirror, capturing your evolving journey, illuminating patterns in your thoughts and behaviors, and pinpointing areas of growth and opportunity.

Emphasizing the "positivity log" during this phase remains instrumental. This aspect of your journaling routine encourages you to identify and celebrate your daily victories, no matter how small they may seem. It's a practice that nurtures gratitude and shifts your focus to positive aspects of your life, contributing significantly to cultivating a more optimistic mindset. This shift is essential for moving away from depressive patterns and cultivating a more fulfilling and balanced life.

Remember, writing down your experiences, thoughts, and feelings can be therapeutic. It helps you process and release the emotions tied to those experiences but also aids in recognizing your strengths and resilience. You're weaving a cohesive narrative of your healing journey by consistently connecting insights from the past weeks with your current experiences. This narrative tracks your progress and serves as a beacon, guiding your path to overcome depression.

Keep this journaling practice as a cornerstone of your daily routine. It's a powerful tool that supports your journey to a healthier, more positive outlook on life, reinforcing your changes.

Week 5 Day 1

Objective: to cultivate self-awareness and connection with oneself through the Eight Cs—Curiosity, Calm, Confidence, Compassion, Creativity, Clarity, Courage, and Connectedness—enabling a foundation for overcoming anxiety.

Prepare Your Space and Mind: Choose a quiet, comfortable space where you won't be disturbed. Take a few moments to settle in, focusing on your breath, allowing your body to relax and your mind to clear. This preparation is crucial for creating a receptive state for introspection.

Engage with Each of the Eight Cs:

- **Curiosity**: Start by cultivating an open, non-judgmental curiosity about your thoughts, feelings, and bodily sensations. Ask yourself, "What am I experiencing right now?" without trying to change anything.
- **Calm**: Focus on invoking a sense of calm within yourself. Deep, slow breathing can facilitate this. Notice areas of tension in your body and imagine your breath flowing into and gently relaxing these areas.
- **Confidence**: Reflect on moments when you felt confident. What did that feel like in your body? How did that confidence influence your thoughts and actions? Try to embody that sensation as you sit with yourself.
- **Compassion**: Turn a compassionate gaze inward. Think of a time you struggled and how you might offer kindness to a friend in a similar situation. Extend that same kindness to yourself.

- **Creativity**: Allow your mind to explore creative thoughts without judgment. This might involve imagining a peaceful scene, thinking about a problem from a new angle, or simply letting your mind wander freely.
- **Clarity**: Seek clarity by asking yourself what you need most right now. This question can help reduce the noise of conflicting thoughts and feelings, revealing your underlying desires or concerns.
- **Courage**: Contemplate the concept of courage, especially in the context of facing internal challenges. Consider a time when you acted bravely despite fear. How can you apply that courage to exploring your internal world?
- **Connectedness**: Reflect on your connection to humanity, the world, and even parts within you. Acknowledge that you are not alone in your experiences; a universal thread of human experience binds us all.

Journaling: After meditating on each of the eight Cs, take some time to journal about your reflections. This can help consolidate your insights and deepen your connection to these qualities of the Self.

Daily Reminder: Choose one of the eight Cs that resonated most with you during this exercise. Set an intention to carry this quality with you throughout the day, reminding yourself of it in moments of stress or disconnection.

Reflection at Day's End: Before going to bed, reflect on how the day's focus on the chosen C influenced your interactions with yourself and the world. What did you notice? How did it feel to embody this quality?

By dedicating time to understand and embody the eight Cs, you begin to forge a stronger connection with yourself, laying a solid foundation for the work ahead in navigating and harmonizing your internal family system. This initial step is essential for creating an internal environment conducive to healing and growth.

Week 5 Day 2

Objective: to deepen your connection with the Self and differentiate it from your parts. This exercise uses visualization to explore self-energy, facilitating understanding and embodying the core qualities of the Self. Here are the expanded and detailed instructions for this transformative exercise:

Detailed Instructions:

1. **Preparation**: Choose a time and place where you are least likely to be interrupted. Create a comfortable and soothing environment, perhaps by dimming the lights, sitting in a comfortable chair, or lying in a peaceful spot. Close your eyes to minimize external distractions.

2. **Breathing and Centering**: Begin with several deep, slow breaths to center yourself. With each inhale, visualize drawing in calm and clarity; imagine releasing tension and distractions with each exhale. Allow yourself to reach a state of relaxed alertness.

3. **Visualization of the Path**: In your mind's eye, imagine standing at the beginning of a path. This path represents your journey of deeper self-awareness and healing. Notice the details of this path —the texture underfoot, the surrounding landscape, the quality of light—and allow a sense of curiosity to emerge.

4. **Meeting Your Parts**: As you reach the path's onset, envision your parts gathering around you. These might include Managers, Firefighters, and Exiles, each with unique energies and emotions. Acknowledge their presence and express your intention to explore the path of self-discovery, asking them to support you by staying here as you proceed alone.

5. **Observing Parts' Reactions**: Consider how your parts react to your request. Some may express fear or reluctance, worried about what you might encounter without their protection. Reassure them that this journey is necessary for growth and healing; their cooperation is invaluable. If any part is particularly resistant, it's okay to pause and acknowledge that today might not be the day to proceed. There's always another opportunity.

6. **Walking the Path**: If you feel ready and your parts will let you proceed, begin walking the path. With each step, visualize yourself moving deeper into a state of pure awareness, where thoughts and parts do not define your experience. Notice any shifts in your internal landscape as you distance yourself from the parts.

7. **Experiencing Self-Energy**: As you advance, allow yourself to embody the qualities of the Self—clarity, calm, compassion, and connectedness. Feel yourself becoming lighter, more present, and filled with inherent well-being. Invite this energy to saturate your being, filling you from within.

8. **Integration and Return**: When you feel self-energy, pause to savor this experience. What does it feel like to have so much Self present within you? Hold onto this feeling, recognizing it as your natural state, unburdened by the parts. When you're ready, gently bring your focus back to the room, taking slow, grounding breaths.

9. **Reflection**: After completing the exercise, take some time to journal about your experience. What did you notice about your parts? How did the journey affect your relationship with them? How can you carry the sense of Self you discovered into your daily life?

10. **Daily Practice**: Throughout the day, try to recall and embody the qualities of the Self you connected with during the exercise. When you notice parts becoming active, gently remind them of your intention to lead with Self-energy.

This exercise is decisive in cultivating a stronger, more compassionate relationship with yourself and your parts. It encourages the differentiation of the Self from the parts, fostering a sense of inner harmony and balance.

Week 5 Day 3

Objective: engage in the "Fire Drill" exercise, a reflective practice designed to explore and understand the protective parts of your internal system—specifically, your Firefighters. This exercise helps to identify the triggers that activate these parts and practice calming and reassuring them, enhancing self-leadership, and fostering a deeper connection between the Self and protective parts. Here are expanded and detailed instructions for this insightful exercise:

Detailed Instructions, *The Fire Drill Exercise:*

1. **Preparation for Reflection**:
   - Choose a quiet, comfortable place where you feel safe and will not be disturbed.
   - Sit or lie down in a relaxed posture. Close your eyes if it feels comfortable, and take a few deep breaths to center yourself.
2. **Identifying a Trigger**:
   - Think of a person from your past or present life who often triggers strong emotional responses in you, such as anger, sadness, or fear. This should be someone who stirs up intense feelings when you think of them or interact with them.
3. **Visualization and Observation**:
   - Imagine this person is in a room they cannot leave, and you are observing them through a one-way mirror. They cannot see you, but you can see them.

- Visualize this person doing or saying things that typically upset you. Pay close attention to your bodily sensations, emotions, and thoughts as this scenario unfolds.

4. **Noticing the Protector's Activation:**
   - Observe the changes in your body and mind as your protective part, the Firefighter activates. You might notice muscle tension, breathing or heart rate changes, and shifts in your emotional state or thought patterns.

5. **Reassuring the Protector:**
   - Now, consciously shift your perspective to view the person through the eyes of your protector part. Recognize and acknowledge the protective intentions of this part.
   - Mentally reassure your protector that you are safe and do not need to engage or confront the person in the room. Ask the protector if it is willing to step aside or relax its protective stance.

6. **Reflecting on Changes:**
   - After asking the protector to relax, notice changes in your physical sensations, emotions, and thoughts. Observe the person in the room again. Do they appear different to you now? How does your body respond?

7. **Exploring the Possibility of Self-Leadership:**
   - Consider how it might feel to interact with the person in the room led by the Self rather than the protector. Can you approach the situation with curiosity, calm, and compassion?
   - Ask the protector if it can begin to trust the leadership of the Self. If the protector hesitates, inquire about its concerns or needs.

8. **Expressing Gratitude and Returning:**
   - Whether or not the protector steps aside, thank it for its protective efforts and the new trust it places in you.
   - Take a few deep breaths to ground yourself and gently open your eyes, returning your focus to your surroundings.

9. **Journaling and Reflection**:
   - Write about your experience with the "Fire Drill" exercise. Reflect on the interaction between your protector and the Self. What did you learn about your protector's intentions and fears? How can you apply these insights to future interactions with triggering situations?

10. **Practice and Integration**:
    - Throughout the day, when you notice emotional triggers or protective responses arising, pause and recall the insights from this exercise. Practice engaging the Self to lead with curiosity, calm, and compassion, aiming to integrate this approach into your daily life.

This exercise is a powerful tool for gaining insight into the dynamics between your protective parts and the Self. Practicing it regularly can enhance your ability to navigate emotional triggers with greater self-awareness and resilience, fostering a sense of inner peace and well-being.

Week 5 Day 4

Objective: Conduct a detailed mapping of your internal system on Day 4, exploring the various parts within, their roles, qualities, and interactions with each other and the Self, to enhance understanding of your internal world, and promote self-awareness and healing.

Instructions, *Mapping Your Internal System:*

1. **Preparation for Mapping**:
   - Find a quiet and comfortable space where you can reflect without interruptions.
   - Gather materials you might need, such as paper, colored pens or pencils, and markers.
   - Take a few deep breaths to center yourself, approaching this exercise with an open heart and mind.

2. **Introduction to Parts Mapping**:
   - Begin by reminding yourself of the concept of parts within the IFS model: Managers, Firefighters, and Exiles, along with the qualities of the Self.
   - Reflect on the notion that each part has a positive intention and that understanding these parts can lead to greater self-compassion and healing.

3. **Drawing the Map**:
   - Start by drawing a circle in the center of your paper. This represents your Self, the core of being characterized by calmness, curiosity, compassion, and clarity.
   - Around the Self, begin to draw other circles or shapes representing your different parts. You might want to use

different colors to distinguish between Managers, Fire-fighters, and Exiles.
- As you identify a part, label it based on its role or the emotion it carries (e.g., "Protector," "Critic," "Insecure One").

4. **Exploring Relationships**:
- Draw lines connecting the parts to the Self and each other. Use arrows to indicate the direction of influence or protection.
- Notice any clusters that form—these may represent parts that frequently work together or conflict with each other.

5. **Adding Details**:
- Within or next to each part, jot down key attributes, feelings, or memories associated with them. You might also note what triggers each part to become active.
- If you sense any parts are particularly linked to certain life events or developmental stages, include this information to deepen your understanding.

6. **Reflecting on the Map**:
- Once your map feels complete for now, take a step back. Reflect on what you see. Are there parts that surprised you? Parts that seem to have a stronger influence than you realized?
- Consider how the Self relates to each part. Are there parts that seem distant from the Self? Parts that the Self might reach out to with curiosity and compassion?

7. **Journaling and Integration**:
- After completing your map, spend some time journaling about the process. What did you learn about your internal system? How might this awareness influence your approach to self-care and healing?
- Think about ways to foster a more harmonious relationship between the Self and the parts. This might include setting intentions to listen more closely to certain parts or practicing self-compassion when difficult emotions arise.

8. **Ongoing Exploration**:
   ○ Keep your map in a place where you can revisit it. As you continue your journey with IFS, you may discover new parts or find that the roles of existing parts shift. Update your map accordingly to reflect your evolving internal landscape.

This mapping exercise is a dynamic tool for self-exploration and healing. It not only aids in visualizing the complex system of parts within you but also serves as a stepping stone for greater self-awareness, self-compassion, and integration.

Week 5 Day 5

Objective: Engage with and begin the unburdening process for your Exiles, facilitating their expression of stories and the release of heavy emotional burdens in a safe and supportive environment, to foster healing and protection of the psyche.

Instructions, *Connecting with and Unburdening Vulnerable Parts*:

1. **Preparation**:
   - Choose a quiet, comfortable space where you feel safe and won't be disturbed.
   - Have your journal or any other form of note-taking tool ready for reflections and insights that may arise.
   - Begin with a few deep breaths, grounding yourself in the present moment, and invite a sense of calm and openness.

2. **Setting an Intention**:
   - Set a clear, compassionate intention for this exercise. You might silently affirm, "I approach my vulnerable parts with kindness, curiosity, and an open heart, ready to listen and heal."

3. **Identifying an Exile**:
   - Reflect on recent times when you felt overwhelmed, distressed, or unusually reactive. These feelings might uncover an active Exile.
   - Gently inquire within, "Which part of me needs attention right now?" Allow any sensations, emotions, or images to surface naturally.

4. **Approaching with Curiosity**:

- Once you identify an Exile, approach it with the curiosity of the Self. Ask this part if it would be willing to share with you: What does it feel? What does it believe? What does it need?

5. **Listening and Validating**:
   - Listen deeply to what the Exile shares, validating its experiences and emotions without trying to change or fix anything immediately. Acknowledge the pain or fear it holds with phrases like, "I see you" or "I hear how hard this has been for you."

6. **Exploring the Burden**:
   - Ask the Exile about the burden it carries. This might involve pain, negative beliefs about itself or the world, or traumatic memories. Note these burdens with compassion, understanding they've been carried in an attempt to protect you.

7. **Offering Reassurance**:
   - Offer reassurance to this part. Let it know that you, as the Self, are here now to help carry its burdens and that it's not alone anymore. Encourage a dialogue about what it needs to feel relieved or lighter.

8. **Visualization of Unburdening**:
   - Invite the Exile to visualize releasing its burdens in a safe and healing way. This could be imagined as placing heavy loads down, washing away pain in a stream, or even transforming the burden into light.

9. **Integrating Insights**:
   - Reflect on the exercise and any new understandings or shifts in feelings about the Exile. How might this part's relief from its burdens change its role within your internal system?

10. **Journaling and Commitment**:

○ Journal about the experience, focusing on insights gained, emotions felt, and any commitments you want to make to this Exile moving forward. This might include more regular check-ins or specific actions to honor its needs and contributions to yourself.

11. **Closing with Gratitude**:
   ○ Close the session by expressing gratitude for the Exile's strength and survival. Acknowledge your courage in engaging with vulnerable parts of yourself.

This exercise is a courageous step, as it allows Exiles to be seen, heard, and relieved of their burdens, often for many years. Remember, this process can evoke strong emotions and should be approached with care, patience, and readiness. If the exercise feels overwhelming, it's okay to pause and seek support from a therapist or trusted person.

Week 5 Day 6

Objective: Cultivate self-compassion, focusing on kindness, understanding, and supportive self-care towards internal parts carrying pain, fear, or shame, to create a nurturing internal environment conducive to healing.

Instructions, *Cultivating Self-Compassion*:

1. **Setting the Stage for Self-Compassion**:
   - Find a quiet, comfortable space where you feel secure and won't be interrupted. Consider creating a nurturing ambiance, perhaps with soft lighting or calming music.
   - Start with a few minutes of deep, grounding breaths to center yourself in the present moment, preparing your heart and mind for self-compassion work.

2. **Guided Self-Compassion Meditation**:
   - Begin by recalling a situation that is causing you distress or pain. Approach this recall with gentleness, ensuring that you do not overwhelm yourself.
   - Acknowledge the discomfort or pain you're feeling. Allow yourself to notice where you might be holding this emotional pain in your body.
   - Now, consciously send compassionate thoughts to this part of yourself. You might use phrases like, "May I be kind to myself in this moment," or "May I give myself the compassion I need."

3. **Writing a Letter to Yourself**:
   - From a place of compassion, write a letter to yourself about the current challenge or pain you're experiencing. Write

this letter from the perspective of a wise, understanding, and compassionate friend.

- In your letter, acknowledge your suffering, validate your feelings, and express kindness and support for yourself.

4. **Practicing Mindful Self-Compassion**:
   - Engage in a mindfulness practice where you observe your thoughts and feelings without judgment. As you notice critical or harsh thoughts, gently remind yourself of your intention to be compassionate.
   - Each time you encounter a judgmental thought, replace it with a compassionate response or simply observe it with kindness and let it go.

5. **Cultivating Compassion through Visualization**:
   - Visualize a being (real or imagined) that embodies unconditional love and compassion. Imagine this being sending you love and kindness, filling you with a sense of warmth, safety, and acceptance.
   - Absorb this compassion into every part of your body and being, especially directing it towards parts that feel unworthy or in pain.

6. **Implementing Self-Compassion in Daily Life**:
   - Identify one action you can take to express self-compassion in your daily life. This could be as simple as taking a few moments to breathe deeply when you notice stress or treating yourself to a nurturing experience like a warm bath or a stroll through nature.

7. **Reflecting on Your Experience**:
   - After completing these exercises, take some time to reflect on what you noticed and how it felt to actively cultivate self-compassion. Journal about your experiences, insights, and any shifts in how you relate to yourself.

8. **Commitment to Ongoing Practice**:

○ Conclude Day 6 by setting an intention to continue practicing self-compassion. Remember that, like any skill, self-compassion grows stronger with practice and patience.

This day's work is about nurturing a compassionate relationship with all parts of yourself, recognizing that self-compassion is not a one-time effort but an ongoing practice. By dedicating time to cultivating self-compassion, you lay a foundational stone in your healing pathway, empowering you to meet your parts with kindness and understanding.

Week 5 Day 7

Objective: to integrate the week's learnings and experiences, focusing on integration and forward movement. This day is about consolidating the self-discovery and healing work you've embarked on, recognizing the shifts within your internal system, and setting intentions for continued growth. Here's how to expand on this final day's activities for a comprehensive wrap-up:

Instructions, *Integration and Moving Forward*:

1. **Review and Reflection:**
   - Review your journal entries, notes, or reflections from the past six days. Pay particular attention to any insights, shifts in perspectives, or significant moments of connection with your parts.
   - Reflect on how your understanding of your internal family system—comprising Managers, Firefighters, Exiles, and the Self—has evolved. Consider how your relationship with these parts has changed through the week.

2. **Mindful Acknowledgment:**
   - Engage in a quiet, contemplative practice to mindfully acknowledge each part you've interacted with over the week. You might visualize sitting in a circle with these parts, thanking each one for what it has shared or for the role it plays in your life.
   - Acknowledge the Self's leadership in this process and its growing capacity to bring healing and harmony to your internal system.

3. **Creating a Vision for the Future:**

- With a clear understanding of your internal dynamics, envision how you'd like your internal family system to operate moving forward. What role do you wish the Self to play? How do you see your parts interacting with each other and the Self?
- Write a vision statement or create a visual representation (e.g., a drawing or collage) that encapsulates your intentions for self-discovery and healing.

4. **Setting Intentions**:
   - Based on your reflections and vision for the future, set specific, actionable intentions for how you will continue to nurture the relationship between the Self and your parts. These might include regular check-ins with your parts, practicing self-compassion daily, or continuing to explore IFS through reading, courses, or therapy.
   - Write these intentions down in a place where you can revisit them regularly, reminding yourself of your commitment to your healing process.

5. **Developing a Practice Plan**:
   - Develop a practical plan for integrating the insights and practices from this week into your daily life. This could include scheduling time for meditation, journaling, or other IFS exercises that you found particularly beneficial.
   - Consider how you can create supportive environments and routines that facilitate ongoing self-exploration and healing.

6. **Celebration and Gratitude**:
   - Take time to celebrate your work this week, recognizing the courage, openness, and effort it has taken to engage so deeply with yourself.
   - Express self-gratitude for undertaking this journey and for any support (people, resources, or practices) that have assisted you along the way.

7. **Closing Ritual**:

○ Conclude Day 7 with a closing ritual that signifies the end of this intensive week and the beginning of your continued journey. This could be a simple meditation, lighting a candle, or spending time in nature—anything that feels meaningful and grounding.

This comprehensive approach to Day 7 helps solidify the week's work and sets a foundation for ongoing growth and healing. Remember, integrating IFS into your life is ongoing, and each day offers new opportunities for self-discovery and inner harmony.

Bridge Week 5

As this week wraps up, take a moment to check in with yourself and your journey across the bridge. Envision where you've reached, consider the strides you've made, acknowledge any emotions you've encountered, and maintain a hopeful gaze toward the future. Please update your position on the bridge to reflect your current state, using this exercise to honor your progress and resilience.

11

Problem-Solving & Solution-Focused Therapy

Entering Week 6 of the self-help guide, we venture into the therapeutic practices of Problem-Solving Therapy (PST) and Solution-Focused Therapy (SFT). This phase of our guide introduces techniques designed not merely for coping but for actively disarming the complexities that fuel our depression. We will focus on actionable strategies that will help to clear the fog of depression.

This week marks a transition from understanding and acceptance to action and change. PST and SFT are our tools for this shift. They offer a dual approach to confronting mental health challenges. With PST, we adopt a structured methodology to dissect our problems, identifying their core and systematically exploring potential solutions. It teaches us to transform our obstacles into manageable tasks, each with a solution waiting to be discovered. Meanwhile, SFT shifts our gaze to be future-focused, encouraging us to envision a life beyond current struggles. It asks us to define what we wish to achieve and to recognize the resources and strengths we already possess to make these aspirations a reality.

The synergy of PST and SFT is profound. Together, they equip us with the means to navigate life's turbulent waters with resilience. This week we will learn to solve problems by focusing on solutions and changing our relationship with challenges. By understanding that we can alter our circumstances, or at least our perspective on them, we begin to see that depression, though formidable, is not insurmountable.

As we begin, let's approach this week with openness and readiness to engage with the tools and exercises provided. This is an invitation to recognize your ability in shaping your journey through, and ultimately beyond, depression. Let's explore these therapies as more than just methods for managing depression—they are pathways to a life defined not by struggles but by strength and resilience.

Problem-Solving Therapy

With Problem-Solving Therapy (PST), we transform our approach to life's challenges and the depression that comes from these struggles. This therapy equips us with a methodical approach, encouraging us to view our problems not as unconquerable monsters but as puzzles that can be solved with patience and strategy. Through PST, we learn to dissect these puzzles, understand their makeup, and approach them with a curiosity that leads to discovery and resolution.

Imagine standing at the edge of a thick forest—the forest representing the problem that clouds life with depression. The dense foliage and dark shadows may seem daunting, but equipped with the tools of PST, you begin to see a path through the thicket. You start by identifying the nature of the forest; what type of trees are these? What creatures live here? Problem-solving therapy prompts us to clearly defining the issue at hand—understanding its boundaries, essence, and its impacts.

With the problem defined, we consider the ways through the forest. Could you find a path that has already been made, or do you need to create a new one? Perhaps there's a way to go around the forest altogether. This stage mirrors the process of brainstorming potential solutions, where all ideas are welcome. The aim here is not to judge or limit your options but to imagine all possible routes that could lead you out of the forest.

Next, you evaluate each potential option. Some may be too difficult, others may take too long, and a few might offer the right balance of challenge and achievability. This is about assessing the feasibility and potential outcomes of each solution you've brainstormed. It involves weighing the pros and cons, considering your resources, and ultimately selecting the most promising path.

With a chosen path, you begin your trek through the forest. This is when you put your solution into action. You move forward with intention, prepared for possible obstacles, and ready to adapt your strategy. Just as a traveler in the forest keeps an eye on the compass and tracks progress, you also monitor how well your chosen solution works, ready to adjust your course if you find it leading you astray.

Upon emerging from the forest, you take a moment to reflect on the journey. Did this path lead you out as you had hoped? What lessons did you learn along the way? This reflection is crucial in PST, allowing you to evaluate the outcome of your problem-solving efforts. If the problem persists, consider what adjustments could be made or whether a different path might offer a better solution.

Problem-solving therapy teaches us that solving problems is a dynamic, ongoing process. It's about engaging with our problems constructively and methodically, leveraging our creativity, and learning from each step we take. This approach not only helps us navigate the immediate challenges that contribute to our depression but also strengthens our overall resilience, preparing us for whatever forests lie ahead on our journey through life.

Solution Focused Therapy

Solution-Focused Therapy (SFT) operates on a principle distinctly different from many traditional therapy models. It encourages individuals to envisage a future free from the constraints of their current issues, focusing specifically on the strengths and resources they already possess. This therapeutic approach doesn't dwell on the origins and causes of depression; instead, it encourages identifying and achieving a state of well-being through practical, forward-looking strategies.

At the heart of SFT is recognizing an individual's inherent abilities and past successes. The therapy asserts that every person has at their disposal a set of tools and experiences that, when correctly identified and utilized, can significantly aid in navigating out of depressive states. The process involves carefully examining those moments in life where the individual felt more capable or successfully navigated challenges. These reflections are not casual reminiscences but are instrumental in constructing a robust foundation for future action.

Applying the *Miracle Question* within SFT is a powerful technique to facilitate this forward-looking perspective. The *Miracle Question* asks individuals to imagine themselves in transformed life. A life where the issues of today no longer exist. This opens up a dialogue about desires, hopes, and possible realities. This question is designed to shift focus from present difficulties to future possibilities, encouraging a detailed exploration of what changes would look like and how they might be achieved.

Furthermore, SFT employs scaling questions to evaluate and monitor progress. These questions help individuals assess their feelings, motivations, and confidence levels regarding their ability to manage depression and make desired changes. By regularly examining where one stands on a scale from one to ten in various aspects of their emotional and psychological well-being, individuals can gain insights into their progress and identify areas requiring more focused attention.

SMART Goals: Setting SMART goals is integral to translating the envisioned future into reality. In SFT, goals are formulated to be specific, measurable, achievable, relevant, and time-bound. This approach ensures that objectives are clear and actionable, providing structured pathways for achieving the desired state of well-being. Each goal is a step in the process, carefully designed to be attainable and directly contribute to overcoming the challenges posed by depression.

In practice, SFT's emphasis on building upon existing strengths and setting clear, attainable goals offers a highly effective framework for individuals seeking to emerge from the shadow of depression. It fosters a sense of empowerment and agency, highlighting the capacity for change and the attainability of a future marked by improved mental health and emotional resilience. Through SFT, individuals learn to navigate their journey, focusing on solutions and outcomes. They are equipped with practical tools and a clear direction for achieving a life defined not by depression but by their strengths and aspirations.

The integration of SMART goals within Problem-Solving Therapy (PST) and Solution-Focused Therapy (SFT) provides a structured and efficient framework for addressing depression. By aligning the pragmatic aspects of PST and the forward-thinking nature of SFT with SMART goal-setting, individuals are empowered to navigate their journey out of depression with clarity and purpose.

SMART goals—Specific, Measurable, Achievable, Relevant, and Time-bound—serve as a bridge between the problem-oriented focus of PST and the outcome-oriented focus of SFT. This synergy allows for a comprehensive approach to managing depression, combining the identification and resolution of problems with the pursuit of a positive future state.

For instance, in PST, an individual might identify "improving daily mood" as a general aim. However, to apply a SMART framework, this goal is refined to be specific ("Spend at least 30 minutes outside in daylight to improve my mood"), measurable ("Track my mood daily on a scale of 1 to 10"), achievable (choosing an activity that is easily accessible), relevant (directly impacting mood and well-being), and time-bound ("For the next two weeks"). This detailed goal-setting enhances the individual's ability to tackle the aspects of life contributing to depression effectively.

Similarly, in SFT, where the focus is on envisioning a preferred future, SMART goals help break down this vision into actionable steps. If the imagined future includes "feeling more connected to others," a SMART goal might be to "Initiate one conversation per day with a friend or family member over the next month." This goal aligns with the broader objective, providing a structured path.

The application of SMART goals in both PST and SFT encourages a proactive and structured approach to managing depression. It transforms vague aspirations into tangible actions, enhancing the sense of control and efficacy. This approach not only supports individuals in dealing with current challenges but also equips them with the skills to manage future hurdles, fostering resilience and a sustained sense of achievement.

By meticulously detailing each goal's 'what,' 'how,' and 'why,' individuals are better positioned to recognize progress, adjust strategies as needed, and maintain motivation throughout their therapeutic journey. Using SMART goals in conjunction with PST and SFT exemplifies a holistic approach to depression management, where problem-solving and future-oriented strategies converge to facilitate meaningful, long-term change.

The art of problem-solving, coupled with a solutions-focused outlook, transcends mere coping mechanisms for depression; it lays the groundwork for a life characterized by resilience, purpose, and fulfillment. Every step forward, no matter how modest, signifies moment toward reclaiming life from the shadows of depression. Applaud your inherent strength and the tangible progress you're capable of achieving.

Moving forward, the next seven days will focus on integrating the skills learned this week into your daily activities. You'll be provided with exercises to practice problem-solving and solution-focused techniques on actual challenges. Each day, you'll work on breaking down a challenge into manageable parts using Problem-Solving Therapy (PST) and envisioning a future without these challenges through Solution-Focused Therapy (SFT), setting SMART goals to achieve desired outcomes.

This period is crucial for applying what you've learned, reflecting on your progress, and fine-tuning your strategies. Active participation in these exercises will solidify your understanding of PST and SFT, enabling you to take practical steps towards change.

Embrace the tools and strengths you've developed, and approach each task with openness and commitment. Progress toward overcoming depression is gradual. Each day's effort is a step towards gaining control over your narrative, leading to a life marked by determination, resilience, and optimism.

Week 6 Self-Help Guide

Looking ahead, we introduce a seven-day homework guide, a continuation of our commitment to embedding the principles of PST, SFT, and SMART goal-setting into the fabric of your daily life. This guide reinforces the skills and insights gained this week, providing structured exercises and reflections further to solidify understanding and application of these transformative strategies.

Week 6 Day 1

Objective: Apply the Problem-Solving Therapy (PST) framework to tackle a specific life challenge, enhance your problem-solving skills, and foster a growth mindset.

Information: Problem-Solving Therapy (PST) offers a structured approach to addressing challenges. By engaging in this exercise, you'll learn to navigate difficulties more effectively, reducing stress and depressive feelings associated with unresolved issues.

Instructions:

1. **Identify the Challenge**: Begin by writing a detailed description of a recent challenge or problem in your life in your journal. Capture the essence of why this issue is a significant source of stress or depression for you.
2. **Brainstorm Solutions**: List all possible solutions you can think of without assessing feasibility. Aim for creativity and openness to different perspectives. This process is about expanding your problem-solving toolkit.
3. **Evaluate Solutions**: For each solution, critically assess its practicality, potential benefits, and drawbacks. Consider how each solution aligns with your current circumstances and well-being goals. This step involves critical thinking to identify the most viable option.
4. **Plan Implementation**: Choose the most promising solution and develop a detailed plan for its implementation. Include specific actions necessary resources, and anticipate potential

obstacles. Approach this with realism, preparing for challenges that may arise.

5. **Reflect on the Outcome**: After implementing your solution, reflect on its effectiveness. Write about whether it met your expectations, what you learned, and how you could adjust your strategy in the future. This reflection enhances your problem-solving capabilities and resilience.

Reflection: Encourage reflection and journaling on the process, focusing on what you learned about your problem-solving skills and how you can apply these insights to future challenges.

Integration: Discuss and encourage ongoing integration of the PST framework into daily life, emphasizing its value in viewing challenges as opportunities for growth and learning.

Week 6 Day 2

Objective: Utilize Solution-Focused Therapy (SFT) to envision a future beyond current challenges, fostering hope and outlining steps to achieving this future.

Information: Solution-Focused Therapy (SFT) is an approach that emphasizes envisioning one's desired future and mapping out practical steps to achieve it. This exercise aims to cultivate optimism and a sense of agency by focusing on potential rather than problems.

Instructions:

1. **Envision Your Future**: Dedicate time to vividly imagine a future where you've overcome a current challenge that contributes to your feelings of depression. In your journal, describe this future in detail, focusing on how your life would differ, the emotions you would feel, the activities you would engage in, and any changes in your daily life.

2. **The Miracle Question**: Engage with the "Miracle Question" to deepen your reflection. Imagine waking up tomorrow to find the challenge resolved. What would be the first sign that things have changed? Reflect on how your interactions with others would differ, activities you'd do more or less, and how you would view yourself.

3. **Identify Steps Toward Your Future**: Reflect on small, concrete actions that can move you closer to this envisioned future. Consider your current strengths and resources that can aid in achieving this vision.

4. **Set a SMART Goal**: To make your envisioned future more tangible, set a Specific, Measurable, Attainable, Relevant, and Time-bound (SMART) goal related to this vision. Detail what you aim to achieve and how you'll measure progress, ensure it's achievable, confirm it aligns with your values, and set a realistic timeframe for accomplishment.

5. **Document Your Vision and Steps**: Writing down your envisioned future and the steps to reach it is a powerful motivational tool that reminds you of your capacity to change.

Reflection: Encourage reflecting on this exercise in your journal, focusing on the sense of hope and agency it brings. Reflect on the importance of believing in your ability to enact change and improve your well-being.

Integration: Discuss and encourage the integration of SFT principles into daily life. Highlight how adopting a solution-focused mindset can inspire a proactive approach to challenges, reinforcing the belief in personal growth and the possibility of change.

Week 6 Day 3

Objective: Create a SMART goal focused on an aspect of your life that significantly influences your mood and overall well-being, aiming to turn intention into actionable improvement.

Information: SMART goals are a structured approach to setting objectives that are Specific, Measurable, Achievable, Relevant, and Time-bound. This methodology helps make aspirations more concrete, actionable, and aligned with your mental health improvement efforts.

Instructions:

1. **Identify an Impactful Area**: Choose an area you want to improve that directly affects your emotional state. This could be enhancing physical activity, social interactions, or dedicating time to a hobby. Be specific in your choice to ensure clarity.
2. **Formulate Your SMART Goal:**
    - **Specific**: Clearly define what you aim to achieve. For example, a specific goal might be to increase physical activity for mood improvement, "I will walk for 30 minutes in the park three times a week."
    - **Measurable**: Add parameters to track progress, such as the activity's duration (30 minutes) and frequency (three times a week).
    - **Achievable**: Ensure the goal fits your current physical, mental, and lifestyle constraints. It should be realistic and attainable.

- **Relevant**: The goal should align with your broader mental health improvement objectives. Choose activities that you enjoy or find meaningful.
- **Time-bound**: Set a deadline or timeframe for achieving your goal, such as maintaining this routine for one month, to encourage accountability and evaluation.
3. **Document Your Goal**: Record your SMART goal in your journal, outlining each aspect and the steps you plan to take. This documentation is a commitment to yourself and a plan of action.
4. **Regular Reflection**: Plan regular check-ins to reflect on your progress, making any necessary adjustments to stay on course. This process is vital for accountability and adapting to challenges.

Reflection: Encourage reflection on setting and working with your SMART goal in your journal. Focus on how this structured approach enhances motivation, discipline, and achievement.

Integration: Discuss how integrating SMART goal-setting into your daily life can impact your mental health. Highlight the importance of turning intentions into actions and how this discipline contributes to navigating out of depression.

Week 6 Day 4

Objective: Employ introspection and scaling questions to evaluate your progress in managing depression, sustain progress, and adapt strategies effectively.

Information: Introspection and assessment are vital components of the therapeutic journey, providing insights into your current state and areas for improvement. Scaling questions are a helpful tool for evaluating progress and determining actionable steps.

Instructions:

1. **Identify Key Areas**: Select key aspects related to your mental health and well-being you have been focusing on, such as mood management, coping strategies, or social interactions.
2. **Formulate Scaling Questions**: For each identified area, create a scaling question that helps assess your progress or current status on a scale of 1 to 10. Example questions could include, "How effective have my coping strategies been in reducing my feelings of anxiety this week?" or "How supported do I feel by my social network?"
3. **Reflect and Score**: Reflect on each question and assign a numerical value to your answer. Delve into why you chose this score, considering what factors contribute to it and how it might be improved.
4. **Identify an Improvement Area**: Choose one area you believe is crucial to improve in the short term. Set a small, achievable goal to increase your score in this selected area for the next week.

5. **Document Your Reflections and Goal**: In your journal, record your scores, the reasoning behind them, and improvement goal. This process enhances self-awareness and guides the action steps.

Reflection: Encourage deep reflection on this process, focusing on the insights gained through scoring and how they inform your understanding of your current state and areas for improvement.

Integration: Discuss how regular use of introspection and scaling questions can be integrated into your daily routine to continuously assess and adapt your strategies for managing depression. Highlight the importance of this dynamic approach in responding to evolving needs and circumstances, underlining the fundamental role of self-evaluation in progressing on your therapeutic journey.

Week 6 Day 5

Objective: Identify and integrate an underutilized personal strength or external resource into your strategy for overcoming depression, aiming to deepen self-awareness and enhance coping mechanisms.

Information: Recognizing and leveraging personal strengths and resources can significantly impact your journey out of depression. This exercise focuses on uncovering capabilities or supports that have not been fully utilized, understanding their potential in managing depression, and integrating them into your daily life.

Instructions:

1. **Identify an Unexplored Strength or Resource**: Reflect on your personal traits, skills, or external supports that you might not have fully leveraged against depression. This could be anything from resilience, empathy, creative talents, or a supportive relationship.
2. **Assess Its Application**: Consider how this identified strength or resource can be effectively applied to manage your depression more effectively. If creativity is your strength, explore how creative expressions like painting, writing, or music can be therapeutic.
3. **Formulate an Integration Plan**: To incorporate this strength or resource into your daily routine or coping strategies. Include specific, actionable steps that are achievable and fit into your current lifestyle. For example, dedicating 30 minutes daily to a chosen creative activity.

4. **Set a SMART Goal**: Establish a SMART (Specific, Measurable, Achievable, Relevant, Time-bound) goal related to using this strength or resource. An example goal could be: "To harness my creativity as a coping mechanism, I will engage in a creative activity for 30 minutes daily over the next two weeks."
5. **Document and Reflect**: In your journal, note your chosen strength or resource, your plan for its integration, and your SMART goal. Reflect on how this process enhances your overall strategy for managing depression, fostering a sense of empowerment and self-efficacy.

Reflection: Encourage journaling on the discovery and planning process, emphasizing the newfound understanding of your capabilities and their potential impact on your mental health and well-being.

Integration: Discuss the importance of regularly revisiting and re-assessing your strengths and resources as part of your ongoing strategy for managing depression. This practice promotes self-awareness and ensures a dynamic, personalized approach to coping and recovery.

Week 6 Day 6

Objective: Evaluate and potentially adjust the SMART goal earlier, emphasizing adaptability and resilience in managing depression.

Information: Setting, pursuing, and reviewing goals is dynamic. Reflecting on your progress with your SMART goal and making necessary adjustments is crucial for maintaining momentum and ensuring the goal remains aligned with your needs and circumstances.

Instructions:

1. **Review Your SMART Goal**: Reflect on the specific SMART goal you set earlier in the week. Consider the actions you've taken thus far and the outcomes observed. Approach this review with honesty, compassion, and recognition of your efforts and any challenges you have encountered.
2. **Reflect on Key Questions**:
    - What steps have I successfully taken?
    - What obstacles or challenges have I faced?
    - How have these challenges impacted my progress?
    - What insights have I gained about myself and my coping strategies?
3. **Decide on Adjustments**: Based on your reflection, determine if any changes to your goal or approach are needed. If obstacles have arisen, brainstorm alternative strategies to address them. Adjustments might include changing the frequency, type of activity, or any other aspect to make your goal more attainable and relevant.

4. **Document Adjustments**: In your journal, record your reflections and any decisions to adjust your goal. If revising your goal, ensure it remains Specific, Measurable, Achievable, Relevant, and Time-bound (SMART). Set a new timeframe to reinvigorate your motivation and commitment.
5. **Outline a Revised Action Plan**: If adjustments are made, draft a revised plan detailing your adjusted steps. This plan should account for the insights gained and any new strategies you intend to implement.

Reflection: Encourage deep reflection on this evaluative process in your journal, focusing on the learning opportunities it presents and how it contributes to your adaptability and resilience.

Integration: Highlight the importance of flexibility in managing depression. Regularly reviewing and adjusting goals supports current well-being and enhances your long-term strategy for a balanced and fulfilling life. This practice demonstrates a commitment to continuous self-improvement and developing coping strategies responsive to your evolving needs.

Week 6 Day 7

Objective: Conduct a thorough review of the past week's journal entries to consolidate learning, identify patterns, and plan future steps in managing depression.

Information: Reflecting on your journal entries provides valuable insights into your thoughts, behaviors, and progress. This exercise aims to highlight recurring themes, assess the strategies' effectiveness, and set the stage for continuous improvement in managing depression.

Instructions:

1. **Review Journal Entries**: Start with Day 1 and carefully read each day's reflections, observations, and goals. Pay attention to recurring themes, challenges faced, and any progress made.
2. **Assess Progress and Challenges**: Reflect on your progress toward your SMART goals. Consider the factors contributing to your success or obstacles hindering your progress, viewing these as learning opportunities rather than failures.
3. **Identify Key Insights**: From the week's exercises, pinpoint at least one significant insight or lesson learned. This could be a beneficial coping strategy, a personal strength you effectively utilized, or an area for potential growth.
4. **Set New Goals for the Coming Week**: Based on this week's reflections and insights, establish one or two new SMART goals for the next week. These goals should build on your current progress and insights, enhancing your problem-solving and solution-focused capabilities.

5. **Document Your Reflections and Goals**: Write down your comprehensive review, the key insights you've identified, and your goals for the upcoming week in your journal. This acts as a reflective exercise and a roadmap for your continued Depression-Free journey.

Reflection: Encourage deep reflection on the entire week's experiences, emphasizing the importance of recognizing patterns, learning from challenges, and acknowledging progress.

Integration: Discuss the importance of integrating the insights and strategies from this week into your ongoing approach to managing depression. Highlight how regular reflection and goal setting can boost self-awareness, personal growth, and sustained progress.

Bridge Week 6

At the end of this week, give yourself a moment to touch base with your progress on the bridge. Visualize your current position, reflect on the week's experiences, hold space for your emotions, and look forward with optimism. Record your spot on the bridge, allowing this act to serve as both recognition and celebration of your journey thus far. This consistent practice helps chart your path toward a brighter, depression-free future.

12

Psychodynamic Therapy

Psychodynamic therapy brings us into the depths of the human mind. It is the enduring legacy of Freudian theory. Since its origins in the early 20th century, this therapeutic approach has evolved remarkably, seamlessly integrating modern psychological insights with its foundational principles. Its essence lies in the understanding that our present selves are inextricably linked to our pasts. The therapy posits that unresolved conflicts, particularly those buried in the unconscious mind from our formative years, cast long shadows over our current emotional and behavioral states. In psychodynamic theory, the symptoms of depression are seen as symptoms of and a manifestation of deep-seated, unresolved issues.

At its core, psychodynamic therapy explores the uncharted territories of the unconscious mind. It is guided by the conviction that by uncovering and confronting these hidden aspects of our psyche, we can achieve an understanding of our depression. This approach seeks to alleviate symptoms and unearth the root causes of our emotional distress, fostering enduring healing and growth.

As we navigate through the complexities of this therapy, it becomes evident that its goals extend beyond immediate relief. Psychodynamic therapy is a holistic journey of self-awareness and self-discovery, challenging individuals to confront deep-seated fears, desires, and conflicts.

It offers a unique lens through which to view our mental health, emphasizing the dynamic interplay between past experiences and present realities.

This evolution from its Freudian origins to a contemporary therapeutic tool underscores a significant shift in how we perceive and treat mental health issues. Psychodynamic therapy represents a bridge between the historical depths of psychoanalytic thought and the cutting-edge of modern psychological practices, maintaining its relevance and efficacy in today's therapeutic landscape. As we delve deeper into this chapter, we will explore the intricate mechanisms of psychodynamic therapy, its application in treating depression, and the transformative journey it facilitates for those brave enough to embark on this path of self-exploration and healing.

Understanding the Unconscious

The unconscious mind is akin to an iceberg's vast, hidden portion beneath the ocean's surface, holding our deepest fears, desires, and memories. These submerged elements shape our actions, feelings, and thoughts in profound, often unrecognized ways. Imagine your mind as a garden, where the seeds of past experiences grow into the behaviors and emotions we exhibit today. Once planted during our early years, these seeds can sprout into patterns that influence our adult lives unexpectedly.

Consider the case of Robert, who always finds himself withdrawing in social situations. Unbeknownst to Robert, this behavior stems from a deep-seated fear of rejection, rooted in a childhood marked by frequent moves and the constant challenge of making new friends. Each attempt at socialization became a potential for disappointment, embedding an aversion for relationships deep within Robert's unconscious mind. As an adult, Robert's unconscious acts as a protective barrier, steering them away from potential social pain but also leading to loneliness and feelings of isolation, which can contribute to depressive states.

Or take Jamie, who is known among friends for their generosity but struggles with feelings of unworthiness and depression. This trait of over-giving might be traced back to Jamie's unconscious belief, formed in early childhood, that they need to earn affection and approval through acts of giving, a belief rooted in their experiences with emotionally distant parents. Without realizing it, Jamie's adult behavior is driven by an unconscious attempt to fulfill a childhood need for love and validation, which, when unmet, exacerbates their depressive feelings.

Psychodynamic therapy helps individuals like Robert and Jamie explore these hidden gardens of their minds, shedding light on the unconscious beliefs and patterns cultivated by past experiences. By bringing these patterns to consciousness, individuals can begin to understand the root causes of their emotional struggles, providing a foundation for healing and change.

Uncovering these unconscious elements is akin to gently excavating around the roots of a tree to understand its growth. It's a delicate journey of self-discovery, guided by the therapeutic relationship, which offers a safe and nurturing space for this exploration. Through this process, individuals can start to untangle the complex interplay between their past experiences and current emotional landscape, paving the way for a deeper understanding of themselves and a more fulfilling life.

Understanding the unconscious is about connecting the dots between our past and present, revealing how hidden memories and unresolved conflicts shape our current selves. By engaging with and integrating these aspects of our unconscious, we can be free from the burdens of the past and become enriched with awareness and emotional resilience.

The Role of Past Experiences

As discussed earlier, psychodynamic therapy suggests a belief in the powerful influence of past relationships and experiences on an individual's current mental and emotional state. This therapeutic approach emphasizes the intricate process of examining these past experiences to uncover their impact on the present. Through the unique and supportive therapist-client relationship, individuals are provided a secure and empathetic environment conducive to this exploration, facilitating profound insights and discoveries.

At its core, psychodynamic therapy seeks to unravel the complex narrative threads woven throughout an individual's life. These threads, comprising past relationships, significant events, and formative experiences, contribute to one's current emotional landscape. By meticulously tracing these threads back to their origins, the therapy helps individuals understand the recurring patterns and themes, shedding light on how these elements shape their feelings, behaviors, and thoughts.

Consider, for example, a person who consistently feels unworthy in their personal and professional relationships. Through the process of psychodynamic therapy, they may discover that this pervasive sense of unworthiness stems from a childhood marked by parental criticism and lack of validation. The treatment would help them see how these early experiences have led to a deeply ingrained belief in their inadequacy, influencing their adult relationships and contributing to feelings of depression.

Similarly, an individual struggling with assertiveness might, through therapy, trace this challenge back to an upbringing where expressing needs or desires was discouraged or met with hostility. Understanding this connection allows the person to recognize the origins of their difficulty with assertiveness, providing a foundation for addressing and transforming this pattern in the present.

The therapist-client relationship plays a crucial role in this exploratory process. It serves as a reflective mirror, offering a safe space to express thoughts and emotions that may have been silenced or ignored. This relationship also models healthy interpersonal dynamics, helping clients learn new ways of relating to others and themselves.

By delving into and understanding these past experiences, psychodynamic therapy illuminates the root causes of current emotional difficulties and empowers individuals to rewrite their stories. It facilitates a shift from being unconsciously driven by the past to consciously shaping the present and future. This journey of discovery and insight can lead to significant emotional healing, fostering a sense of liberation from the constraints of past experiences and opening the door to a more fulfilling life.

In essence, the role of past experiences in psychodynamic therapy is pivotal, both the key to understanding present difficulties and the gateway to emotional growth and change. Through this therapeutic journey, individuals are given the tools to transform their relationship with their past, enabling them to move forward with greater self-awareness, resilience, and emotional well-being.

Mechanisms of Change in Psychodynamic Therapy

Psychodynamic therapy provides a toolkit for navigating the complex landscape of the mind, employing various techniques to facilitate change. These methods aim to bring the unconscious into the conscious, allowing individuals to understand and heal from their emotional wounds. Let's delve deeper into these mechanisms with straightforward examples to illuminate their transformative power.

Imagine a process akin to unlocking a diary that holds the secrets of your mind. *Free association* encourages you to speak whatever comes to mind, no matter how trivial or disconnected it may seem. This technique is like following a trail of breadcrumbs that leads back to your unconscious. For instance, Sarah starts talking about her day at work, meanders through memories of her childhood pet, and reflects on feelings of abandonment. This seemingly random pathway of thoughts can reveal connections between past experiences and current emotional issues, offering insights into the roots of Sarah's anxiety or depression.

Dreams are often considered the window to the unconscious. In *dream analysis*, therapists help you decode the symbolic language of your dreams to uncover hidden desires and fears. Think of it as translating a foreign film into your native language. For example, Tom dreams of being trapped in a maze, unable to find the exit. Through analysis, he realizes the maze represents his feeling trapped in his career, mirroring his fear of making a wrong turn. Recognizing this can be the first step in addressing helplessness and dissatisfaction.

Defense mechanisms are the mind's invisible armor, protecting us from emotional pain and anxiety. However, they can also prevent us from confronting the issues that cause us distress. Identifying and understanding these mechanisms are crucial steps in psychodynamic therapy. For example, Emma frequently uses humor to deflect severe discussions about her feelings, a defense mechanism known as "humor." By recognizing this pattern, Emma and her therapist can work together to explore the painful emotions she's avoiding, paving the way for genuine emotional healing.

Transference occurs when clients project feelings about significant people in their past onto their therapist. *Countertransference* is the therapist's emotional reaction to the client's transference. Consider James, who starts feeling angry with his therapist, similar to his anger toward his father. This projection can uncover unresolved issues with parental figures, offering a pathway to healing. Similarly, a therapist's countertransference can provide valuable insights into the therapy dynamics, further facilitating the therapeutic process.

The *therapeutic alliance* is at the heart of these techniques—the collaborative and trusting relationship between the therapist and the client. This bond is the foundation upon which the journey of self-discovery and healing is built. It's like having a skilled guide when navigating unfamiliar territory, providing support, insight, and encouragement at every step.

Psychodynamic therapy facilitates a complex exploration of the self through these mechanisms. It's a journey of uncovering the hidden influences of the past on present emotions and behaviors, leading to profound understanding and lasting change. By engaging with these techniques, individuals can begin to heal from the inside out, transforming their relationship with themselves and the world around them.

The Journey to Self-Discovery

The journey to self-discovery in psychodynamic therapy is a voyage into one's psyche, marked by introspection, confrontation, and, ultimately, transformation. This path is not for the faint of heart; it demands courage to face one's innermost fears, desires, and conflicts. However, the rewards of such bravery are immeasurable, offering relief from psychological pain and a richer, more nuanced understanding of oneself.

The initial step on this journey involves turning inward, examining thoughts, feelings, and behaviors with a curiosity that transcends surface-level understanding. Imagine someone like Lisa, who always feels responsible for others' happiness. Through introspective exploration in therapy, she discovers this pattern stems from her childhood role as the family peacemaker. Understanding this dynamic allows Lisa to see her behavior differently, acknowledging her needs and boundaries.

As individuals delve deeper, they often encounter unconscious conflicts silently shaping their lives. John, for example, might unearth a deep-seated belief that he is unworthy of success, a theme that underlies his pattern of self-sabotage in personal and professional arenas. By confronting this belief in the safe space of therapy, John can challenge and reshape his self-perception, opening the door to new possibilities for growth and fulfillment.

The journey is not without its emotional turbulence. Encountering buried pain, grief, or trauma can evoke strong emotional responses. It's liken to navigating a stormy sea; therapeutic guidance is the lighthouse, providing direction and support through rough waters. This process, while challenging, is essential for healing. Through facing their pain, individuals like Emma, who has always avoided discussing her grief over losing a parent, can begin to process and integrate these deep-seated emotions, moving toward a place of peace and acceptance.

Amidst the challenges, moments of insight often emerge, illuminating previously obscured aspects of the self. These epiphanies can be life-changing, offering clarity and direction. For instance, James might suddenly understand how his fear of vulnerability has kept him from forming deep, meaningful relationships. This insight becomes a turning point, motivating him to take risks in intimacy that enrich his life immeasurably.

The stories of transformation through psychodynamic therapy are as varied as those who embark on this journey. Many find profound relief from depressive symptoms as they resolve their unconscious conflicts. Others discover a newfound sense of purpose or direction in life. The common thread in these stories is the experience of emerging from the process with a deeper, more compassionate understanding of oneself and a renewed capacity for joy, resilience, and connection.

Self-discovery through psychodynamic therapy is not a destination but a lifelong journey. The insights and growth attained through this process lay the foundation for continued self-exploration and development. Individuals learn to navigate life's challenges with greater self-awareness and emotional agility, equipped with the tools for enduring psychological well-being.

Personal Growth and Beyond

Psychodynamic therapy, with its plunge into the unconscious and exploration of past experiences, offers benefits that extend far beyond the alleviation of depression. This therapeutic journey fosters profound personal growth, touching every aspect of an individual's life. Let's explore how this transformative process contributes to increased self-awareness, healthier relationships, and greater fulfillment, ultimately leading to a resilient, depression-free life.

The journey through psychodynamic therapy illuminates the hidden parts of the self, enhancing self-awareness. This heightened understanding allows individuals to recognize their patterns of thoughts, emotions, and behaviors, many of which have been previously automatic or unconscious. For example, someone may realize that their tendency to isolate when feeling overwhelmed is a defense mechanism rooted in early childhood experiences of neglect. With this insight, they can choose different, more constructive ways to cope with stress, leading to a more engaged and active life.

As individuals gain insight into their behaviors and emotional triggers, they also develop a deeper understanding of their relationships. Psychodynamic therapy can reveal how past experiences shape current interactions with others, often in subtle or unconscious ways. It starts with recognizing patterns. For instance, Maria might discover that her fear of abandonment causes her to push people away before they can get too close, a pattern stemming from early losses. Armed with this knowledge, she can build trust and openness in her relationships, enhance her connection with others, and reduce feelings of loneliness and disconnection.

The self-discovery facilitated by psychodynamic therapy often leads to a clearer sense of what brings joy and meaning to one's life. This may involve reevaluating priorities, discovering new interests, or reconnecting with long-neglected passions. For example, through therapy, Tom realizes that his relentless pursuit of career success has been driven by a need to prove his worth to his critical parents. Understanding this dynamic, he feels free to explore what he truly values and finds fulfillment in, such as creative pursuits or volunteering, leading to a more balanced life.

The insights and emotional skills developed through psychodynamic therapy contribute to a stronger, more resilient self. Individuals learn to navigate life's ups and downs more easily, knowing they have the tools to understand and manage their emotions effectively. This resilience is key to maintaining a depression-free life, as it enables people to face challenges without being overwhelmed and to recover more quickly from setbacks.

The impact of psychodynamic therapy is lasting. Emotional healing and understanding do not simply disappear once therapy concludes. Instead, the growth and changes individuals experience become integrated into their sense of self, providing a sturdy foundation for navigating the future. This ongoing journey of growth ensures that the benefits of therapy—increased self-awareness, healthier relationships, and a greater sense of fulfillment—continue to enrich the individual's life long after the therapeutic process has ended.

Psychodynamic therapy offers a pathway to recovery from depression. It also leads to a life of greater depth, meaning, and connection. By engaging in this process of self-exploration and change, individuals open themselves to the possibility of a truly transformed life marked by emotional health, resilience, and a deep sense of personal fulfillment.

Incorporating these principles into your daily existence, remember that the quest for self-discovery and growth is continuous. Every day is a fresh chance to deepen your self-understanding and to embrace life more fully. The obstacles you encounter will test your resilience and fortify it. Through each challenge, you are crafting a more genuine and emotionally sound life.

For those embarking on or currently navigating this path, may this chapter—and the subsequent exercises—act as a GPS. The journey might be lengthy and sometimes arduous, yet the possibilities for transformation and healing are limitless. You possess the tools and the inner strength required to traverse this path; trust in the journey and remain open to the remarkable changes.

As you journey through psychodynamic therapy, consider it a cornerstone for sustained self-care, enabling you to preserve and enhance the progress made during therapy. We encourage a week with structured activities, reflections, and exercises tailored to enrich your comprehension and integrate psychodynamic principles into your daily routines.

We strongly advocate for continuing your journaling practice, encouraging you to document your thoughts and experiences as you progress through this guide. Maintaining a consistent practice with your "positivity journal" is also essential. This journal is a powerful tool designed to shift your focus to the optimistic aspects of your life, promoting a mindset of growth and well-being.

Week 7 Self-Help Guide

Psychodynamic therapy provides a foundation for ongoing self-help, empowering you to maintain and build upon your therapeutic gains. To facilitate this, we introduce a week of structured activities, reflections, and practices designed to deepen your understanding and apply psychodynamic concepts in daily life.

Week 7 Day 1

Objective: Engage in Reflective Journaling for Self-Discovery and Emotional Healing.

Information: Reflective journaling is a powerful tool for self-discovery and healing, serving as a mirror to your inner world. This practice goes beyond simply recording the day's events; it's an invitation to delve into your thoughts, emotions, and reactions, uncovering insights into yourself and your journey through life.

Getting Started

1. **Choose Your Medium**: Select a journal that resonates with you. This could be a traditional notebook, a digital app, or even voice recordings. The key is choosing a comfortable and inviting format that you'll look forward to using daily.
2. **Create a Routine**: Set aside a specific time each day for journaling. Early morning or late evening can be ideal times for reflection. Consider this a sacred time for self-care, a moment to connect with yourself without distractions.
3. **Set the Scene**: Find a quiet, comfortable space where you won't be disturbed. You might want to create a calming atmosphere with soft music, candles, or whatever helps you feel relaxed and open.

Journaling Prompts

Here are some prompts to explore in your journal to kickstart your reflective journey. These prompts are designed to guide your introspection and uncover the layers of your unconscious mind:

- **Today, I felt...**: Start with identifying and exploring your emotions throughout the day. Don't just name the emotions; delve into what triggered these feelings and how you responded to them.
- **A situation that challenged me today was...**: Reflect on any challenges or conflicts you encountered. What thoughts and feelings arose? How did you deal with the situation, and what might it reveal about your patterns or triggers?
- **I noticed a pattern...**: Identify any recurring themes or behaviors in your day. These could be reactions to certain people, situations, or internal triggers. What might these patterns suggest about your underlying beliefs or unresolved issues?
- **A moment of joy/gratitude was...**: Recognizing positive moments is just as crucial as exploring challenges. What brought you joy, comfort, or gratitude today? Reflecting on these moments can help balance your perspective and foster positivity.
- **My body felt...**: Tune into your physical sensations and experiences throughout the day. Often, our bodies hold emotional tensions and truths that our minds overlook. What might your body be communicating?

Reflecting and Connecting

As you journal, allow your thoughts and feelings to flow without censorship. This is your private space for honesty and exploration. After writing, take a moment to read through your entry. Notice any insights, patterns, or surprises that emerge. Over time, these reflections can provide valuable clues to your inner workings.

Remember, reflective journaling is not about perfection or finding immediate solutions. It's about creating a dialogue with yourself, learning to listen deeply to your voice, and honoring your journey with compassion and curiosity. Continuing this practice becomes a cornerstone of your daily routine, offering clarity, insight, and profound personal growth.

Week 7 Day 2

Objective: To uncover insights into the unconscious mind by interpreting symbols and narratives in dreams, reflecting deep-seated fears, desires, and conflicts, and connecting these insights to conscious life experiences for personal growth and emotional healing.

Dream analysis in psychodynamic therapy aims to tap into the unconscious mind by interpreting the symbols and narratives that emerge in dreams. Dreams can act as a mirror, reflecting our deepest fears, desires, and conflicts, often revealing insights our conscious mind may overlook or suppress.

Instructions for Detailed Dream Analysis

- **Immediate Recording**: Upon waking, make it a habit to record every detail you can recall about your dreams, no matter how insignificant or bizarre they may seem. Use a dedicated dream diary for this purpose. Describe the setting, characters, events, and especially your feelings during the dream.
- **Symbol Identification**: After recording the dream, go back and underline or highlight symbols or themes that stand out. Symbols in dreams are often highly personal and subjective. For instance, water might symbolize emotions, while a house might represent oneself or one's psyche.
- **Emotional Response and Context**: Note your emotional responses within the dream and after waking. Ask yourself how these emotions relate to your current life situations. Are there any recent events, stressors, or emotions the dream might be processing?

- **Recurring Dreams and Symbols**: Pay attention to any dreams or symbols that recur over time. Recurring dreams can indicate unresolved issues or conflicts in your unconscious mind that need attention.
- **Connecting Dreams to Daytime Experiences**: Reflect on how the themes or emotions of your dreams might relate to your daytime thoughts, feelings, or experiences. This can provide insight into how your unconscious mind works through issues or conflicts in your waking life.
- **Interpretation Resources**: While personal reflection is key, sometimes external resources can offer additional perspectives on common symbols or dream themes. Consider consulting reputable dream dictionaries or psychology resources, but always weigh these interpretations against your feelings and experiences.
- **Discussion with a Therapist**: Bring your dream journal to your sessions if you're working with a therapist. Discussing your dreams can provide valuable insights and facilitate the exploration of your unconscious mind. Your therapist can help you connect the dots between your dreams and your inner emotional world.

Practical Tips

- Keep your dream diary and a pen beside your bed to minimize the time between waking and recording, as dreams are often quickly forgotten.
- If you struggle to remember your dreams, try setting a gentle alarm to wake you during REM sleep phases, when dreams are more likely to occur and be remembered.
- Approach dream analysis with an open mind and curiosity rather than seeking concrete answers. The goal is to explore and understand, not to judge or diagnose.

Dream analysis is a powerful tool in the journey of self-discovery and healing. By paying attention to the narratives and symbols your unconscious mind communicates through dreams, you can gain insights into your deepest self, fostering personal growth and emotional healing. Remember, the value of dream analysis lies in interpreting individual dreams and the ongoing practice of listening to and engaging with your unconscious mind.

Week 7 Day 3

Objective: to delve into the subconscious strategies, known as defense mechanisms, that we employ to protect ourselves from emotional pain and anxiety. These automatic responses can often mask our true feelings and prevent us from confronting our underlying issues, thereby influencing our behavior in ways we might not fully understand.

Detailed Instructions for Reflection and Identification

- **Morning Reflection**: Begin your day with a brief meditation or quiet reflection. Set an intention to observe your interactions and reactions with mindfulness, particularly when you might be using defense mechanisms.
- **Identify and Record**: Keep a small notebook or digital note-taking device handy to jot down instances where you catch yourself employing defense mechanisms such as denial, projection (attributing your unacceptable feelings to someone else), rationalization (justifying behavior with logical reasons, ignoring the real reasons), or repression (pushing uncomfortable thoughts into the unconscious). Note the situation, your initial feelings, and the defense mechanism you believe was at play.
- **Evening Analysis**: Dedicate time in the evening to review your notes. For each noted instance, ask yourself:
    - What was the emotion I was trying to avoid?
    - Why might this emotion feel threatening or uncomfortable to me?
    - Can I trace this pattern back to earlier experiences in my life?

- **Deep Dive into One Defense Mechanism**: Select one defense mechanism you identified during the day and write a more detailed exploration. When you first remember using this mechanism, consider how it has served you in the past and what it might cost you regarding emotional growth and relationships.
- **Alternative Responses**: For the defense mechanisms you've identified, brainstorm healthier ways to deal with the emotions you're trying to avoid. For instance, if you're using projection to avoid acknowledging your feelings of insecurity, consider ways you might openly address and work through these insecurities instead.

Practical Tips for Recognizing Defense Mechanisms

- **Mindfulness Practice**: Regular mindfulness can enhance your ability to observe your thoughts and feelings without immediately reacting, making it easier to identify when using defense mechanisms.
- **Seek Feedback**: Sometimes, it's difficult to see our defense mechanisms. Trusted friends, family members, or therapists can offer valuable perspectives on patterns we might not recognize.
- **Educational Resources**: Familiarize yourself with common defense mechanisms by reading psychological texts or reputable online resources. Understanding these concepts theoretically can help you recognize them in your behavior.

Understanding and reflecting on your defense mechanisms is a crucial step. This will facilitate emotional maturity and healthier coping strategies. By recognizing these patterns, you're better equipped to confront and process your emotions directly, fostering deeper self-awareness and more authentic relationships.

Week 7 Day 4

Objective: to examine the dynamics of your most significant relationships to uncover how they may reflect deeper patterns or unresolved issues from your past and how they influence your current emotional state and behavior. This exploration is crucial for understanding the impact of interpersonal relationships on your well-being and for identifying areas where growth and change are needed.

Detailed Instructions

- **Mapping Your Relationships**: Start by listing significant relationships in your life. This list can include family members, partners, close friends, or colleagues. For each relationship, briefly describe the nature of your interaction, the emotions they evoke in you, and any recurring patterns or conflicts.
- **Identifying Patterns**: Once you've mapped out these relationships, look closely to identify recurring themes or patterns. Do you notice tendencies toward certain types of people or relationships? Are there common issues that arise, such as conflicts around trust, communication, or boundaries? Reflecting on these patterns can reveal insights into your needs, fears, and relationship behaviors.
- **Connecting Past to Present**: Consider how these patterns might be linked to your past experiences, particularly those from childhood. For instance, if you consistently find yourself in relationships where you feel undervalued, this might echo earlier experiences of not feeling seen or heard in your family. Drawing connections between your past and present can help you understand the origins of your relational patterns.

- **Emotional Impact Assessment**: Reflect on the emotional impact of these relationships on your current state. How do they contribute to or alleviate your feelings of depression? Understanding these relationships' emotional toll or support can highlight areas where changes might be beneficial.
- **Envisioning Healthy Relationships**: Based on your reflections, consider what a healthy relationship would look like for you. What qualities would it have? How would conflicts be handled? What boundaries would be in place? This vision can serve as a guide for fostering healthier relationships moving forward.
- **Action Steps for Growth**: Finally, identify specific steps you can take to improve the health of your relationships. This might involve initiating difficult conversations, setting clearer boundaries, seeking therapy to work through past traumas, or even reconsidering the place of certain relationships in your life.

Practical Tips

- **Journaling**: Use your journal to document your reflections, making it a safe space to explore your feelings and thoughts about your relationships without judgment.
- **Seeking Feedback**: Consider openly discussing your relationship dynamics with trusted individuals if appropriate. External perspectives can offer valuable insights and validation of your feelings.
- **Self-Compassion**: Remember to approach this process with kindness and compassion for yourself. Recognizing and addressing unhealthy patterns in relationships is challenging work and requires courage and self-compassion.

Day 4's focus on relationship reflections helps with understanding the complex interplay between your past experiences, current relational dynamics, and emotional well-being. By critically examining the nature of your significant relationships, you empower yourself to make conscious choices that support your growth, healing, and happiness in interpersonal connections.

Week 7 Day 5

Objective: To utilize the Free Association technique to access and articulate unconscious thoughts, feelings, and memories, thereby enhancing self-awareness and facilitating deeper psychological insight.

Information: Free Association is a core psychodynamic exercise that encourages a stream-of-consciousness approach to uncover hidden thoughts, feelings, and memories. This technique allows you to bypass the critical, censoring parts of your mind to access deeper, unconscious aspects of your psyche, providing valuable insights into your inner workings.

Detailed Instructions

- **Setting the Stage**: Choose a quiet, comfortable spot where you won't be disturbed. Have a journal or digital document open and ready for your thoughts. Set aside a specific time for this exercise, preferably 20-30 minutes.
- **Starting the Process**: Begin by writing down or speaking aloud (if recording) the first thing that comes to your mind. It doesn't matter how trivial, nonsensical, or disconnected it seems. The key is not to censor or judge what arises but to let your thoughts flow freely.
- **Following the Thread**: As you note your thoughts, let each lead you to the next without intervention. If you are hesitating or censoring, note this down as part of the process and move on. This can include random memories, sensory experiences, fantasies, or even parts of songs and dialogues.

- **Embracing Whatever Comes**: You might encounter uncomfortable thoughts or memories or evoke strong emotions. Acknowledge them as part of your experience and continue the process. The aim is not to analyze or understand these thoughts at the moment but to allow them a space to be expressed.
- **Concluding the Session**: Once your time is up, gently conclude your session. You might want to take a few deep breaths to center yourself after this deep dive into your psyche.
- **Reflection and Analysis**: After a break, return to your recorded thoughts. Read through them and note any themes, surprising elements, or recurrent thoughts that catch your attention. Reflect on how these might relate to your current feelings, challenges, or life situations.

Tips for Effective Free Association

- **Regular Practice**: Free association becomes more effective with regular practice. Try incorporating it into your routine, noticing how the process and content evolve.
- **Non-Judgmental Stance**: Approach this exercise with curiosity and an open mind. The goal is to observe and record, not to critique.
- **Use of Prompts**: If you find yourself stuck, you can use a prompt to get started. This could be a word, an image, or a question. However, once you begin, let go of the prompt and follow wherever your mind leads.
- **Integration into Therapy**: If you're working with a therapist, consider sharing some of your free association sessions. These can provide rich material for exploration in your therapy work.

Day 5's focus on Free Association is designed to deepen your self-awareness and enhance your connection with your unconscious mind. By allowing thoughts and feelings to surface without censorship, you're opening a direct line to your inner self, offering profound insights and aiding the therapeutic process.

Week 7 Day 6

Objective: To establish personal goals informed by a deepened self-understanding, applying insights from values clarification and relationship reflections into SMART (Specific, Measurable, Achievable, Relevant, Time-bound) objectives, and to create actionable plans for authentic growth and fulfillment.

Information: On Day 6, we focus on setting personal goals that align with the deeper understanding of ourselves we've cultivated through the week. The aim is to translate insights into actionable steps, grounding our aspirations in our uncovered values and desires, thereby creating pathways for authentic growth and fulfillment.

Detailed Instructions

- **Reflection and Identification**: Begin with a reflective session where you revisit the insights gathered from the previous days, especially from the exercises on values clarification and relationship reflections. Identify which aspects of your life you're most eager to develop or change based on your newfound understanding of your values and desires.
- **SMART Goal Setting**: Utilize the SMART criteria (Specific, Measurable, Achievable, Relevant, Time-bound) to frame your goals. For instance, if you discovered a value around creativity but have neglected this area, a SMART goal could be: "Dedicate 30 minutes each day to creative writing, aiming to complete a short story within the next month."
- **Creating an Action Plan**: Break down each goal into smaller, manageable actions. Detail what steps you'll take daily, weekly,

or monthly to progress. This could include scheduling specific times for activities, identifying resources you'll need, or outlining how you'll overcome potential obstacles.

- **Visualizing Success**: Spend time visualizing what achieving these goals will look like and how it will feel. Visualization can be a powerful motivator, helping to solidify your commitment to your goals and the positive changes they represent.
- **Accountability Measures**: Consider ways to hold yourself accountable for pursuing your goals. This could involve regular check-ins with a supportive friend or family member, maintaining a progress journal, or setting up reminders and alarms.
- **Adaptability and Flexibility**: Acknowledge that goals and priorities can change. Stay open to reassessing and adjusting your goals based on your growth, changes in circumstances, or new insights you may gain.
- **Celebrating Milestones**: Identify milestones within your goal-setting plan and decide how to celebrate reaching them. Recognizing and celebrating progress is crucial for maintaining motivation and recognizing your achievements, no matter how small.

Practical Tips

- **Prioritize**: If you have multiple goals, prioritize them based on which are most important or urgent. Trying to achieve too many goals simultaneously can lead to overwhelm.
- **Incremental Steps**: Start with small, achievable steps to build momentum. Success in smaller goals can boost confidence and motivation for larger challenges.
- **Seek Support**: Don't hesitate to seek support from friends, family, or professionals who can offer encouragement, advice, or accountability.

Week 7 Day 7

Objective: To prepare for potential future challenges by identifying likely obstacles, analyzing triggers, and developing tailored coping strategies that leverage the insights and skills acquired throughout the week, aimed at fostering resilience, ensuring continued progress, and managing setbacks effectively.

Information: The focus for Day 7 is on anticipating future obstacles and developing strategies to navigate these challenges with resilience. This day is about leveraging the insights, self-awareness, and skills you've cultivated throughout the week to prepare for life's inevitable ups and downs. The goal is to create a proactive plan that allows you to maintain your progress, continue your growth, and manage setbacks effectively.

Detailed Instructions

- **Identifying Potential Challenges**: Start by reflecting on potential challenges that might arise. Consider various aspects of your life, such as personal relationships, work, health, and your inner emotional landscape. Describe scenarios that could derail your progress or trigger emotional distress.
- **Analyzing Triggers and Patterns**: For each identified challenge, delve into the triggers or patterns contributing to its occurrence. This involves understanding the situations, thoughts, or feelings that precede and accompany these challenges. Recognizing these patterns can help you become more aware of early warning signs and effectively implement coping strategies.

- **Developing Coping Strategies**: Create a list of coping strategies for each challenge. These strategies should be actionable and tailored to address the specific nuances of each obstacle. Consider techniques that have worked in the past and new strategies you've learned through psychodynamic therapy and self-help exercises. Strategies might include mindfulness practices, seeking support from your social network, engaging in physical activity, or using cognitive reframing techniques.
- **Creating a Support Plan**: Identify individuals who can support you when facing challenges. This could be friends, family members, therapists, or support groups. Outline how and when you will reach out to these sources of support and how they can best assist you.
- **Building Flexibility and Resilience**: Acknowledge that setbacks are a natural part of growth and healing. Incorporate flexibility into your plan by identifying alternative strategies or adjustments that can be made if your initial plan doesn't work as expected. This might include setting aside time for reflection and reassessment, being open to changing your approach or seeking additional resources.
- **Implementing a Routine Check-In**: Schedule regular check-ins with yourself to assess your progress, evaluate the effectiveness of your coping strategies, and adjust your plan as needed. Depending on your needs and challenges, these check-ins can be daily, weekly, or monthly.
- **Journaling for Reflection and Adjustment**: Use your journal to document your reflections during these check-ins. Note any new insights, successes, difficulties, and how you're feeling emotionally and physically. This record can be invaluable for tracking your progress, understanding your evolving needs, and making informed adjustments to your plan.

Day 7 wraps up the week with a focus on preparedness and resilience, equipping you with a comprehensive plan to face future challenges head-on. By anticipating obstacles and developing tailored strategies, you're not just reacting to difficulties but actively engaging in your ongoing journey of growth and healing. Remember, resilience is not about avoiding setbacks but navigating them with grace, learning from each experience, and emerging stronger on the other side.

Bridge Week 7

Pause for a brief reflection as you close another chapter of your journey. Picture where you now stand on the bridge, ponder the week's journey, embrace the emotions you've encountered, and anticipate the path ahead with optimism. Update your position on the bridge, marking this week's passage as a step forward in your ongoing quest for healing. This simple act is a vital part of your progress, aiding in visualizing the strides you're making towards a life of greater balance and joy.

13

Emotional Intelligence

Welcome to Week 8 of *DEPRESSION FREE*. This week, we delve into the pivotal realm of Emotional Intelligence (EI), an indispensable skill set in mastering the management of depression and enhancing your overall mental health. Emotional intelligence transcends the mere recognition of our feelings; it involves the adept manipulation and utilization of emotions to alleviate stress, foster effective communication, empathize with others, surmount obstacles, and mitigate conflicts. It beckons us to discern our emotional states and those of the people around us, embarking on a journey through this emotional landscape with a spirit of awareness, comprehension, and benevolence.

The significance of emotional intelligence in our quest to transcend depression cannot be overstated. At its core, depression often distorts our emotional compass, leading to overwhelming feelings of sadness, despair, and apathy. However, by cultivating a robust emotional intelligence, we equip ourselves with the tools necessary to navigate these turbulent waters gracefully. EI guides us through the fog of depression by enhancing our self-awareness, teaching us to manage distressing emotions, improving our social skills, and ultimately helping us build more meaningful and supportive relationships.

Moreover, emotional intelligence is intricately linked to being depression-free because it directly influences our capacity to cope with life's stressors. Individuals with high EI are better equipped to recognize the onset of depressive thoughts and feelings, enabling them to employ effective strategies to counteract these negative patterns before they spiral out of control. By understanding and managing our own emotions, we can prevent the kind of rumination and negative thinking that often exacerbates or triggers depressive episodes.

Furthermore, emotional intelligence fosters resilience—the ability to bounce back from setbacks and challenges. Resilience is crucial in the battle against depression, as it imbues us with the strength to face adversity without losing hope. By enhancing our EI, we learn to manage our emotions and view challenges as opportunities for growth rather than insurmountable obstacles. This shift in perspective is vital for anyone on the path to overcoming depression.

Lastly, the connection between EI and being depression-free lies in the profound impact emotional intelligence has on our relationships. Depression can often feel isolating, creating barriers between us and those we care about. However, by developing our emotional intelligence, we improve our ability to communicate our feelings, empathize with others, and maintain strong, supportive connections. These relationships are the bedrock upon which we can build a foundation for lasting mental health and well-being.

As we embark on this week's exploration of emotional intelligence, remember that the depression-free journey is about mitigating symptoms and fostering a deep, nuanced understanding of our emotional selves. By honing our emotional intelligence, we unlock the door to a life characterized not just by the absence of depression but also by a profound sense of emotional richness and fulfillment.

Understanding Emotional Intelligence

Understanding Emotional Intelligence in managing depression and improving mental well-being involves a look into the nature of our emotional processes and how they influence our interactions with ourselves and others. At its core, EI represents a sophisticated blend of self-perception, self-regulation, social insight, and relational dynamics, each aspect contributing uniquely to the mastery of emotional landscapes.

Self-awareness, the cornerstone of EI, involves insight and introspection into one's emotional world, unveiling the layers of feelings, thoughts, and behaviors that shape our daily lives. It's an internal dialogue where you're both the speaker and the listener, constantly engaging with your emotional self to understand your essence.

Imagine a scenario where you've had a long, stressful day at work, and upon returning home, you find yourself snapping at a loved one over a minor issue. The immediate reaction might be anger or frustration, but with self-awareness, you take a step back to reflect. You recognize that your response wasn't about the minor issue but a manifestation of the day's accumulated stress and exhaustion. This moment of reflection allows you to understand the underlying cause of your reaction, leading you to address the real issue which is your need for rest and decompression rather than misdirecting your emotions toward your loved one.

In another example, consider the feelings of sadness that can envelop you out of the blue, casting a shadow over your mood without an apparent reason. With self-awareness, you embark on a reflective process, exploring these feelings rather than pushing them aside. You might realize that this sadness is a response to an unmet need or a longing for connection, prompting you to take constructive steps toward fulfilling these needs, such as reaching out to a friend or engaging in a beloved hobby.

Self-awareness also shines through in moments of joy and contentment. When you feel a surge of happiness from engaging in a particular activity, self-awareness helps you pinpoint what about this activity resonates so deeply with you. Is it the creativity it allows, the sense of achievement, or the connection with others? Understanding what brings you joy empowers you to incorporate more of these elements into your life, enhancing your overall well-being.

In the context of depression, self-awareness becomes a powerful tool. It enables you to recognize the signs and symptoms of your depressive states, distinguishing between fleeting sadness and deeper, more persistent feelings. This awareness is the first step toward seeking help and implementing coping strategies. By understanding your emotional triggers—such as specific environments, interactions, or thoughts—you can begin to navigate your way through depression with greater clarity and purpose.

Self-awareness encourages you to acknowledge your feelings without judgment and address them constructively. For instance, if you recognize that isolation exacerbates your depression, this awareness can motivate you to seek social connections, even when it feels daunting. Similarly, understanding that certain activities lift your spirits can inspire you to integrate these actions into your daily routine, fostering moments of joy and lightness amidst the challenges of depression.

In cultivating self-awareness, you're learning to identify and understand your emotions and how to respond to them in ways that support your mental health and well-being. It's a constant learning and adaptation journey, where each insight brings you closer to a life of emotional balance and resilience.

Self-Management: Steering Your Emotional Ship: Self-management acts as your compass and rudder when navigating complex emotions. It helps you to harness the power of self-awareness to actively guide your emotional and behavioral responses. This ensures they align with your long-term values and goals rather than being reactive to the moment's whims.

Consider a situation at work where you're faced with a project deadline. The pressure mounts and you feel a wave of anxiety threatening to overwhelm you. At this moment, self-management comes into play by recognizing the anxiety for what it is—a natural stress response. Instead of succumbing to panic or procrastination, you employ stress-reduction techniques such as deep breathing, breaking the project into manageable tasks, or scheduling short breaks to clear your mind. This approach helps manage your immediate stress and keeps you on track toward your goal, demonstrating resilience in the face of pressure.

Another example of self-management is dealing with the impulse to withdraw during depressive episodes. While isolation might feel comforting in the short term, you recognize through self-awareness that connection with others supports your mental health. Using self-management, you motivate yourself to reach out to a friend or attend a support group, even when it feels difficult. This action doesn't negate your feelings but represents a conscious choice to engage in behaviors that align with your well-being.

Self-management also plays a crucial role in managing negative self-talk, a common challenge in depression. For instance, when you catch yourself spiraling into a pattern of self-criticism after a minor mistake, self-management allows you to pause and shift your inner dialogue. Instead of criticizing yourself, you remind yourself that mistakes are opportunities for learning and growth. This positive affirmation is a self-management tool, redirecting your thoughts toward a more compassionate and constructive mindset.

Self-management equips you with the skills to actively counter depressive thoughts and behaviors with actions that promote healing and growth. For example, recognizing the onset of a depressive episode can trigger self-management strategies such as engaging in physical activity, practicing mindfulness, or reaching out to your support network. These actions don't erase depression but can significantly mitigate its intensity and duration.

Furthermore, self-management involves setting realistic, achievable goals that provide a sense of purpose and direction. For someone battling depression, setting a goal to take a daily walk, practice a hobby for a few minutes each day, or cook a healthy meal can be empowering. These goals, grounded in self-management, foster a sense of achievement and progress, key elements in the journey out of depression.

Self-management transforms self-awareness into action, guiding you through the emotional storms with a steady hand and a clear vision. It's about making choices that support your mental health and well-being, even when depression makes those choices challenging. Through practice and perseverance, self-management becomes a powerful ally in navigating the complexities of depression, steering you toward a life marked by resilience, purpose, and emotional balance.

Social Awareness: Navigating the Emotional Landscape of Others: Social awareness, a critical component of Emotional Intelligence, involves the understanding and empathizing with the emotional landscapes of those around us. It's about moving beyond our own experiences to connect with others on a deeper level, recognizing their feelings, needs, and perspectives. This skill is particularly important in the context of depression, where isolation can intensify feelings of disconnection.

Imagine you're at a family gathering and notice a relative sitting quietly, withdrawn from the lively conversation. Your initial thought might be to engage them directly in conversation to bring them into the fold. However, with social awareness, you tune into the subtler cues they're presenting—body language that suggests they're not simply shy but perhaps overwhelmed or in need of space. Instead of urging them into a social situation that might increase their discomfort, you choose a gentler approach. You sit beside them, offering a calm presence and an open invitation to talk if they wish, without the pressure to engage more broadly. This action, rooted in social awareness, acknowledges their emotional state and offers support on their terms, fostering a connection that respects their needs and boundaries.

For individuals navigating the complexities of depression, social awareness can serve as both a bridge and a barrier to connection. On the one hand, heightened sensitivity to the emotions of others can foster deep empathy and understanding, creating strong bonds of support and companionship. These connections are invaluable, offering a sense of belonging and shared experience that can alleviate the isolation often accompanying depression.

On the other hand, this same sensitivity can sometimes be overwhelming, making it difficult to separate one's emotions from those of others. This is where the balance of EI comes into play—using self-awareness and self-management to recognize when you need to set boundaries for your emotional well-being. It's about finding the equilibrium between connecting with empathy and protecting your emotional space, ensuring that social awareness enriches rather than exhausts your emotional reserves.

Social awareness also plays a crucial role in recognizing the support networks available to you. Understanding the emotional states of those in your support circle can help you identify who might be best equipped to offer the kind of support you need at any given time. It allows for a reciprocal exchange of support, where you can be both a giver and receiver of empathy and understanding, strengthening the bonds that contribute to a supportive and nurturing environment.

In the journey out of depression, social awareness is a skill that can illuminate the path toward deeper connections and a stronger support network. It's about engaging with the world around you with empathy, understanding, and a keen sense of the emotional landscapes of others, enriching your relationships and enhancing your emotional well-being. Through practice and mindfulness, social awareness can be a powerful tool in navigating the emotional complexities of life, offering a compass for connecting with others in meaningful, supportive ways.

Relationship Management: The Art of Connection: Relationship Management, the harmonious blend of self-awareness, self-management, social awareness, and the ability to navigate and nurture interpersonal relationships, is a pinnacle of Emotional Intelligence. This intricate dance of emotional and social skills is pivotal in creating and sustaining meaningful connections and fostering environments of mutual respect, understanding, and support.

Relationship management is about the dynamic interplay between understanding oneself and effectively engaging with others. It involves a active approach to communication, where listening becomes just as important as speaking, and empathy is the thread that weaves through every interaction. Effective relationship management enables you to express your own needs and boundaries with clarity and confidence and to hear and respect those of others, building bridges of mutual support and understanding.

Imagine you're navigating a challenging period of depression and find communication within your closest relationships strained. You recognize the need to share your feelings and seek support, yet you're also mindful of the emotional toll your depression might take on your loved ones. Employing relationship management skills, you choose a moment of calm to initiate a conversation, starting with expressing gratitude for their support. You share your experiences, clarifying that while you value their care, you also understand the importance of boundaries and self-care for both parties. Together, you explore ways they can support you that are healthy and sustainable for everyone involved.

This approach, rooted in relationship management, not only fosters a deeper understanding and connection but also empowers both you and your loved ones to navigate the complexities of depression with compassion and resilience. It transforms potential conflicts into opportunities for growth, deepening the bonds of trust and support essential during challenging times.

For those dealing with depression, mastering relationship management can indeed be transformative. It opens the door to creating a supportive network that understands your journey and contributes positively to it. By effectively managing relationships, you can ensure that your interactions with others are sources of strength and encouragement rather than stress or misunderstanding.

Moreover, relationship management skills allow for the constructive resolution of conflicts, fostering an environment where challenges can be addressed openly and collaboratively rather than avoided or left to fester. This proactive approach to conflict resolution can significantly reduce the relational stress that might otherwise exacerbate feelings of depression.

Developing your relationship management skills involves continuous learning and practice. It starts with the willingness to engage in honest self-reflection and extends to the consistent practice of empathy, active listening, and constructive communication in your interactions. It's about consciously understanding and appreciating the perspectives and feelings of those around you and navigating your shared emotional landscapes with care and respect.

As you strengthen your relationship management skills, you'll find that your ability to connect with others, even in the midst of depression, becomes more profound and fulfilling. This not only aids in your journey out of depression but also enriches the lives of those around you, creating a virtuous cycle of emotional support and growth.

Developing Your Emotional Intelligence

Developing your Emotional Intelligence is to embark on a journey of self-discovery and growth, where each step forward is a stride to understanding and managing your emotions more effectively. This journey is particularly crucial for individuals dealing with depression, as it arms them with the tools necessary to navigate their emotional landscape, fostering resilience and a deeper connection with themselves and others.

Enhancing Emotional Intelligence is a deeply personal and transformative process rooted in the understanding that emotional growth and resilience are cultivated through consistent practice and unwavering patience. The development of EI is not a linear path but a rich, multifaceted exploration into the depths of one's emotional being, offering profound insights into how we perceive, interact with, and ultimately shape our emotional landscape.

The practices that facilitate the development of EI are varied, encompassing a range of activities from journaling, which offers a reflective space for exploring emotions and thoughts, to mindfulness, a practice that encourages present-moment awareness and acceptance of one's emotional state. These activities are an active self-exploration toward cultivating a deeper, more complete understanding of oneself and one's emotional responses.

Ultimately, the development of EI is a lifelong journey that enriches the individual's emotional landscape and enhances their capacity for emotional well-being. By committing to the practices that foster EI, individuals open themselves up to a world of emotional growth, improved relationships, and a deeper, more meaningful connection with themselves and those around them. While uniquely personal, the path to enhanced EI offers universal rewards—a more fulfilling, emotionally balanced life.

Journaling: Journaling is a potent vehicle for enhancing self-awareness and navigating the emotional complexities of depression. It creates a sanctuary where thoughts and feelings can unfold freely, allowing for an intimate dialogue with oneself. This reflective practice offers more than just an outlet for emotional expression; it serves as a tool for discovery and insight, shedding light on the inner workings of one's mind and heart.

At its core, journaling is about laying bare the intricacies of your emotional landscape. It's an exercise in honesty and vulnerability, where you can voice your deepest fears, joys, sorrows, and hopes without fear of judgment. This act of writing becomes a form of self-therapy, a way to untangle and make sense of the emotions and thoughts within. For individuals grappling with depression, journaling provides a unique opportunity to confront their feelings directly to recognize patterns in their thoughts and behaviors that may be contributing to their state of mind.

Regular engagement with journaling can illuminate the triggers and cycles of depression, offering crucial insights into the personal dynamics that fuel depressive episodes. By documenting daily experiences, emotions, and reactions, patterns emerge, revealing the specific circumstances, interactions, or thoughts that precipitate sadness, anxiety, or hopelessness. This awareness is the first step toward change, empowering individuals with the knowledge to address and alter these patterns.

The process of writing itself can be incredibly therapeutic. It allows for a cathartic release of pent-up emotions, providing relief and lightness. As words flow onto the page, they carry the weight of unspoken emotions, leaving behind a clearer mind and a more serene heart. Moreover, journaling offers a tangible record of one's emotional journey, enabling individuals to track their progress over time, celebrate their victories, however small, and better understand the ebbs and flows of their emotional state.

Ultimately, journaling is a personal guide that enhances emotional intelligence. It cultivates a deep, introspective awareness essential for effectively understanding and managing one's emotions. By committing to this practice, individuals embark on a journey of self-discovery, unlocking new pathways to emotional well-being and resilience. In the context of depression, journaling emerges not just as a mirror reflecting the soul's depths but as a map guiding the way toward healing and emotional balance.

Mindfulness: Mindfulness, the practice of being fully present and engaged in the moment, unfolds as a sanctuary for those navigating the complexities of depression. This discipline teaches the art of observing thoughts, emotions, and bodily sensations without judgment, fostering an environment where one can experience the present moment, free from the distractions of past regrets or future anxieties.

For individuals experiencing depression, mindfulness offers a reprieve from the relentless cycle of negative thoughts and worries that often characterize this condition. It provides a space where emotions can be acknowledged and felt without the pressure to immediately change or judge them. This acceptance is key to breaking the cycle of negative self-evaluation and rumination that feeds depressive states, allowing for a more compassionate relationship with oneself.

Mindfulness encourages an intimate awareness of the here and now, grounding individuals in their current experience with a sense of acceptance and peace. Practicing mindfulness teaches one to observe their thoughts as transient phenomena, not facts that define reality or self-worth. This shift in perspective can significantly alter how emotions are experienced, reducing their overwhelming power and providing a sense of control and peace amidst emotional turmoil.

Engaging in mindfulness meditation or mindfulness-based exercises can help stabilize the mind, bringing a sense of balance and calm to the emotional chaos of depression. Techniques such as focused breathing, body scans, or mindful walking are gateways to cultivating a present-moment awareness, each offering a method to anchor oneself in the now. These practices teach the valuable skill of returning to the present moment, again and again, building resilience crucial for managing depression.

Mindfulness is a practice of returning to the simplicity of the present moment, offering a powerful antidote to the complexities of depression. It fosters a deepened sense of awareness and acceptance, providing a pathway out of the darkness of depression into a space of light, balance, and emotional resilience. By embracing mindfulness, individuals open themselves to a process of healing and discovery, where each moment is an opportunity for growth, connection, and peace.

Emotion Naming: Emotion Naming is a transformative practice in Emotional Intelligence. It transcends mere recognition, inviting an exploration and understanding of one's emotional landscape. This simple yet profound act of identifying and naming emotions as they surface is critical to mastering them. It is rooted deeply in the principles of self-awareness, acting as a gateway to a more nuanced comprehension of how our emotions color our thoughts, actions, and overall mental state.

The process of emotion naming is like shining a light on shadows. It involves pausing to acknowledge what we feel at any given moment and giving it a label. This practice does more than categorize our emotional experiences. It brings them into the realm of the tangible, where they can be examined, understood, and managed. By articulating what we feel, we demystify our emotions, stripping away their power to overwhelm us and instead turning them into signals that guide our responses.

Naming our emotions is a step in acknowledging their presence and impact on our lives. This acknowledgment is not about judgment or suppression but about observation and acceptance. It is through this acceptance that we can begin to develop strategies to navigate our emotions more effectively. For instance, recognizing and naming feelings of sadness or anxiety when they arise can prompt us to employ coping mechanisms, such as breathing exercises or mindfulness, to soothe these emotions before they escalate.

One of the most significant benefits of emotion naming is its ability to reduce the intensity of our emotional experiences. Identifying and labeling our feelings creates a psychological distance between ourselves and our emotions. This distance allows us to view our emotions as separate from our core selves, making them less overwhelming and more manageable. It transforms vague feelings of discomfort into identifiable emotions that we can address and work through.

As we become more adept at identifying and naming our emotions, we cultivate emotional mastery that supports our journey toward mental health, resilience, and a deeper connection with ourselves and the world around us.

Empathy Practice: Empathy Practice is essential to developing deep social awareness and a critical skill in fostering meaningful connections. It is the immersion of oneself in the emotional experience of another, truly grasping the depth and breadth of what they're going through. This practice is invaluable for anyone, and it holds particular significance for those navigating the complexities of depression, as it can significantly enhance the quality of support networks and diminish the intense feelings of isolation that often accompany this condition.

Practicing empathy involves a conscious effort to engage in active listening, where the goal is to simply hear and understand the other person's perspective, without offering solutions. It's about being present with another's emotions, without judgment or bias, and offering compassion and support that is attuned to their needs. This level of empathetic engagement can transform relationships, building a foundation of trust, mutual understanding, and respect that is both healing and empowering.

For individuals experiencing depression, the sense of being understood on a deep, emotional level can be profoundly impactful. It breaks through the walls of isolation, offering a sense of solidarity and connection that is often lost amidst the struggles with mental health. Empathy allows for creating a shared space where vulnerabilities can be exposed without fear of judgment, fostering a supportive environment that encourages openness and healing.

Developing empathy is a skill that can be honed through practice. It starts with cultivating genuine curiosity about others' experiences and perspectives. This means asking open-ended questions, listening attentively to the answers, and reflecting on what you've heard to ensure understanding. It also involves recognizing and setting aside one's biases or preconceived notions to fully appreciate the unique experiences of others. Empathy becomes a bridge to deeper, more meaningful relationships through such practices.

Effective Communication: Effective communication is necessary for those navigating the complexities of depression. It involves the ability to express one's feelings and needs in a manner that is both clear and calm, fostering constructive dialogues and strengthening the fabric of interpersonal relationships. This skill is crucial in establishing supportive connections that significantly contribute to healing.

In the vast landscape of human interaction, the art of communication manifests in various styles, each with its unique characteristics and impact on relationships. These styles—passive, aggressive, passive-aggressive, and assertive—serve as the mediums through which individuals express their thoughts, feelings, and needs.

Imagine someone consistently avoiding expressing their true opinions or feelings, always deferring to others' preferences to avoid conflict. This passive communication style, while seemingly non-confrontational, often comes at the expense of one's rights and needs. Picture a scenario where this person says, "It doesn't matter to me; whatever you think is best," even though they harbor a strong preference. This approach can lead to internal resentment and dissatisfaction as their desires remain unvoiced and unacknowledged.

Conversely, aggressive communication stands at the other end of the spectrum. This style is marked by a tendency to express one's opinions and feelings in a manner that encroaches upon the rights of others. An individual adopting this approach might forcefully assert their will with little regard for others' feelings, declaring, "I don't care what you think; we're doing it my way!" This approach can create an environment of tension and hostility, as it prioritizes one's needs over mutual respect and understanding.

Then there's the passive-aggressive communication style, where individuals might outwardly appear passive but are, in fact, expressing their anger and dissatisfaction in subtle, indirect ways. This could manifest through sulking, the silent treatment, or delivering backhanded compliments, all of which serve to express discontent without engaging in direct confrontation. This style complicates relationships by masking the true source of conflict under a veneer of passivity, making resolution more difficult.

Among these varied styles, assertive communication emerges as the most effective and balanced approach. It embodies the ability to express one's needs, feelings, and thoughts clearly and respectfully while also considering the perspectives and needs of others. An individual practicing assertive communication might seek common ground in disagreements, saying, "I understand your point of view, but I feel differently about this situation. Can we find a middle ground?" This style fosters an environment of open, honest dialogue where both parties feel heard and respected, paving the way for healthier, more supportive relationships.

Each communication style carries distinct consequences for interpersonal dynamics, influencing relationships' depth, quality, and health. Understanding and navigating these styles, particularly the shift toward more assertive communication, can significantly enhance one's ability to connect with others, manage conflicts constructively, and cultivate a supportive network, especially crucial for those navigating the challenges of depression.

Assertive communication is particularly significant in the context of EI and managing depression. It empowers individuals to express their needs and boundaries clearly without encroaching on the rights of others, thereby reducing misunderstandings and conflicts. Assertive communication fosters open, honest dialogues where both parties feel heard and respected, contributing to stronger, more supportive relationships.

For example, someone dealing with depression might use assertive communication to express their need for space or support: "I'm feeling overwhelmed right now and need some time alone. I appreciate your understanding and support through this." This approach ensures their needs are communicated effectively, fostering a supportive environment conducive to healing.

Developing assertive communication skills involves practicing self-awareness, empathy, and emotional regulation. It requires understanding one's emotions and the ability to express them in a balanced and respectful way. For instance, before engaging in a potentially difficult conversation, one might take a few deep breaths to center themselves, reflect on their feelings and needs, and consider the other person's perspective. This preparation paves the way for an assertive and empathetic conversation, enhancing the quality of the interaction and the relationship overall.

Effective communication, particularly assertive communication, is a cornerstone of EI that is crucial in managing depression. By expressing oneself clearly and calmly, individuals can build and maintain supportive relationships, navigate conflicts constructively, and create a solid foundation for healing and emotional well-being.

This chapter has illuminated the EI skills needed to navigate the emotional waters of depression, emphasizing the importance of self-awareness, self-management, social awareness, and relationship management. Each skill contributes uniquely to understanding and managing our emotions, enhancing our interactions, and nurturing our relationships.

As we move forward, I encourage you to continue the practices you've started in the previous weeks, especially your journaling and the maintenance of your "positivity journal." These tools are invaluable. They provide a space for reflection, learning, and acknowledgment of your progress, no matter how small.

In the spirit of building upon our foundation, I invite you to dedicate yourself to the seven days of self-help homework. These exercises are designed to further enhance your EI skills, offering practical applications that integrate seamlessly into your daily life. Whether it's a journal entry that dives deeper into your emotional landscape, a mindfulness practice that brings you into the present, or an exercise in empathy that connects you with another's experience, each task is a step toward a more emotionally intelligent you.

Week 8 Self-Help Guide

This week, we will explore practices such as journaling, mindfulness, emotion naming, empathy practice, and effective communication. These practices are not just exercises but lifelines that can guide us toward a more emotionally intelligent and fulfilling life. We've seen how journaling acts as a mirror to our soul, providing clarity and catharsis. Mindfulness has taught us the art of being present, offering a sanctuary from the storm of negative thoughts. Through emotion naming, we've learned to identify and manage our feelings more effectively, while empathy practice has opened our hearts to the experiences of others, strengthening our connections. Finally, effective communication has empowered us to express ourselves clearly and constructively, reducing misunderstandings and deepening our relationships.

Week 8 Day 1

Objective: To cultivate self-awareness and enhance emotional resilience through practical exercises focused on mindfulness, reflective journaling, and relaxation techniques, aimed at improving stress and emotion management skills essential for navigating depression.Day 1, focusing on Self-Management, is designed to be introspective and practical. This day is dedicated to enhancing your ability to manage stress and emotions, crucial skills for navigating depression with greater resilience.

Day 1: Self-Management Focus

- **Morning:** Begin your day with a mindfulness exercise. Find a quiet place where you can sit comfortably without distractions. Spend 10 minutes focusing on your breath. Inhale deeply through your nose, feeling your abdomen expand, and exhale slowly through your mouth. If your mind wanders, gently redirect your focus back to your breath. This practice aims to ground you in the present moment, reducing stress and enhancing emotional clarity.

- **Afternoon:** Reflect on a recent situation where you felt overwhelmed by stress or negative emotions. Write about this experience in your journal, focusing on what triggered these feelings and how you reacted. Identify one strategy you could use to manage similar situations more effectively. This could be a stress-reduction technique, a way to reframe negative thoughts, or an action to address the root cause of the stress.

- **Evening:** Engage in a relaxing activity that brings you joy and comfort, such as reading, listening to music, or taking a warm bath. As you do so, pay attention to how your stress levels and emotions change. Note these observations in your journal.

Today's exercises aim to enhance your self-awareness and develop practical skills for managing stress and emotions. By practicing mindfulness, reflecting on your experiences, and engaging in activities that promote relaxation, you're taking important steps toward building emotional resilience and navigating depression more effectively.

Week 8 Day 2

For Day 2, the focus is on enhancing self-awareness through journaling. This involves a reflective practice where you'll dedicate parts of your day to actively noting and exploring your emotions and their triggers. Start your morning by setting a goal to be mindful of your emotional states throughout the day. Carry a notebook or use a digital journal to record significant emotions as they arise, noting what triggered these feelings and how you responded to them. In the evening, allocate time to review your notes, reflecting on the patterns of your emotional responses and considering what these might indicate about your needs or areas for growth. This process of observation and reflection is designed to deepen your understanding of yourself, fostering a heightened sense of self-awareness crucial for emotional intelligence.

Week 8 Day 3

Objective: To enhance social awareness and empathy through engaging in a meaningful conversation with a chosen individual, focusing on understanding their perspective without judgment, and practicing active listening skills.

Action Steps:

1. **Select a Partner:** Choose someone you trust and feel comfortable with for an open conversation. It could be a friend, family member, or even a colleague.

2. **Prepare Mentally:** Before the conversation, take a moment to clear your mind and focus on the intention behind this exercise. Remember that the purpose is to listen and understand, not offer advice or judgment.

3. **Engage in Conversation:** Initiate the conversation with an open-ended question that encourages sharing, such as "How have you been feeling about the changes happening lately?" Practice active listening, which means focusing fully on the speaker, making eye contact, and nodding to show understanding. Avoid interrupting or planning your response while they're speaking.

4. **Reflect:** After the conversation, spend some time reflecting on the experience. Consider the emotions they expressed, how it felt to connect on this level, and what you learned about their perspective and your ability to empathize.

Journaling: Write down your reflections in your journal. Note any new insights into the person's feelings and thoughts, your emotional reactions during the process, and how the exercise impacted your understanding of empathy and social awareness.

This exercise aims to enhance your EI by practicing empathy and active listening, crucial skills for building strong, supportive relationships.

Week 8 Day 4

Objective: To focus on resolving a recent conflict or misunderstanding through assertive communication. Reflect on an incident that led to a disagreement or miscommunication with someone close to you.

Action Steps:

1. **Reflect and Plan:** Take some time to reflect on the conflict. Consider your feelings, the other person's perspective, and the root cause of the misunderstanding. Write down your thoughts and feelings about the situation.

2. **Develop a Communication Plan:** Create a detailed plan for addressing the issue based on your reflection. Your plan should include expressing your feelings and needs clearly and respectfully, listening actively to the other person's perspective, and finding a mutually acceptable resolution.

3. **Initiate the Conversation:** Reach out to the person involved to have a conversation. Use your plan as a guide, but remain open to the conversation's natural flow. Focus on being assertive yet respectful, ensuring you both feel heard and understood.

Journal Reflection: After the conversation, spend some time journaling about the experience. Reflect on what went well, what could have been improved, and any insights gained about yourself and your relationship management skills.

This exercise enhances emotional intelligence by applying assertive communication strategies to real-life conflicts, fostering healthier and more supportive relationships.

Week 8 Day 5

Objective: To cultivate present-moment awareness and enhance sensory and emotional connection through a mindfulness walk, followed by reflective journaling, fostering a practice of presence beneficial for individuals managing depression.

Task: Engage in a mindfulness walk to enhance present-moment awareness, focusing on the sensory experiences and emotions that arise, followed by a reflective journaling session.

Instructions:

- **Preparation:** Choose a safe and quiet environment for your walk. Before starting, take a few deep breaths to center yourself, setting the intention to be fully present during the walk.
- **Mindfulness Walk:** Begin your walk at a comfortable pace. Direct your attention to the sensory experiences around you—the sights, sounds, smells, and the feeling of movement. Notice the details of your environment, the texture of the ground under your feet, the temperature of the air, and any smells or sounds that you encounter. If your mind wanders, gently acknowledge this and bring your focus back to the sensory experience of walking.
- **Journal Reflection:** After completing your walk, take some time to journal about the experience. Reflect on what you noticed, how it made you feel, and any emotions or thoughts that arose during the walk. Consider how this exercise affected your sense of presence and any insights you gained about your emotional state.

This day's exercise aims to deepen your mindfulness practice, enhancing your ability to stay present and connected to your experiences. Through mindful walking and reflective journaling, you're invited to explore the richness of the present moment, cultivating a sense of peace and grounding that can support emotional well-being.

Week 8 Day 6

Objective: Cultivate a deeper emotional awareness by consciously identifying and recording your emotions throughout the day. This exercise aims to enhance your understanding of how different situations impact your emotional state.

Information: For Day 6, focusing on the Emotion Naming Exercise, your goal is to enhance your emotional awareness by actively identifying and recording your emotions throughout the day. Start by carrying a small notebook or using a digital note-taking app where you can easily jot down your feelings. Each time you notice a significant emotion, pause for a moment. Note the emotion, describe the context or situation that elicited it, and briefly reflect on how it affected your thoughts or behavior. This practice improves self-awareness and helps recognize patterns in emotional responses, contributing to better emotional regulation and understanding.

Instructions:

1. **Preparation:** Begin your day by setting an intention to remain emotionally attentive. Equip yourself with a notebook or a digital app for easy access to jot down your observations.
2. **Observation:** Stay alert to your emotional shifts as you move through your day. Each time you encounter a noticeable emotion, take a moment to pause. Identify the emotion as precisely as you can. Is it joy, frustration, anxiety, contentment, or something else?

3. **Recording:** Write down the emotion you've identified in your notebook or app. Include a brief description of the context or situation that elicited this emotion. Note any specific thoughts or external events that may have triggered this emotional response.
4. **Reflection:** At the end of the day, review your entries. Reflect on the variety of emotions you experienced, the contexts that prompted them, and any patterns you notice. How do different environments, interactions, or activities influence your emotional landscape?

Journal Reflection: Expand on your reflections by journaling about the insights gained from this exercise. Consider how this increased awareness of your emotions and their triggers can inform your approach to emotional regulation and interpersonal relationships.

This structured exercise is designed to build your self-awareness and emotional intelligence by making you more mindful of your emotional responses and the stimuli that trigger them. Through diligent observation and reflection, you'll better understand your emotional self, contributing to your overall emotional well-being.

Week 8 Day 7

Objective: focusing on Empathy Practice, your task is to enhance your understanding and connection with others through deliberate empathy. The aim is to deepen your empathetic understanding by actively engaging in a conversation where you fully grasp another person's perspective and emotions without judgment.

Instructions:

1. **Selection:** Choose a friend, family member, or colleague you know is going through a challenging time or with whom you wish to connect deeply emotionally.
2. **Engagement:** Initiate a conversation with them, consciously approaching the discussion with an open heart and mind. Utilize active listening skills—hearing what they're saying, acknowledging their feelings, and asking open-ended questions to encourage deeper sharing.
3. **Reflection:** After the conversation, take some time for personal reflection. Consider how the conversation made you feel, what you learned about the other person's experiences and feelings, and how this exercise in empathy might impact your relationship with them and others in the future.

Journaling: Conclude the day by journaling about your experience. Write about the insights you gained from trying to understand another's perspective fully and any emotions that arose during the process. Reflect on how practicing empathy can enhance your emotional intelligence and the quality of your relationships.

This structured approach to practicing empathy fosters genuine under-standing and connection, reinforcing the importance of emotional intelligence in enhancing interpersonal relationships and personal growth.

Bridge Week 8

As you conclude the week, take a moment to align with your journey's progress. Visualize your location on the bridge, reflect on the changes and challenges faced, acknowledge all feelings, and remain hopeful about the journey ahead. Adjust your marker on the bridge to signify this week's experiences. This quick but meaningful reflection is crucial in navigating your way toward healing, offering a clear view of the progress you're making each step of the way.

14

Exploring Mindfulness and Acceptance

Welcome to Week 9, where we deepen our exploration into mindfulness, with a special focus on acceptance. Mindfulness, a practice of present-moment awareness, serves as our guide through the complexities of emotions and thoughts, teaching us the importance of observing without judgment. This week, we venture into understanding acceptance not as passive resignation, but as a dynamic engagement with our experiences, fostering compassion and openness towards ourselves.

Acceptance: The Essence of Mindfulness

At the core of mindfulness, acceptance acts as a foundational element, inviting us to embrace our immediate experiences—our thoughts, emotions, and bodily sensations—without the impulse to modify them. This principle of acceptance is not about passive resignation but an active, deliberate choice to be present with our experiences as they unfold, observing them with curiosity and openness. By doing so, we engage in a form of self-compassion, acknowledging our suffering and discomfort with a gentle, accepting stance, rather than meeting them with denial or resistance.

The power of acceptance in mindfulness extends beyond mere tolerance of our inner states; it facilitates a deeper understanding and connection with ourselves. In acknowledging our feelings and thoughts without judgment, we create a space where healing can commence. This doesn't imply that we desire or endorse our negative states but recognize them as part of our current reality, transient and not defining our essence.

Moreover, practicing acceptance empowers us to break the cycle of chronic negativity and self-criticism by shifting our perspective towards one of kindness and self-support. It helps dismantle the barriers we've erected against our own compassion, encouraging us to meet our own vulnerabilities with the same empathy and understanding we would offer a dear friend. This shift not only alleviates our own suffering but also enhances our capacity for empathy and connectedness with others, fostering a sense of common humanity and shared experience.

In essence, the practice of acceptance within mindfulness is transformative, offering us a pathway to navigate life's challenges with more grace and resilience. It teaches us that peace and well-being lie not in changing our external circumstances or suppressing our inner experiences, but in altering our relationship with them. Through acceptance, we learn that the serenity we seek is accessible not in the distant future, but in the depth of our present moment experience, woven into the fabric of our daily lives.

Acceptance plays a transformative role in managing depression. It encourages us to embrace our mental states without labeling them as 'good' or 'bad,' reducing the suffering that comes from resisting reality. By acknowledging our pain without the urge to immediately change it, we open ourselves to healing, emotional resilience, and growth.

The Practice of Acceptance in Mindfulness

Incorporating acceptance into mindfulness is a nuanced process that enhances our capacity to navigate life's ups and downs with greater ease and resilience. This integration involves a structured approach, each step building upon the other to cultivate a deep, transformative practice:

Observation: This initial step involves a conscious effort to pay attention to your moment-to-moment experiences. Observation in mindfulness is not passive; it's an active process of engaging with your thoughts, feelings, and bodily sensations as they arise. The key here is to maintain an attitude of openness, curiosity, and non-judgment. Imagine yourself as a neutral witness to your own experience, observing without getting caught up in the narrative of your thoughts or the intensity of your emotions. This detachment helps create a space between you and your experiences, offering clarity and a sense of calm amidst the chaos of the mind.

Acknowledgment: Following observation, acknowledgment involves recognizing and mentally noting your experiences. This step goes beyond mere awareness; it's about validating your feelings and thoughts without attaching undue significance or power to them. For instance, if you notice feelings of anxiety, you might silently note to yourself, "This is anxiety." Acknowledgment is a way of honoring your experience without letting it define or overwhelm you. It fosters a balanced perspective, where you're neither dismissing your feelings nor amplifying them. This balanced acknowledgment encourages a healthier relationship with your emotions and thoughts, one that's rooted in acceptance rather than avoidance or overidentification.

Allowing: At the heart of acceptance is the practice of allowing. This step is about letting your experiences be exactly as they are, without trying to change, suppress, or escape them. Allowing is a form of surrender to the present moment, but it's far from passive. It requires a conscious decision to give space to your thoughts and emotions, to say "Yes, this is happening" without judgment or resistance. This doesn't mean you have to like what's occurring, but rather you accept it as part of your current reality. Allowing creates an environment where emotions and thoughts can arise and pass without creating additional turmoil. It's an acknowledgment of the transient nature of our experiences and a step toward greater emotional freedom.

Compassion: The culmination of incorporating acceptance into mindfulness is the cultivation of compassion, particularly self-compassion. This involves treating yourself with the same kindness, care, and understanding that you would offer a good friend. Compassion means recognizing that suffering, failure, and imperfection are part of the shared human experience. It encourages a gentle, supportive dialogue with yourself, especially in moments of struggle. Compassion softens the often harsh self-criticism that can accompany difficult emotions and thoughts. By extending compassion to ourselves, we open the door to healing, self-acceptance, and a more loving relationship with our inner world.

Each of these steps represents a fundamental aspect of mindfulness practice focused on acceptance. Together, they form a comprehensive approach to embracing our moment-to-moment experiences with openness, kindness, and a deep sense of presence.

Transforming Our Relationship with Ourselves

Embracing acceptance is a transformative practice that reshapes our relationship with ourselves, steering us towards a path of self-discovery and growth. This process involves seeing our experiences, whether challenging or joyful, as catalysts for personal development rather than obstacles blocking our happiness. By adopting acceptance, we engage in a mindful cultivation of our inner landscape, akin to tending a garden. This metaphorical gardening encourages us to nurture seeds of peace and contentment, allowing them to flourish into a state of well-being. It fosters a compassionate connection with ourselves, where every thought, emotion, and sensation is met with kindness rather than criticism.

This approach doesn't just change how we interact with our thoughts and feelings; it fundamentally alters our perception of life's ups and downs, enabling us to find wisdom in adversity and serenity in turmoil. As we deepen our practice of acceptance, we learn to navigate life's complexities with grace, viewing each moment as an opportunity to grow and enrich our understanding of ourselves. This journey towards acceptance is not always easy, but it is incredibly rewarding, offering us a more peaceful, content, and compassionate way of being.

Daily Practices for Integrating Mindfulness and Acceptance

To embed these principles into your daily life, we propose a seven-day self-help guide, each day focusing on different aspects of mindfulness and acceptance, from mindful observation to cultivating compassion, and mindful listening. These exercises are designed not just as tasks but as gateways to deeper presence and understanding. Embracing these practices invites us into a journey of self-discovery, healing, and profound connection with the essence of who we are.

Let this guide serve as a beacon as you continue to weave mindfulness and acceptance into the fabric of your daily experiences, moving forward with resilience, peace, and a heart open to the full spectrum of life's experiences.

Week 9 Self-Help Guide

The seven-day self-help homework guide is a carefully structured journey designed to deepen your understanding and practice of mindfulness and acceptance. Each day, you'll engage in exercises that focus on different aspects of mindfulness, starting with the simple act of observing your present experiences in a non-judgmental way. From mindful observation to the naming of thoughts and emotions, allowing them space to simply be, and cultivating compassion towards oneself, the guide invites you to explore the transformative power of acceptance in daily life. You'll learn to integrate these practices into your routine, whether it's through engaging fully in everyday activities, enhancing connections through mindful listening, or fostering self-compassion in moments of discomfort. As you progress, the guide encourages reflection, helping you to see challenges as opportunities for growth and fostering a deeper, more compassionate relationship with yourself. This seven-day journey promises to enrich your daily experiences, offering insights into how mindfulness and acceptance can lead to a more peaceful, resilient, and fulfilling life.

Week 9 Day 1

Objective: The goal of today's exercise is to infuse an ordinary activity with mindfulness, transforming it into a rich experience of awareness and presence. By choosing an everyday task and engaging with it fully, you'll practice observing your immediate experience with fresh eyes, noticing the subtleties and nuances that are often overlooked.

Choosing Your Activity: Select an activity that is part of your daily routine but doesn't require intense concentration or effort. This could be drinking a cup of tea or coffee in the morning, taking a shower, eating a meal, or going for a walk. The simplicity of the activity allows you to focus more on the practice of mindfulness itself.

Practicing Mindful Observation:

1. **Prepare**: As you begin your chosen activity, take a moment to center yourself. Take a few deep breaths to bring your attention to the present moment.
2. **Engage Fully**: Engage in the activity with your full attention. If you're drinking a cup of tea, for instance, notice the weight of the cup in your hand, the steam rising, the aroma of the tea, and the warmth as you take a sip. Observe each sensation as it occurs, from the visual aspects to the tastes, sounds, and textures.
3. **Observe Your Thoughts**: As you engage in this activity, you'll likely notice thoughts arising. Instead of following these thoughts or making judgments about them, simply observe them as they pass. Imagine your thoughts as leaves floating down a stream, observing each one without getting caught up in its current.

4. **Gently Redirect**: Whenever you find your attention wandering away from the activity, gently acknowledge this and bring your focus back to the sensations of the moment. This act of redirecting your attention is where the practice of mindfulness lies.

5. **Embrace Each Moment**: Try to remain open and curious about the experience, as if you're encountering it for the first time. Notice any new details or aspects you may have previously overlooked.

Reflection: After completing the activity, spend a few minutes reflecting on the experience. Consider writing about it in a journal. How did the practice of mindful observation affect your experience of the activity? Did you notice anything new or unexpected? How did it feel to engage with an ordinary task consciously and mindfully?

This exercise is not just about the activity itself but about cultivating an attitude of mindfulness that you can carry into other aspects of your life. By practicing mindful observation, you learn to live more fully in the present moment, enriching your daily experiences with a deeper sense of awareness and appreciation.

Week 9 Day 2

Objective: Today's focus is on developing a mindful relationship with your thoughts and emotions through the practice of naming. This technique involves observing your inner experiences and gently labeling them, which can help create a helpful distance between you and these experiences, allowing for greater clarity and reduced intensity.

Understanding the Power of Naming: Naming our thoughts and emotions is a powerful mindfulness practice that helps us to step back and observe our internal states without getting caught up in them. It fosters awareness and recognition of our habitual thought patterns and emotional responses, encouraging a stance of curiosity rather than judgment.

How to Practice Naming:

1. **Prepare**: Find a quiet moment in your day to begin this practice. You can choose to sit quietly in a comfortable space or integrate this practice into your daily activities.
2. **Observe**: Start by bringing your attention inward observing your current thoughts and feelings. Allow your mind to settle and become aware of whatever arises without trying to change it.
3. **Name Gently**: As you notice thoughts or emotions, gently name them. For example, if you recognize a feeling of anxiety, you might mentally note, "This is anxiety," or simply, "anxiety." If a thought about the future arises, you could label it as "planning" or "worrying." The key is to use simple, neutral labels without getting involved in the narrative of the thought or emotion.

4. **Non-Identification**: Remember, the practice of naming is not about identifying with the thoughts or emotions ("I am anxious") but rather recognizing their presence ("This is anxiety"). This subtle shift helps create a space where you can observe your experiences without being defined by them.

5. **Return to Observation**: After naming your thoughts and emotions, return to a state of open observation, ready to name the next experience that arises. This continuous cycle of observation and naming helps to cultivate a deep sense of presence and mindfulness.

Reflection: After practicing the naming technique, take some time to reflect on the experience. How did it feel to name your thoughts and emotions? Did you notice any changes in your relationship with these experiences as you practiced naming? Reflecting on these questions can enhance your understanding of how naming influences your mindfulness practice.

This practice of naming is a step toward disentangling ourselves from the automatic identification with our thoughts and emotions. It offers a pathway to observing our internal landscape with greater clarity and equanimity. As you become more adept at naming, you may find that it becomes a valuable tool for navigating daily life with mindfulness and presence, helping to create a sense of calm and centeredness amidst the flux of internal experiences.

Day 3: Allowing Space

Objective: The essence of today's practice is to cultivate a mindful acceptance of your thoughts and emotions by allowing them the space to exist without resistance. This approach helps acknowledge and make peace with your experiences, recognizing them as temporary and not defining who you are.

Embracing the Concept of Allowing: Allowing is a gentle yet powerful mindfulness practice that teaches us to meet our internal experiences with openness and acceptance. Rather than trying to control, judge, or escape our thoughts and feelings, we learn to let them be. This practice can significantly shift our relationship with difficult emotions and thoughts, leading to greater peace and resilience.

Steps to Practice Allowing:

1. **Find a Comfortable Space**: Begin by finding a quiet and comfortable place where you can sit or lie down without interruptions. Take a few deep breaths to center yourself and prepare for the practice.
2. **Notice and Acknowledge**: Bring your awareness to your current thoughts and emotions. Notice what's present for you right now without trying to alter your experience. Acknowledge whatever arises, be it a sense of tension, a specific thought, or an emotion.
3. **Create Space**: Once you've acknowledged your experiences, imagine creating a spacious environment around them. Visualize giving your thoughts and emotions room to breathe, existing without the need for them to be different. This visualization can help foster a sense of acceptance and peace.
4. **Practice Non-Resistance**: If you find yourself wanting to push away or resist any thoughts or emotions, gently remind yourself of the intention to allow. Non-resistance doesn't mean you want or endorse these experiences; it simply means you're willing to let them be a part of your current reality.
5. **Observe Changes**: As you practice allowing, observe any changes in your thoughts, emotions, or bodily sensations. Often, simply giving space to these experiences can lead to a natural shift or softening.

Reflection: After completing the allowing practice, take some time to reflect on your experience. How did it feel to consciously allow your thoughts and emotions space? Did you notice any resistance to this practice, and if so, how did you address it? Reflecting on these aspects can deepen your understanding and appreciation of the power of cultivating mindfulness and acceptance.

Integrating Allowing into Daily Life: As you become more comfortable with this practice, try integrating it into your daily activities. When you encounter challenging situations or difficult emotions, remind yourself of the practice of allowing. By doing so, you can navigate life's ups and downs with greater ease and equanimity, fostering a more mindful and accepting relationship with yourself and your experiences.

Day 4: Cultivating Compassion

Objective: The focus for today is on cultivating compassion towards oneself, particularly in moments of difficulty or discomfort. This practice involves directing kindness and understanding inward, recognizing our common humanity and the universal experience of suffering.

Understanding Self-Compassion: Self-compassion is an essential component of mindfulness and acceptance, offering a soothing balm to the wounds of critical self-judgment and harshness. It encourages us to treat ourselves with the kindness and care we would provide a dear friend in distress. Cultivating compassion towards ourselves can significantly alter our emotional landscape, introducing a sense of warmth and safety that fosters healing and growth.

Steps to Practice Self-Compassion:

1. **Prepare Your Mind and Body**: Find a quiet, comfortable place where you won't be disturbed. Begin by taking several deep, calming breaths to ground yourself in the present moment.

2. **Recognize Your Suffering**: Bring to mind a recent situation or ongoing circumstance that causes you distress or suffering. Acknowledge this difficulty openly, without judgment or minimization.

3. **Connect with Your Humanity**: Remind yourself that suffering is a part of the human experience—that you are not alone in feeling this way. This recognition can help you feel connected to others in their struggles, reducing feelings of isolation.

4. **Direct Kindness Inward**: Imagine directing words of kindness and compassion towards yourself. You might use phrases such as "May I be kind to myself," "May I accept myself as I am," or "May I learn to accept my suffering with compassion." Feel free to create phrases that resonate deeply with you.

5. **Embrace Compassion Fully**: Allow yourself to fully receive this compassion. Notice any areas of resistance and, if possible, offer these parts of yourself compassion as well. If emotions arise, permit them to be present, surrounding them with your compassionate attention.

Reflection: After engaging in the self-compassion meditation, spend some time reflecting on the experience. How did it feel to offer yourself compassion? Were there parts of the practice that felt particularly challenging or especially soothing? Writing about these reflections can enhance your understanding of self-compassion and its role in your life.

Integrating Compassion into Daily Moments: As you move through your day, look for opportunities to practice self-compassion. It might be in moments of self-criticism, disappointment, or when facing challenges. Pause, offer yourself a compassionate phrase, and notice the impact this has on your experience.

Week 9 Day 5

Objective: Today's practice centers on mindful listening, a powerful aspect of mindfulness that enhances our ability to connect with others and the world around us. By engaging in mindful listening, we learn to be fully present with someone else's words, fostering deeper understanding and empathy.

The Essence of Mindful Listening: Mindful listening involves giving complete attention to the person speaking, free from distractions, judgments, or the preparation of our subsequent response. It's about hearing not just the words but also the emotions and intentions behind them. This practice can transform our interactions, making them more meaningful and connected.

Steps to Practice Mindful Listening:

1. **Set an Intention**: Before entering a conversation, set the intention to listen mindfully. Remind yourself of the importance of truly hearing the other person and the value of your presence in the conversation.
2. **Full Presence**: Engage in the conversation with your full presence. Put away any distractions such as phones or other devices. Position your body to show you are fully engaged, making eye contact if appropriate and nodding to acknowledge you are listening.
3. **Listen Beyond Words**: Pay attention not just to the words being spoken but also to the tone of voice, facial expressions, and body language. These non-verbal cues can provide a deeper understanding of the speaker's message and emotions.

4. **Notice Your Reactions**: Be aware of your reactions and thoughts as you listen. If you find yourself planning what to say next or judging what's being said, gently bring your attention back to simply listening. Practice holding space for the speaker's words and experiences without inserting your own.
5. **Respond with Empathy**: When it's time to respond, do so with empathy and understanding. Reflect what you've heard to ensure you've understood correctly and show that you value the speaker's perspective.

Reflection: After engaging in mindful listening, take some time to reflect on the experience. How did practicing mindful listening change the dynamic of the conversation? Did you notice anything new about how you listened or the person you were engaging with? Reflecting on these questions can deepen your appreciation for mindful listening and its impact on your relationships.

Integrating Mindful Listening into Everyday Interactions: Try to incorporate mindful listening into various interactions throughout your day, whether it's a deep conversation with a friend or a casual exchange with a colleague. Notice how this practice affects your connections with others and your sense of presence and engagement in your interactions.

Week 9 Day 6

Objective: Today, we focus on the body scan meditation, a practice aimed at promoting acceptance and awareness of the body. This exercise encourages a mindful exploration of bodily sensations, fostering a deeper connection with and acceptance of our physical selves.

Understanding the Body Scan Meditation: The body scan is a foundational mindfulness practice that involves mentally scanning your body from head to toe, noticing any sensations, tensions, or discomfort without judgment. It teaches us to be present with our bodies, recognizing our physical experiences as they are, which can lead to greater acceptance and kindness towards ourselves.

Steps to Practice Body Scan for Acceptance:

1. **Find a Quiet Space**: Begin by finding a comfortable and quiet place where you can lie down on your back, perhaps on a mat or a bed. Allow your arms to rest by your sides, palms facing up, and let your feet fall gently apart.
2. **Start with a Few Deep Breaths**: Take a moment to breathe deeply, inhaling through your nose and exhaling through your mouth. Allow each breath to ground you further into the present moment, preparing your mind and body for the body scan.
3. **Begin the Scan at Your Feet**: Direct your attention to your feet. Notice any sensations you feel—warmth, coolness, tingling, or maybe nothing at all. Whatever you observe is perfectly fine. Practice accepting these sensations without trying to change them.

4. **Gradually Move Upwards**: Slowly move your attention up through your body— to your ankles, legs, hips, abdomen, chest, back, arms, hands, neck, and finally, your head. At each part of your body, pause to notice any sensations, tensions, or discomfort. Approach each observation with curiosity and openness, without judgment.

5. **Acknowledge and Allow**: As you notice areas of tension or discomfort, acknowledge them and imagine breathing into them with acceptance. Visualize your breath, creating space around any tightness or pain, offering a sense of ease and compassion.

6. **Complete the Scan with Gratitude**: Once you've scanned your entire body, take a few moments to feel a sense of gratitude for your body and all it does for you. Acknowledge the complex and beautiful vessel that carries you through life with all its imperfections and strengths.

Reflection: After completing the body scan, reflect on your experience. How did it feel to approach your body with acceptance rather than judgment? Were there parts of your body that were more challenging to accept? Writing about your experience can help solidify your practice of acceptance and awareness.

Integrating the Body Scan into Daily Life: The body scan can be a valuable tool for moments when you feel disconnected from your body or when physical discomfort arises. By practicing acceptance towards your body regularly, you cultivate a more compassionate and understanding relationship with yourself, which can enhance your overall well-being and mindfulness practice.

The body scan for acceptance is a powerful reminder that mindfulness extends beyond the mind, encompassing our physical selves. By embracing our bodies with acceptance and kindness, we support our journey toward a more integrated sense of self rooted in mindfulness and compassion.

Week 9 Day 7

Objective: On this final day, the goal is to bring together all that you've learned about mindfulness and acceptance, applying these practices to a specific challenge or aspect of your daily life. This integration is a culmination of your week's journey, embodying mindfulness and acceptance in action.

Choosing Your Challenge: Reflect on your week and identify a situation, interaction, or aspect of your daily routine that you find challenging. This could be a task you've been avoiding, a difficult conversation you need to have, or even a personal habit you're trying to change. The key is to choose something that feels significant to you and where you can consciously apply mindfulness and acceptance.

Preparation: Before engaging with your chosen challenge, take a few moments to ground yourself in the present. Find a quiet space to sit comfortably, close your eyes, and take several deep breaths. Remind yourself of the practices of observation, naming, allowing, and cultivating compassion. Set an intention to approach your challenge with mindfulness and acceptance.

Mindful Engagement:

1. **Approach with Observation**: As you begin to engage with your challenge, maintain an attitude of mindful observation. Notice your thoughts, emotions, and bodily sensations without getting caught up in them. Remember, you are not your thoughts or feelings; you are the awareness that observes them.

2. **Practice Naming and Allowing**: Use the naming practice to label your experiences as they arise ("This is anxiety," "I am feeling frustrated," etc.). Then, practice allowing these experiences to be present without resistance. Imagine giving them space to exist alongside you.

3. **Apply Compassion**: Be especially mindful when applying compassion towards yourself during this challenge. Acknowledge that it's okay to find this situation difficult and remind yourself that you're doing your best. Use compassionate self-talk and remember that everyone faces challenges.

4. **Reflect on Your Experience**: After engaging with your challenge, take time to reflect on the experience. How did applying mindfulness and acceptance change your approach or experience of the challenge? What did you learn about yourself in the process?

Integration into Daily Life: Consider how you can continue to integrate mindfulness and acceptance into your daily life beyond this exercise. Mindfulness is not just a practice for the meditation cushion, but a way of being that can transform our relationship with ourselves, others, and the world around us.

By choosing to engage mindfully and acceptingly with our challenges, we not only find new ways to navigate them but also open ourselves to growth and transformation. This practice of integrating mindfulness and acceptance into our daily challenges is a powerful tool for cultivating resilience, peace, and a deeper sense of connection to the present moment.

Bridge Week 9

As this week draws to a close, afford yourself a moment of introspection regarding your traversal of the bridge. Contemplate where you find yourself along this metaphorical journey, mull over the week's insights and obstacles, hold your emotions gently, and cast a hopeful eye towards what lies ahead. Adjust your symbolic marker on the bridge to denote your current stance, capturing the essence of this week's navigation.

15

Self-Care and Social Connections

This week we find ourselves at looking at the realms of self-care and the nurturing of social connections. This chapter unfolds a broader perspective on self-care, transcending the conventional indulgences often highlighted in popular culture. Self-care is an intricate blend of daily actions and decisions to support our physical, mental, and emotional health. From setting boundaries that safeguard our peace to engaging in activities that replenish our spirits, self-care emerges as a dynamic and multifaceted practice essential for our well-being.

Moreover, this chapter illuminates the profound significance of cultivating supportive and enriching social connections. In a world where isolation can easily creep into our lives, the art of building and maintaining relationships stands as a beacon of hope and healing. It's about cherishing the bonds that bring joy and comfort and seeking new connections that inspire growth and understanding. Through these relationships, we find mirrors reflecting our humanity, offering compassion, empathy, and mutual support that nourish our souls.

This week is an invitation to explore the layers of self-care and embrace the beauty of human connection. It's a call to action to prioritize ourselves in a society that often demands we place others first, reminding us that in nurturing our hearts, we are better equipped to extend our love and support to those around us. As we venture through this chapter, let us hold dear the principle that caring for oneself and forging solid relationships are not mere acts of self-preservation but radical acts of self-love that have the power to transform our lives and the lives of those we touch.

The Core of Self-Care

The essence of self-care extends far beyond the surface-level practices often depicted in media. It is a deeply personal journey, an ongoing dialogue with oneself about what is needed to thrive, not just survive. The core of self-care lies in understanding and honoring your unique needs, desires, and circumstances. It's about cultivating a relationship with yourself rooted in kindness, respect, and understanding.

As we delve into the intricacies of self-care, we find it encompasses a spectrum of practices that cater to our physical, mental, emotional, and spiritual well-being. Setting boundaries is a critical aspect of self-care, serving as a protective barrier that guards our energy against the demands and stresses of daily life. It's about learning to say no, to prioritize your well-being, and to recognize that your needs are valid and important.

Committing to a regular sleep schedule is another cornerstone of self-care, recognizing sleep as a foundational element of health. Quality sleep rejuvenates the mind and body, enhancing our ability to think clearly, manage emotions, and maintain physical health. It's a commitment to honoring the body's need for rest and regeneration.

Finding joy in movement is a celebration of the body's capabilities and a form of self-care that nourishes both the body and soul. Movement is a powerful way to connect with your body and release tension and stress, whether it's a gentle yoga session, a brisk walk in nature, or dancing to your favorite songs.

Moreover, self-care involves the quieter, introspective practices that allow us to connect with our inner selves. Starting a journal offers a space for reflection, a place to process thoughts and emotions, and to celebrate victories, no matter how small. Meditation, even for a few minutes each day, can be a profound practice of self-care, providing a moment of peace, grounding, and connection to the present.

Enjoying a cup of tea in quiet reflection embodies the simplicity at the heart of self-care. It's an act of slowing down, savoring the moment, and being present with oneself. This simple practice can remind us of the beauty in stillness and the importance of pausing in our fast-paced lives.

Self-care is indeed a necessity. It is the bedrock upon which we can build a life of stability, fulfillment, and resilience. This week, as you explore the various facets of self-care, remember that it's about finding what works for you, what brings you joy, and what helps you to feel balanced and ready to face the world. It's an individualized practice that evolves with you over time, adapting to your changing needs and circumstances. Let this exploration be guided by self-compassion and a deep commitment to your well-being.

Fostering Social Connections: Fostering social connections is an essential aspect of our well-being, deeply rooted in our innate nature as social creatures. The warmth of companionship, the strength of shared experiences, and the comfort of belonging are important for mental and emotional health. Amid life's rapid pace, the significance of these connections can sometimes fade into the background, overshadowed by the demands of our daily routines and responsibilities. Yet, it is precisely in these moments that reaching out and reinforcing our bonds becomes most vital.

This week presents an opportune moment to rekindle the spark of social interaction and deepen the ties that bind us to others. Emphasizing the quality of these connections rather than the quantity can transform our social landscape. It's about making intentional choices to engage in interactions that are rich in meaning and satisfaction.

Sending a thoughtful message to a friend, a simple gesture that may seem small, can have profound effects. It's a way of saying, "I'm thinking of you," which can brighten someone's day and reinforce the bond you share. It's about acknowledging the value of the relationship and showing that, despite the busyness of life, you make time for those who matter to you.

Planning a family dinner is another way to strengthen connections. It's a chance to come together, share stories, and enjoy each other's company in a relaxed setting. These moments of togetherness foster a sense of belonging and create memories that can be a source of comfort and joy.

Joining a community class that interests you is a fantastic way to expand your social network while engaging in activities you love. Whether it's a cooking class, a photography workshop, or a fitness group, these settings provide unique opportunities to meet new people who share your interests. The shared learning experience and growing together can lay the foundation for meaningful and supportive relationships.

The goal of fostering social connections is to cultivate genuine, enriching, and supportive interactions. It's about creating a social environment where you feel uplifted and where you can also uplift others. This week, let us embrace the beauty of connection, recognizing that each interaction, no matter how small, is a step toward a more connected and supportive community. Let's cherish the relationships we have and remain open to the new ones that may come our way, knowing that each connection has the potential to enrich our lives in immeasurable ways.

Strategies for Improving Relationships: The path to sustaining healthy relationships is woven with intention and effort. Imagine walking alongside someone, where the ground beneath is paved with understanding, trust, and genuine connection. This goes beyond being physically present. It calls for a deeper engagement with those we care about.

Consider the act of active listening a foundational stone in this path. It's when you truly immerse yourself in listening to someone, setting aside the urge to craft your reply while they're still sharing their thoughts. Imagine the scene: two friends sitting across from each other, one sharing a story, the other listening intently, nodding, and responding at just the right moments. This kind of listening communicates a powerful message: "Your thoughts and feelings matter to me." It's a testament to the value you place on the relationship, showing care and respect for the other's perspective.

Empathy is the bridge that connects two souls, allowing one to cross into the realm of the other's experiences and view the world through their eyes. It's about more than just understanding someone's feelings; it's about feeling with them. Picture a moment when a loved one is going through a tough time. Instead of offering solutions or dismissing their feelings, you sit with them in their moment of vulnerability, acknowledging their pain and letting them know they're not alone. This shared emotional space fosters a deep bond, a trust that says, "I see you, I hear you, and I'm with you."

Open communication is the lifeline of any relationship. It's about sharing your thoughts and feelings in a manner that's both honest and respectful. Imagine navigating a misunderstanding with a partner. Instead of letting assumptions and frustrations build up, you choose to have an open conversation. You share your perspective, listen to theirs, and together, find common ground. This openness prevents the build-up of resentment and misunderstandings, laying the groundwork for a relationship that can withstand the tests of time.

Finally, the essence of quality time. It's not about the duration spent together but the depth of the connection during those moments. Imagine a day spent with a family member doing something you both enjoy, free from the distractions of daily life. It could be as simple as a walk in the park, immersed in nature and each other's company, where conversations flow freely and laughter fills the air. These moments of undivided attention and shared experiences are the threads that strengthen the fabric of your relationships.

In the pages that follow, you'll discover the self-help guide designed to enhance your self-care practices and equip you with valuable tools for nurturing deeper social connections. This guide serves as a companion on your journey toward a more fulfilling and connected life, offering practical steps to cultivate well-being and strengthen relationships with those around you. Embrace this opportunity to transform your approach to self-care and foster meaningful connections, setting the stage for a richer, more vibrant life experience.

Week 10 Self-Help Guide

Week 10 Day 1

Objective: The objective of today is to initiate a reflective process that sets the foundation for this week's journey toward enhancing self-care and deepening social connections. It's a day dedicated to introspection and goal-setting, aiming to create a balanced approach to nurturing oneself and fostering meaningful relationships.

Information: Balancing self-care with social interaction is crucial for mental health and well-being. Today's exercise encourages you to reflect on your current practices and aspirations in these areas. By setting clear, achievable goals, you're laying the groundwork for a week of intentional actions aimed at improving your quality of life.

Instructions:

1. **Prepare Your Space:** Find a quiet, comfortable spot where you can reflect without interruptions. Have your journal and a pen ready, or open a new document on your digital device if you prefer typing.
2. **Reflect on Your Current Balance:** Spend the first 10 minutes thinking about how you currently manage self-care and social interactions. Consider the following questions:
   - How do I prioritize self-care in my daily routine?
   - What types of social interactions do I engage in regularly? Are these fulfilling?
   - Are there aspects of my self-care or social life that feel neglected or unbalanced?
3. **Set Your Goals:** Based on your reflection, set two specific goals for the week:

- One goal related to enhancing your self-care. This could be anything from incorporating a new self-care activity into your routine to improving your sleep hygiene.
- Another goal is to deepen or broaden your social connections. Think about reaching out to a friend you haven't spoken to in a while, joining a new group or club, or simply spending more quality time with family.

4. **Write in Your Journal:** Spend the next 10 minutes writing about your reflections and the goals you've set. Describe why these goals are important to you and how achieving them will impact your well-being.

Reflection: After completing today's task, reflect on the process for a few moments. How did it feel to dedicate time to introspection? Do your goals feel aligned with your desires for personal growth and social fulfillment?

Integration: Consider how you can integrate today's reflections and goals into the upcoming days. Keep your journal handy throughout the week to jot down any thoughts, progress, or challenges related to your goals. This ongoing reflection will enhance your awareness and commitment to self-care and nurturing social connections.

Today is just the beginning. As you move forward, remember that the journey toward a balanced and fulfilling life is ongoing. Your reflections and goals set today will serve as a compass, guiding your actions and decisions in the days to come.

Week 10 Day 2

Objective: Today's focus is on taking proactive steps to strengthen your social network by reaching out to someone you've been meaning to connect with but haven't had the opportunity to do so recently. This exercise emphasizes the importance of maintaining and nurturing relationships, recognizing that reconnecting can bring joy and a renewed sense of community.

Information: Social connections play a crucial role in our overall well-being. Reaching out to others reinforces our social bonds and fosters a sense of belonging and support. Today, you're encouraged to bridge the gap that time and circumstances may have created in your relationships. This task is about making the first move toward rekindling a connection demonstrating the value you place on your relationships.

Instructions:

1. **Select Someone to Reach Out To:** Think of a friend, family member, or colleague you've lost touch with or haven't spoken to in a while. Choose someone whose company you've missed or have been thinking about recently.

2. **Decide on Your Method of Communication:** Depending on your relationship with this person and your personal preference, choose whether to send a message (text, email, social media) or make a phone call. Consider what method of communication they would most appreciate.

3. **Craft Your Message or Conversation Starters:** If sending a message, take a moment to write something heartfelt and genuine. Express your desire to reconnect and perhaps share a fond

memory or a thoughtful inquiry about their life. If calling, mentally prepare a few points you'd like to discuss or simply express your wish to catch up.

4. **Reach Out:** Send your message or make the call. Remember, the goal is to open the door to reconnection without expecting immediate response or engagement.

5. **Reflect in Your Journal:** After reaching out, spend some time writing about the experience in your journal. Note who you decided to reach out to, the method you chose, and why. Reflect on your feelings before, during, and after the process. If they respond, note their reaction and how the reconnection made you feel. If there's no response, reflect on your feelings about that as well.

Reflection: Consider the emotional impact of reaching out to someone you've missed. How did it feel to take that step? Reflect on the importance of maintaining connections and the role they play in your life.

Integration: Think about how you can make reaching out and reconnecting with others a more regular part of your life. Integrating this practice into your routine can enhance your social well-being and strengthen your support network. Moving forward, consider setting a regular schedule, perhaps once a month, to reach out to someone you haven't spoken to in a while, thereby continuously nurturing your relationships.

Week 10 Day 3

Objective: The goal for today is to inject novelty into your self-care routine by exploring new practices or revisiting activities you haven't engaged in for a while. This exploration aims to broaden your self-care repertoire, potentially uncovering new sources of joy, relaxation, and fulfillment.

Information: Self-care is a dynamic and personalized process involving a range of activities that nurture your physical, mental, and emotional well-being. By introducing new practices into your routine, you challenge yourself to step out of your comfort zone, promoting growth and self-discovery. Today's task encourages you to embrace the unfamiliar, recognizing that new experiences can offer fresh perspectives and enhance your overall quality of life.

Instructions:

1. **Identify a New Self-Care Activity:** Reflect on activities you've been curious about but haven't tried, or consider past interests you've not pursued in a long time. This could be anything from starting a creative project, like painting or writing, to physical activities such as a dance class or hiking in a new location. Even simpler actions qualify, like trying a new cooking recipe or taking a different route on your walk.

2. **Prepare for the Activity:** Once you've chosen your new self-care practice, take any necessary steps to prepare. This might involve gathering materials, finding a recipe, or researching a new walking path. Approach this preparation as part of the self-care

experience, allowing yourself to fully engage in the anticipation and planning.

3. **Engage in the Activity:** Dedicate time to immerse yourself in this new experience. Do your best to be present, letting go of judgments or expectations about how it should go. Allow yourself to simply enjoy the process, regardless of the outcome.

4. **Reflect on the Experience:** After completing the activity, take some time to reflect on the experience. How did engaging in something new make you feel? Did you discover any unexpected sources of joy or relaxation? Were there any challenges, and how did you feel about overcoming them?

5. **Journal Your Reflections:** Write about the activity you chose, why you chose it, and your experience engaging with it. Include your emotional reactions, any surprises you encountered, and whether you'd like to incorporate this into your regular self-care routine.

Reflection: Reflect on the value of incorporating new and varied practices into your self-care routine. How does trying new things contribute to your sense of self and well-being?

Integration: Consider how you can continue to explore new self-care practices in the future. Think about setting a regular interval, maybe once a month, to try something new or revisit a long-forgotten hobby. This ongoing commitment to self-exploration and care can lead to a more enriched and fulfilling life.

Week 10 Day 4

Objective: Today's objective is to enhance your empathy skills by engaging in a conversation to fully understand the other person's perspective. This exercise is designed to deepen your connections and foster a greater understanding within your relationships, particularly in unfamiliar or challenging contexts.

Information: Empathy, the ability to understand and share the feelings of another, is a cornerstone of meaningful relationships. It requires setting aside our viewpoints to fully immerse ourselves in another's experience. By practicing empathy in our conversations, we enrich our relationships and cultivate a supportive and compassionate community around us. Today, you're encouraged to choose a dialogue that challenges you to stretch your empathetic understanding, providing an opportunity for personal and relational growth.

Instructions:

1. **Select the Conversation:** Think of a person you can have a meaningful conversation with today. This might be someone with a different background, belief system, or life experience that you find challenging to understand. The conversation could be scheduled, like a meet-up or call, or it could happen organically.
2. **Prepare Yourself Mentally:** Before the conversation, take a few moments to center yourself and set the intention to listen deeply. Remind yourself that the goal is to understand the other person's perspective without judgment or needing to offer advice unless asked.

3. **Engage Fully:** During the conversation, focus your attention entirely on the other person. Listen to their words, observe their nonverbal cues, and ask open-ended questions to encourage them to express themselves more fully. Practice active listening by summarizing what you've heard and asking for clarification to ensure you've understood correctly.

4. **Reflect on the Experience:** After the conversation, spend some time reflecting on the experience. Consider how focusing on empathy affected the dynamic of the conversation. Did you discover anything new about the person or their perspective? How did the effort to empathize impact your feelings toward them and the relationship as a whole?

5. **Journal Your Reflections:** Write about the conversation in your journal, focusing on your process of trying to understand the other person's perspective. Include your initial feelings, challenges you faced in maintaining an empathetic stance, and insights gained from the experience.

Reflection: Reflect on the role empathy plays in enhancing relationships and fostering understanding. Consider how practicing empathy can change the way you relate to others, especially in conversations that challenge your perspectives.

Integration: Think about how you can continue to cultivate empathy in your daily interactions. Commit to approach conversations with an open heart and mind, striving to understand rather than to be understood. This ongoing practice can transform your relationships and contribute to a more compassionate world.

Week 10 Day 5

Objective: The focus of Day 5 is to actively foster and enjoy your social connections by organizing a small gathering or a one-on-one meet-up. The essence of this task is to spend quality time with someone, emphasizing the importance of being fully present and engaged during the interaction. This endeavor aims to strengthen bonds, create shared experiences, and enhance relationships.

Information: Quality time is a crucial component of maintaining and deepening relationships. It allows for meaningful interactions that can reinforce the bonds we share with others. By dedicating focused time to someone, free from the usual distractions of daily life, we communicate their importance in our lives. Today, you're encouraged to initiate an activity that facilitates this kind of connection, whether it's a simple coffee date, sharing a meal, or taking a leisurely walk together.

Instructions:

1. **Choose Your Activity:** Decide the type of get-together you want to organize. Consider activities that both you and the other person enjoy, and that will allow for uninterrupted conversation and interaction. This could be as simple as meeting for coffee, having lunch or dinner together, going for a walk in a park, or visiting a museum.

2. **Invite Your Guest(s):** Reach out to the person or people you want to spend time with. Provide them with the details of your planned get-together, including the date, time, and location. Make sure to communicate the casual and relaxed nature of the meet-up, emphasizing your desire to spend quality time together.

3. **Prepare for the Meet-Up:** Make any reservations or preparations required for your chosen activity. Consider any special touches that could make the get-together more enjoyable, such as selecting a venue with a great atmosphere or bringing a thoughtful item to share.

4. **Be Fully Present:** During the get-together, make a conscious effort to be fully present. This means putting away your phone and any other potential distractions. Focus on engaging in meaningful conversation, actively listening, and sharing openly with your companion(s).

5. **Reflect on the Experience:** After the meet-up, take some time to reflect on the experience. How did spending quality time with this person or these people feel? What did you learn about them that you didn't know before? How has this experience impacted your relationship?

6. **Journal Your Reflections:** Write about the get-together in your journal, detailing the activity you chose, who you spent time with, and how the experience made you feel. Note any changes or deepening in your relationship due to this quality time spent together.

Reflection: Reflect on the significance of quality time in building and sustaining relationships. Consider how making time for others enriches your connections and contributes to your well-being.

Integration: Think about how you can incorporate regular meet-ups into your routine to ensure you're continually nurturing your relationships. Whether scheduling a monthly dinner with a friend or organizing family gatherings, prioritize quality time with loved ones.

Week 10 Day 6

Objective: The objective for Day 6 is to explore the harmonious blend of self-care and social interaction by combining these elements into a single activity. This approach aims to enhance your enjoyment and engagement with both the self-care practice and the interpersonal connection, showcasing the synergistic potential of integrating these aspects of your life.

Information: Self-care and social interactions are essential components of a well-rounded life, contributing significantly to our mental and emotional well-being. By merging these elements, we double the benefits and create unique opportunities for shared experiences that can deepen our relationships. This exercise encourages you to select an activity that serves as a self-care practice and a means of connecting with someone important to you, reinforcing the idea that taking care of ourselves and nurturing our relationships can be a simultaneous, mutually reinforcing process.

Instructions:

1. **Choose an Activity:** Select a self-care activity that can be shared with a friend or loved one. This could be attending a yoga class together, participating in a joint meditation session online, crafting, cooking a meal together, or even going for a nature walk. Ensure it's something both of you will enjoy and find rejuvenating.

2. **Plan and Coordinate:** Reach out to the person you've chosen to share this experience with and coordinate the details. Discuss

the activity, decide on a time and place (if applicable), and make any necessary preparations or reservations.

3. **Engage in the Activity:** Participate in the chosen activity together, making a conscious effort to be fully present. Focus on the experience itself, as well as the joy of sharing this time with someone else. Allow yourself to be open to the dual benefits of the activity—nurturing your well-being while strengthening your bond with the other person.

4. **Reflect on the Experience:** After completing the activity, take some time to reflect on how the integration of self-care and social interaction influenced your experience. Consider how the shared aspect of the activity affected your enjoyment and engagement. Did it enhance the self-care practice? How did it impact your relationship with the person you shared it with?

5. **Journal Your Reflections:** Document your chosen activity, the planning process, your experience during the activity, and your reflections afterward. Include any insights on how combining self-care with social interaction contributed to your overall well-being and relationship quality.

Reflection: Reflect on the value of integrating self-care practices with social interactions. How does sharing self-care activities affect your relationships? What did you learn about the balance between nurturing yourself and nurturing your relationships?

Integration: Based on today's experience, consider how you might continue incorporating shared self-care activities into your routine. Think about other activities you can enjoy with friends or loved ones that contribute to your well-being and strengthen your connections. Commit to regularly schedule such activities, recognizing them as vital components of a balanced, fulfilling life.

Week 10 Day 7

Objective: The focus of today is to reflect thoughtfully on the week's journey, examining the insights gained from each day's activities. This process of reflection aims to solidify your understanding and appreciation of the roles that self-care and social connections play in your life. Based on your reflections, you'll set a concrete action plan for the upcoming week to continue nurturing your well-being and enriching your social interactions.

Information: Reflection is a powerful tool for personal growth, allowing us to recognize our progress, understand our experiences, and identify areas for future development. Reviewing your journal entries and contemplating the impact of this week's exercises will give you a deeper understanding of your relationship with self-care and social connections. This day is about synthesizing your experiences and using your insights to inform your path forward, ensuring that the lessons learned translate into continued growth and enrichment.

Instructions:

1. **Review Your Journal Entries:** Read your journal entries from the past week. Pay particular attention to your observations, feelings, and any changes you've noticed in your approach to self-care and your interactions with others.

2. **Reflect on Your Growth:** Reflect on the insights you've gained throughout the week. Consider the following questions:
   ○ How have my views on self-care and social connections evolved over the week?

- What activities or practices did I find most beneficial for my well-being?
- How have this week's exercises impacted my relationships?

3. **Identify Key Insights:** Summarize the key insights or revelations that have emerged from your reflections. These might relate to the importance of self-care, the value of empathy in conversations, the joy found in reconnecting with others, or any other significant realizations.

4. **Plan One Action:** Based on your reflections and the insights you've gathered, plan one specific action to take in the coming week. This should be something that builds on what you've learned and aims to further enhance your self-care practice or deepen your social connections. Be as concrete and detailed as possible in your planning.

5. **Journal Your Plan:** Document your reflective process and the action you've decided to take. Include your reasoning behind the chosen action and how you expect it to contribute to your ongoing growth and fulfillment.

Reflection: Reflect on the value of periodic reflection in your life. How does taking the time to review and plan help you to live more intentionally and align your actions with your values and goals?

Integration: Consider how you can incorporate regular reflection and planning into your routine. Setting aside time each week to review your experiences and set intentions for the coming week can be a powerful practice for sustained personal development and well-being.

By dedicating today to reflection and planning, you're acknowledging the progress you've made and committing to continued growth. This process is essential for applying the lessons learned to your life, ensuring that the insights gained during this week lead to lasting changes in your approach to self-care and social connections.

Bridge Week 10

As you reach the end of the week, take a brief pause to connect with your position on the journey's bridge. Visualize precisely where you stand, reflect on the events and emotions of the week, and consider your anticipation for the path that lies ahead. Then, update your marker on the bridge to accurately reflect this moment in your journey. This act of marking your progress serves as a straightforward reminder of the steps you're taking towards your goals.

16

Setting Goals and Taking Action

Depression can often feel like a dense fog, obscuring your path and making even the thought of taking action seem daunting. However, this week, we arm you with strategies to cut through this fog with clarity and determination. We will explore how to set goals that are not only meaningful and aligned with your values but also realistic and achievable within the context of your current circumstances. This pragmatic approach acknowledges the challenges of depression while empowering you to move forward, one step at a time.

The journey of recovery from depression is punctuated by small yet profoundly significant victories—moments when you choose action over inertia, hope over despair. This week is dedicated to fostering those victories. We will guide you through breaking down your overarching goals into manageable, actionable steps, anticipating potential obstacles, and cultivating resilience in the face of setbacks.

As we embark, consider this a warm invitation to embrace the transformative power of setting goals and taking action. This week is about more than just planning for the future; it's about actively constructing the foundation of a life where depression no longer dictates your capabilities or limits your horizons. Let's take this step forward, armed with determination and guided by the values that make you uniquely you.

Understanding the Power of Goals

In the realm of healing and personal development, goals are not merely tasks to be checked off. They are, indeed, the stepping-stones of a fulfilling and meaningful life. These goals offer direction in times of uncertainty, purpose amidst the chaos, and a profound sense of accomplishment upon their realization. When your goals align with your values, they become a powerful roadmap, charting a course through the often murky waters of depression.

Goals have the unique ability to transform your outlook on life. They shift your focus from what is currently lacking to what is possible. This shift is not trivial—it's foundational to overcoming the inertia that depression can create. By setting goals, you engage in an act of hope, projecting your intentions into the future and taking control over the direction of your life.

The most impactful goals resonate with your core values—the principles that give your life meaning and guide your decisions. When goals are aligned with these values, they not only provide motivation but also enrich your sense of self and purpose. This alignment ensures that each step reflects your goals and reinforces your identity and what you stand for, making the journey as meaningful as the destination.

Depression can cloud your vision of the future, making it difficult to see beyond the current moment of despair. Goals act as a light in this fog. They help partition the overwhelming expanse of recovery into manageable segments, making progress tangible and measurable. This roadmap is not rigid; it's adaptable, allowing you to navigate the challenges of depression with flexibility and resilience.

The journey out of depression is marked by small victories and moments of clarity that, over time, accumulate into profound transformation. The satisfaction and sense of achievement derived from reaching your goals—even the smallest ones—are powerful antidotes to the feelings of worthlessness and despair that accompany depression.

The Importance of Realistic Goal Setting

The significance of setting realistic and achievable goals cannot be overstated. While ambitious goals may initially seem motivating, they often lead to a cycle of feelings of inadequacy and frustration, especially when the pervasive effects of depression impede our ability to gather the energy and motivation needed to pursue them. On the other hand, realistic goals offer a sequence of small victories that significantly boost your confidence and motivation. This positive feedback loop is instrumental in propelling you forward, creating momentum that can carry you through the challenges of depression.

Achieving these realistic goals builds confidence. With each goal met, you provide yourself with concrete evidence of your capabilities, challenging the negative self-perceptions that depression often fosters. This growing confidence fuels motivation, encouraging continued progress and engagement with your recovery process.

The positive experiences gained from achieving realistic goals create a feedback loop that reinforces your motivation and commitment to your journey. This loop is vital for maintaining momentum, as the sense of accomplishment derived from meeting goals energizes you to set and achieve new ones, gradually generating higher aspirations.

Strategies for Setting Goals

Reflecting on your values is foundational; it's the essential groundwork upon which everything else is built. Before diving into the specifics of goal setting, it's crucial to pause and engage in an introspective journey to discover what truly matters to you. Seek to uncover the core values that define you as a person. What principles do you hold dear? What kind of life do you envision for yourself? What activities bring you a sense of fulfillment and joy?

Imagine Anna, a graphic designer who has been struggling with depression. She feels lost, unable to pinpoint a direction for her personal or professional life. Through reflection, Anna realizes that creativity, connection, and contribution are her core values. Creativity is a fundamental aspect of her identity, whether designing, painting, or decorating her space. Connection relates to her deep need for meaningful relationships with family, friends, and clients. Contribution speaks to her desire to impact the world through her art and volunteer work.

With these values in mind, Anna sets a goal to launch a community project that combines her design skills with her wish to contribute. She plans to create a series of free workshops for young people interested in graphic design to foster a supportive, creative community. This goal is aligned with her values, providing her with a clear direction and a sense of purpose she had been missing.

Aligning your goals with your values ensures that your efforts lead to meaningful and satisfying outcomes. It transforms the goal-setting process from a mere exercise into a powerful tool for personal growth and fulfillment. When goals are rooted in your values, they carry a deeper significance, motivating you to overcome obstacles and persist even when faced with the challenges of depression. This alignment also provides a sense of congruence and integrity, making your journey feel authentic and rewarding.

As you embark on this reflective process, consider the different areas of your life—career, relationships, personal growth, health—and ask yourself what values are most important to you in each of these areas. This holistic approach ensures that your goals are balanced and reflect all aspects of your life, contributing to a well-rounded sense of well-being and satisfaction.

Taking the time to reflect on your values is not just a preliminary step in setting goals; it's a critical investment in your future happiness and fulfillment. By ensuring that your goals reflect what matters most to you, you set the stage for a life that is not only successful by your standards but also deeply satisfying and meaningful.

SMART GOALS

Utilizing the SMART criteria is a tool for setting and achieving goals in a structured and flexible manner, allowing for clarity, progress, and adaptability.

Specificity: The Compass of Goal Setting: The journey begins with specificity. Imagine standing at the crossroads of where you are and where you want to be. A specific goal acts as a clear, unambiguous sign-post directing you on the path to take. Instead of saying, "I want to be healthier," you define what health means to you: "I want to incorporate a 30-minute workout into my daily routine." This clarity transforms a vague aspiration into a tangible target.

Measurability: The Milestones of Progress: Measurability introduces checkpoints along your journey. It's the difference between wandering in a forest and walking a well-marked trail with distance markers. You can track your progress and adjust your pace by setting measurable goals. For instance, if your goal is to enhance your mental well-being through meditation, you might decide to practice for 15 minutes a day, five days a week, allowing you to concretely measure your adherence and adjust as needed.

Achievability: The Realm of the Possible: Achievability ensures that your goals are within your reach, taking into account your current resources, constraints, and abilities. It's about finding the sweet spot between a goal that's too easy and one that's beyond reach. If you aim to read more books, setting a goal to read one book a week might be more achievable than aiming to read one book a day. This principle helps maintain motivation by setting you up for success rather than frustration.

Relevance: The Alignment with Your Values: Relevance ensures that your goals are aligned with your larger life plans and values. It's about making sure the goals you set are not just another task on your list but are stepping stones toward a larger vision of who you want to be and the life you want to live. If fostering close family relationships is important, a relevant goal might be establishing a weekly family game night.

Time-Bound: The Power of Deadlines: Setting your goals to be time-bound introduces a sense of urgency and commitment. It's the difference between saying "someday" and "by this date." This principle helps you to prioritize, focus, and find the motivation to start. For example, if you aim to improve your writing skills, you might aim to complete a short story by the end of the month.

Imagine you're plotting a course through uncharted waters. The SMART criteria serve as your map, compass, and navigational tools, guiding you through setting goals that are clear and achievable and deeply aligned with your values and aspirations. By applying this framework, you're charting a course that is aligned with purpose, fulfillment, and achievement.

Breaking down your goals into smaller, more manageable tasks transforms an overwhelming journey into a series of achievable steps. This approach is a strategy that builds momentum, fosters a sense of accomplishment, and systematically propels you toward your larger objectives.

Imagine you're embarking on a journey to write a novel, a goal that at first glance seems daunting. The thought of drafting hundreds of pages can freeze any writer in their tracks. However, the task becomes less intimidating by breaking this monumental goal into smaller tasks, such as outlining the plot, developing characters, and writing a set number of words daily. Each completed chapter becomes a milestone, a small victory in the broader campaign of writing your novel.

This method applies universally, whether your goal is to improve your mental health, enhance your physical fitness, or achieve a personal ambition. For instance, if your goal is to improve your mental well-being, start by incorporating brief, daily mindfulness exercises into your routine, gradually increasing the duration as you become more comfortable. This approach makes starting easier and provides a scaffold for building more complex habits over time.

Moreover, breaking down goals enables you to celebrate small successes along the way. Each task completed is an affirmation of your progress, boosting your confidence and motivation to tackle the next challenge. This positive reinforcement is crucial, especially when navigating the complexities of depression, as it provides tangible evidence of your capabilities and progress.

Furthermore, this strategy allows for flexibility and adaptability. Smaller tasks are easier to adjust or realign with your overarching objectives if you encounter obstacles or setbacks. This adaptability is essential in maintaining momentum and ensuring your goals remain achievable, even when circumstances change.

Planning for obstacles is a proactive approach to acknowledging the reality of challenges in achieving your goals. It's about foreseeing potential roadblocks and devising strategies to navigate or overcome them before they even arise. This foresight prepares you for the hurdles and empowers you to maintain your course even when the going gets tough.

Imagine embarking on a journey through a dense forest. The path is unclear, and obstacles are inevitable. Planning for these obstacles is like having a map that notes potential pitfalls and a compass that helps you find your way around them. For instance, if your goal is to improve your physical health by jogging every morning, inclement weather could be potential obstacles. A plan to overcome this might involve identifying an indoor alternative, such as a treadmill or a set of home exercises, ensuring that external conditions don't halt your progress.

Another example could involve setting a goal to spend more quality time with family. A potential obstacle here might be your work schedule. Planning for this obstacle could involve negotiating flexible working hours with your employer or dedicating specific times during weekends exclusively for family activities, thus ensuring that your professional commitments don't overshadow your personal goals.

This goal-setting approach is not about fearing challenges but embracing them as part of the journey. By anticipating and planning for obstacles, you're better prepared to face them and more likely to stay committed to your goals, fostering a sense of resilience and adapt-ability. This strategic foresight can make the difference between goals abandoned at the first sign of difficulty and goals pursued with deter-mination, regardless of the challenges encountered along the way.

Celebrating your achievements, no matter how small, is crucial to overcoming depression. This practice of acknowledgment and celebra-tion is a strategy to reinforce your progress, boost your morale, and sustain momentum in your recovery process.

Imagine you're on a long hike to a distant mountain peak. Each step forward, no matter how small, is a step closer to your destination. Celebrating these steps—each milestone reached—serves as a reminder of how far you've come, energizing you for the journey ahead. For instance, if your goal is to manage your time better, acknowledging the first day you successfully prioritize your tasks and stick to your planned schedule can be immensely empowering. This could be as simple as treating yourself to a favorite coffee or reflecting on the achievement and its significance in your larger journey.

Another example is the goal of improving one's mental health through daily mindfulness practice. After completing a week of con-sistent practice, taking time to recognize this accomplishment can significantly impact your sense of self-efficacy and motivation. This cel-ebration could involve sharing your progress with a supportive friend or family member, which reinforces your achievement and encourages your community's accountability and support.

Celebrating achievements acts as a beacon of light, illuminating your progress, often in ways you might not immediately recognize. It's a powerful antidote to the discouragement and stagnation that can accompany depression. These moments of celebration build a positive feedback loop, where each success, no matter how minor it may seem, fuels the drive and confidence to tackle the next goal, creating a cycle of positive reinforcement that propels you forward on your path to recovery.

Incorporating celebration into your journey is about recognizing the strength and resilience you're building with each forward step. It's a practice that not only enhances your motivation but also deepens your connection to the journey itself, making the process of overcoming depression a series of moments worth celebrating.

Taking Action

With your goals thoughtfully set and aligned with your values, embarking on the journey of taking action becomes the next step. Often seen as the bridge between intention and realization, this phase calls for commitment and a strategic approach to initiating and sustaining momentum.

The essence of starting small cannot be overstressed. Imagine cleaning a house that hasn't seen a broom in months. The thought alone can be daunting. However, by beginning with just one corner, the task gradually becomes less intimidating, and small progress begins to unfold before your eyes. This principle applies directly to goal setting. By initiating your journey with manageable tasks, you ease into the process and build the confidence and momentum essential for tackling larger challenges ahead.

Incorporating these tasks into a daily or weekly routine is akin to weaving a new thread into the fabric of your life. Consistency, much like the steady hands of a skilled weaver, is key to integrating new behaviors and practices into your life. This routine serves as a scaffold, providing structure and regularity that supports your progress.

The role of a support system in this endeavor cannot be overstated. Just as a tree relies on a sturdy trellis to climb upward to the sunlight, so too can you lean on friends, family, or a therapist for support, encouragement, and accountability. This network of support acts as a safety net, ready to catch you should you stumble, and a cheering squad, celebrating each step forward.

Flexibility in your approach is equally crucial. Consider the journey of a river as it makes its way to the sea; when it encounters an obstacle, it doesn't cease to flow—it finds a new path. Similarly, being willing to adjust your goals and plans is not a sign of failure but an acknowledgment of growth and learning. What matters most is not an unwavering adherence to a plan but the continuous movement forward, adapting and growing with each new challenge.

By embracing these strategies, you're not merely setting out to achieve your goals but cultivating a lifestyle of growth, resilience, and fulfillment. Taking action, therefore, becomes less about ticking boxes and more about living intentionally, guided by your values and supported by the structures and people you've put in place to ensure your journey is both successful and enriching.

Reflection and Integration

As you navigate through this week, you must pause and reflect on your journey thus far. Keeping a journal becomes a sanctuary for your thoughts, feelings, and achievements, serving as a mirror reflecting your progress. This act of reflection is not merely about recording events but understanding the significance of each step you've taken. It's about acknowledging the challenges you've faced, the resilience you've shown, and the victories, no matter how small, that you've achieved.

Reflection is a tool that helps you appreciate the distance you've traveled from where you began. It allows you to see your growth, understand the shifts in your perspective, and integrate these successes into your sense of self. This integration is crucial as it solidifies your achievements as external accomplishments and intrinsic parts of your identity.

Setting goals and taking action is inherently a dynamic process. It embodies the essence of learning, growing, and adapting. As you journey through this process, it's important to recognize that there will be days filled with progress and days where progress seems distant. Yet, regardless of size, each step you take is a step away from the shadows of depression and toward a life that resonates deeply with your values and aspirations.

This journey of reflection and integration is akin to weaving a tapestry of your experiences, where each thread represents a goal, challenge, lesson learned, or victory. As you continue to weave this tapestry, you create a vibrant depiction of a defined by the richness of your experiences, the depth of your growth, and the clarity of your aspirations.

Remember, the path to overcoming depression and achieving your goals is not linear. It is filled with twists and turns, ups and downs. But with each reflection, with each moment of integration, you build a stronger, more resilient, and more hopeful version of yourself, capable of navigating the complexities of life with grace and determination.

This week is about empowering yourself to set goals and take meaningful action. It's about recognizing your ability to shape your life, even in the face of depression. By setting realistic goals and actively working on them, you're not just dreaming about a better future but building it, one step at a time.

Week 11 Self-Help Guide

This week's focus is on envisioning your life free from the grips of depression and setting concrete goals and action plans to manifest this vision. Through a series of reflective and proactive exercises, you will begin to carve out a future that resonates with your deepest values and aspirations.

Envisioning a future where you are no longer held back by depression is a powerful first step in the depression-free journey. This process allows you to dream of a better tomorrow and start laying down the practical steps necessary to achieve it. By identifying what a depression-free life looks like for you, you create a target to aim for—a beacon of hope and motivation.

Week 11 Day 1

Objective: Vividly imagine what a depression-free life would look like for you. This exercise is designed to create a clear and compelling vision that will serve as your north star throughout this healing journey.

Information: Envisioning a future free from the weight of depression is a powerful exercise in hope and direction-setting. It allows you to see beyond the current challenges and limitations, painting a picture of a life filled with possibilities and joy. This envisioned future will guide your actions and decisions.

Instructions:

1. **Preparation:** Choose a quiet, comfortable space where you can relax without interruptions. Consider using calming music or nature sounds to create a serene atmosphere.
2. **Visualization:** Close your eyes and take a few deep breaths to center yourself. Begin to imagine your life without the burden of depression. Visualize waking up feeling rested and looking forward to the day. Picture yourself engaging in activities you enjoy, spending time with loved ones, and pursuing goals with energy and optimism.
3. **Detailing Your Vision:** Think about the different areas of your life—personal growth, relationships, career, hobbies, health, and spirituality. For each area, ask yourself:
   - How do I feel in this depression-free future?
   - What am I doing differently?
   - Who am I spending time with?
   - What achievements or milestones have I reached?

4. **Journaling:** Open your eyes and begin to journal your vision. Describe in detail what you've envisioned, focusing on how it feels to live this life. Be as specific as possible, capturing the emotions, activities, and changes you see in yourself.

5. **Emotional Connection:** Try to connect emotionally with your vision as you write. Allow yourself to feel the joy, peace, and fulfillment that comes with this envisioned future.

Reflection: After completing your journal entry, spend a few moments reflecting on the experience.

- How does it feel to imagine a life free from depression?
- Were there any surprises or insights that emerged as you envisioned your future?
- Which aspects of your envisioned future are most important to you?

Integration:

- **Daily Reminder:** Place your journal or a summary of your vision somewhere you will see it every day. This could be a note on your mirror, a background on your phone, or a small card in your wallet.
- **Affirmations:** Create affirmations based on your vision that reinforce your ability to achieve this future. For example, "I am capable of creating joy and fulfillment in my life."
- **Visualization Practice:** Dedicate a few minutes each day to close your eyes and revisit your vision. The more you connect with this future, the more it will guide and motivate your daily actions.

Week 11 Day 2

Objective: to distill your envisioned future without depression into precise, actionable goals using the S.M.A.R.T. framework, ensuring they are specific, measurable, achievable, relevant, and time-bound. This step involves documenting these goals to crystallize your commitment and employing reflection to prioritize them, ultimately creating a vision board or detailed list for continual motivation. This approach aims to convert your envisioned future into a practical, step-by-step action plan.

Instructions: After envisioning your depression-free future, it's time to translate this vision into tangible goals. Reflect deeply on the life you pictured during Day 1. What are the key elements that stood out to you? Was it a career aspiration, improved relationships, or a personal development goal like mastering a new skill or hobby?

1. **Identify Specific Goals:** Start by identifying specific goals that, once achieved, would bring your vision to life. These should be direct contributors to the depression-free future you envision. For instance, if part of your vision includes a healthier lifestyle, a specific goal might be to establish a regular exercise routine.
2. **Apply the S.M.A.R.T. Criteria:** To ensure your goals are actionable and realistic, refine them using the S.M.A.R.T. criteria:
   - **Specific:** Your goals should be clear and specific enough to guide your actions. Ask yourself: What exactly do I want to achieve?
   - **Measurable:** Determine how you will measure progress and know when you have achieved your goal.

- ○ **Achievable:** Considering your current resources and constraints, your goals should be attainable.
- ○ **Relevant:** Ensure that each goal is relevant to your vision and meaningful to your life.
- ○ **Time-bound:** Assign a deadline to each goal to create a sense of urgency and motivation.

3. **Writing Your Goals Down:** Document each goal using the S.M.A.R.T. criteria. This helps clarify your goals and serves as a commitment to yourself.

Reflection: After setting your goals, take a moment to reflect on them. Which goals resonate with you the most? Which ones make you feel excited or motivated? This reflection can help prioritize your goals based on their impact on achieving your vision.

Integration: Create a vision board or a detailed list of your goals. This visual representation constantly reminds you of what you're working toward. Place it next to your vision statement from Day 1. Seeing your vision and goals together can be a powerful motivator, keeping you focused on the path ahead.

By carefully selecting goals aligning with your vision and applying the S.M.A.R.T. criteria to make them actionable, you lay a solid foundation for a depression-free life. This step is about transforming your dreams into plans, setting the stage for the actionable steps that will follow in the days ahead.

Week 11 Day 3

Objective: To transform your S.M.A.R.T. goals into actionable steps, facilitating the transition from vision to reality.

Instructions: With a clear vision for a depression-free future and specific S.M.A.R.T. goals set, today's focus shifts to turning these goals into a reality through actionable steps. This phase is crucial; it's where planning meets execution. The process of breaking down your goals into smaller tasks is akin to mapping out the route for a journey, identifying each step needed to reach the destination.

1. **Select a Goal to Focus On:** Begin by selecting one of the goals you identified on Day 2. Choose a goal that feels particularly significant to you or perhaps one that seems most attainable in the near term. This will be your focus for today.

2. **List the Necessary Steps:** Break this goal down into all the necessary steps required to achieve it. For instance, if your goal is to engage in physical activity for 30 minutes a day, steps might include researching different types of exercises, scheduling a specific time of day for your workouts, and preparing a space in your home for exercise.

3. **Assign Realistic Timelines:** For each step, assign a realistic timeline. Consider your current commitments, energy levels, and any potential obstacles. Setting deadlines helps create a sense of urgency and commitment, but be sure these timelines are flexible enough to accommodate the unpredictability of life.

4. **Prioritize Your Steps:** Look at your outlined steps and prioritize them. Identify which steps are foundational and need to be accomplished first. This might involve setting up a workout area

before you can begin exercising or purchasing healthy groceries before starting a new diet plan.

5. **Document Each Step:** Write down each step, its timeline, and its priority level. This documentation acts as a blueprint, guiding your daily actions. It's also a tangible reminder of your commitment to a depression-free future.

Reflection: After breaking down your goal into actionable steps, take a moment to reflect on the process. How do you feel about the goal now that you see the steps laid out before you? Do you feel more confident in your ability to achieve it, or are some aspects still daunting?

Integration: To integrate today's work into your ongoing journey, consider how you might begin to incorporate these steps into your daily or weekly routine. Is there a step you can take immediately, even if it's small? Look for opportunities to align these steps with your existing habits and commitments to make the process as seamless as possible.

Breaking down your goals into actionable steps demystifies the path to achieving them. It transforms lofty aspirations into a series of manageable tasks, each one bringing you closer to your vision of a depression-free life. Today's exercise sets the stage for tangible progress and reinforces your agency and capability to navigate your recovery journey.

Week 11 Day 4

Objective: to proactively identify and plan for potential obstacles that may hinder your progress towards your goals, particularly in overcoming depression. This involves recognizing both internal and external barriers, devising strategies to navigate or overcome these challenges, and incorporating flexibility into your approach. By documenting anticipated obstacles and corresponding solutions, you prepare yourself to face and manage difficulties effectively, enhancing your resilience and commitment to achieving a depression-free future. This strategic planning fosters a more realistic and empowered mindset towards the attainment of your goals.

Instructions: The path toward achieving your goals, especially in the context of overcoming depression, is seldom without its hurdles. Day 4 is dedicated to identifying potential obstacles that could impede your progress and strategizing how to navigate or overcome them. This proactive approach prepares you for the unexpected and empowers you to maintain momentum even when faced with challenges.

1. **Identify Potential Obstacles:** Reflect on the goal and the actionable steps you've outlined thus far. Consider what might stand in your way. Obstacles can be internal, such as fear of failure, lack of motivation, or depressive symptoms that make it hard to get started. They can also be external, like time constraints, financial limitations, or lack of support from those around you.

2. **Strategize Solutions:** For each obstacle identified, brainstorm possible solutions or strategies to overcome it. If fear of failure is a concern, your strategy might involve setting smaller, more manageable goals to build confidence. For external challenges

like time constraints, solutions could include adjusting your schedule, seeking assistance from others, or prioritizing tasks differently.

3. **Plan for Flexibility:** Not all obstacles can be fully anticipated or avoided. Part of your strategy should include developing flexibility in approaching your goals. This might mean being open to adjusting your goals, timelines, or methods as needed.

4. **Document Your Strategies:** Write down the obstacles you anticipate and your strategies to overcome them. This documentation serves as a roadmap, guiding you through potential challenges and reminding you of your plan to navigate them.

Reflection: After planning for potential obstacles, take a moment to reflect on how this exercise has impacted your outlook on achieving your goal. Do you feel more prepared, less anxious, or perhaps more realistic about the journey ahead? Reflecting on these feelings can further solidify your commitment and adaptability.

Integration: Integrate this anticipatory planning into your overall action plan. By acknowledging that obstacles are part of the process and having a plan to deal with them, you reinforce your resilience and determination. Consider sharing your anticipated obstacles and strategies with a trusted friend or mentor who can offer support, advice, and accountability.

Planning for obstacles is not about expecting the worst; it's about empowering yourself to face and overcome the challenges that may arise on your path to a depression-free future. By anticipating and strategizing for potential hurdles, you equip yourself with the tools and mindset to navigate your journey confidently and resiliently.

Week 11 Day 5

Objective: to actively build and engage with a support network that will bolster your efforts towards achieving a depression-free future.

Instructions: Cultivating a support network is invaluable as you work toward a depression-free future. Today, focus on identifying and engaging with individuals who can provide you with support, encouragement, and accountability. This step acknowledges that the path to achieving your goals is not meant to be walked alone and that seeking and accepting help is a sign of strength, not weakness.

1. **Identify Potential Supporters:** Reflect on the people in your life who could serve as pillars of support. These could be friends, family members, colleagues, or even members of support groups or online communities who share similar goals or experiences. Consider who among them would be understanding, encouraging, and constructive in their support.

2. **Determine the Type of Support You Need:** Support can come in many forms – emotional, practical, informational, or motivational. Pinpoint what kind of support would be most beneficial for you in achieving your goals. For instance, a workout buddy could provide motivational and practical support if your goal is to exercise more.

3. **Reach Out for Support:** Once you've identified potential supporters and the type of support you need, take the step to reach out to at least one person. Be open and honest about your goals and the vision you're working on. Share why their support is important to you and how they can help.

4. **Establishing a Support Agreement:** If they are willing to support you, discuss and agree on what this support will look like. This might involve regular check-ins, sharing updates on your progress, or them providing reminders or encouragement. Setting clear expectations helps ensure the support is beneficial and aligned with your needs.

Reflection: After reaching out for support, reflect on the experience. How did it feel to share your goals and ask for support? Did the response from the person you reached out to change your feelings about your goals or about asking for help?

Integration: Integrating this support is crucial. Consider how you will maintain communication with your supporters. Will you schedule regular check-ins? Share milestones and setbacks? Determine how best to keep your support network informed and engaged in your progress. This integration reinforces your commitment to your goals and strengthens your relationships with those who are rooting for your success.

Seeking and securing support is a strategic step in achieving your goals and moving closer to your envisioned future. It reinforces the notion that you are not alone in your journey and that the strength and encouragement of others can be a powerful catalyst for change.

Week 11 Day 6

Objective: to catalyze your transition from planning to taking tangible action towards your goals, marking a critical shift towards realizing your envisioned future.

Instructions: After envisioning your future, setting goals, planning for obstacles, and securing support, the time has come to transition from planning to action. Day 6 is about taking that first step. No matter how small, this step represents a significant leap toward your envisioned future. It's about breaking the inertia often accompanying depression and taking tangible action that aligns with your values and aspirations.

1. **Choose an Actionable Step:** Look at the list of actionable steps you identified for your goal. Select one step that you can realistically accomplish today. This step should be small enough to be approachable yet significant enough to mark the beginning of your journey. For instance, if your goal involves incorporating exercise into your daily routine, your first step might be as simple as a 10-minute walk around your neighborhood or a short home workout.

2. **Prepare for Action:** Before taking this step, mentally and physically prepare yourself. Gather any resources or materials you might need, and carve out time in your day dedicated to this activity. Preparation reduces the barriers to getting started, making it easier to take action.

3. **Visualize Success:** Spend a few moments visualizing yourself successfully completing this step. Visualization is a powerful tool

that can boost your confidence and motivation, helping to over-come any initial resistance or anxiety about getting started.

4. **Take the Step:** Now, it's time to act. With preparation and visualization complete, engage in the step you've chosen. Remember, the focus is on the act of starting, not on perfection or even completion. Permit yourself to explore this step with curiosity and openness, free from judgment.

Reflection: After taking your first step, reflect on the experience. How did it feel to take action? What did you learn about yourself in the process? This reflection is crucial for acknowledging your courage and for integrating this experience into your depression-free future.

Integration: To integrate today's action into your ongoing journey, consider the next steps you can take in the coming days. How can you build on this initial action to maintain momentum? Also, think about how you can incorporate this practice of taking small, manageable steps into other areas of your life.

Taking the first step is often the hardest part of any journey, especially when facing the challenges of depression. However, by breaking down your goals into actionable steps and courageously engaging with them, one at a time, you begin to create a pattern of proactive behavior that can significantly impact your depression-free journey. Remember, each step, no matter how small, is a victory in its own right, marking progress on the path to realizing your vision.

Week 11 Day 7

Objective: to engage in a comprehensive reflection of the week's progress, measuring successes, understanding challenges, and assessing how well actions align with the vision of a depression-free future.

Instructions: On the final day of this week's journey, it's time to pause, reflect, and assess the progress you've made. This reflective practice is about measuring success and understanding the learning and growth that have occurred along the way. It's a day to celebrate your achievements, recognize your challenges, and consider adjustments to better align with your vision of a depression-free future.

1. **Reflect on Your Progress:** Take some time to review the goals and steps you've identified and taken this week. Consider each action you've implemented and the obstacles you've navigated. Reflect on the support you've sought and received. How have these elements contributed to your progress toward your vision?

2. **Evaluate Achievements and Challenges:** Identify what you've achieved this week, no matter how small these achievements may seem. Equally, acknowledge the challenges you've encountered. Reflecting on successes and hurdles offers a balanced perspective on your journey and your resilience.

3. **Assess the Alignment with Your Vision:** Revisit your depression-free future vision outlined on Day 1. How do the goals and steps you've taken this week align with this vision? Are you moving closer to realizing this future, or are there areas where adjustments are needed?

4. **Consider Necessary Adjustments:** Based on your reflections, identify any adjustments that may be necessary to better align

your actions with your vision. This could involve setting new goals, modifying existing ones, or changing your approach to overcoming obstacles. Remember, flexibility is a strength that allows for growth and adaptation on your journey.

5. **Plan for Continued Action:** With your reflections and adjustments in mind, outline a plan for continuing to work on your goals in the coming weeks. Consider what additional support you might need, what obstacles you anticipate, and how you can integrate the lessons learned this week into your ongoing efforts.

Reflection: Reflect on the overall experience of this week. How has engaging in this structured process of envisioning, planning, acting, and reflecting impacted your outlook on overcoming depression and achieving your goals? What insights have you gained about yourself and your journey?

Integration: To integrate the insights and adjustments from today into your ongoing journey, update your goals and action plans to reflect any changes you've decided to make. Consider how you can maintain the practice of regular reflection and adjustment as part of your routine. This ongoing process of reflection and integration is key to staying aligned with your vision and adapting to the challenges and opportunities that arise.

Day 7 is about embracing growth and goal achievement as an evolving process. By reflecting on your progress, celebrating your achievements, and making necessary adjustments, you reinforce your commitment to a life defined not by depression but by fulfillment and well-being. This practice of continuous reflection and adjustment is about achieving specific goals and cultivating a lifestyle of intentional living and resilience.

Bridge Week 11

At week's end, allow yourself a quiet moment to assess your progress along the bridge. Identify your current location, think about this week's journey with its highs and lows, recognize your feelings, and maintain a forward-looking perspective. Next, relocate your marker on the bridge to represent where you are right now.

17

Finding Meaning and Purpose

As we embark on Week 12 of our self-help guide, we delve into one of the most profound and enriching aspects of the human experience: the quest for meaning and purpose. This chapter is not just another step in our journey. It's a deep dive into the essence of leading a fulfilling life. It's about going beyond the ephemeral joys and accomplishments to touch the core of our existence—our intrinsic values, our character, and the legacy we wish to leave behind.

In a world that often measures success in material wealth and external achievements, this chapter guides us back to the fundamental truths that resonate with our innermost selves. It's an invitation to pause and reflect on the questions that define our existence: Who am I? What do I stand for? What is truly important to me? These are not questions with easy answers, nor should they be. They are the questions that prompt us to look inward, to dig deep into the fabric of our being, and to discover the values and principles that give our lives direction and meaning.

Finding meaning and purpose is a journey that transcends the boundaries of conventional success. It's about identifying what genuinely drives us, what brings us authentic joy and fulfillment, and how to align our daily actions with these deeper aspirations. This exploration is critical because it shapes how we perceive the world, how we interact with others, and, most importantly, how we view ourselves. It's about building a life that reflects our true selves, grounded in our values, morals, and character.

This chapter is structured to guide you through this introspective process, offering tools and exercises designed to help you articulate your values, examine your character, and challenge the cognitive distortions that may cloud your understanding of your worth and purpose. Through reflective practices, personal stories, and actionable advice, we will navigate the complex landscape of our internal value systems, uncovering the beliefs that propel us forward and those that hold us back.

As we embark on this journey of self-discovery, remember that finding meaning and purpose is a continuous process of growth and understanding. It requires patience, openness, and a willingness to embrace the complexities of our human experience.

Let us progress with courage and curiosity, ready to explore the vast landscapes of our inner worlds. Together, we will discover the unique purpose within each of us, forging a path leading to a life of genuine meaning and heartfelt satisfaction. Welcome to Week 12: Finding Meaning and Purpose.

Exploring Personal Values: Embarking on a journey to understand and articulate your values is akin to setting the compass for your life's journey. This profound exploration lays the foundation for constructing a life imbued with joy, fulfillment, and a deep resonance with the essence of who you truly are. Personal values, the bedrock of your character, serve as the guiding stars that influence your decisions, shape your behaviors, and color your interactions with the world around you. They are the silent architects of your destiny, subtly steering your reactions to life's myriad challenges and sculpting your path to success and contentment.

Why Values Matter: In the labyrinth of life, where uncertainty often clouds the way, understanding your values shines a beacon of clarity, guiding you through the fog. Knowing the principles you stand by empowers you to make choices that are in harmony with your true self, fostering a life of authenticity and reduced inner turmoil. Values act as a personal code of conduct, a moral compass that directs actions and decisions reflective of your core beliefs and integrity. They are the silent affirmations of what you deem most important in life, shaping your priorities and guiding your course through the tempests of existence.

The Vitality of Personal Values: In the intricate journey of life, where every path is woven with challenges and choices, your values stand as your guiding light. Imagine walking through a dense forest where the canopy above is thick, and the directions are unclear. In such a scenario, your values are like the compass that points you in the correct direction, offering clarity amidst the complexity. They are the steady beacons that illuminate your path, allowing you to move forward with confidence and grace, knowing that each step you take is aligned with the essence of who you are.

Consider the story of Eric, who values honesty above all. In a situation where Eric finds a wallet full of cash on the street, the choice to seek out the owner rather than keep the money is driven by this core value. This decision brings a sense of satisfaction that far outweighs the temporary gain of finding the money, illustrating how values serve as a source of inner strength and resilience. This unwavering adherence to one's values empowers individuals like Eric to face life's challenges head-on, armed with the conviction of their beliefs and the courage to act accordingly.

Values shape our relationships. Like a magnet, they attract others who resonate with the same principles, fostering connections rooted in mutual understanding and respect. Imagine two friends, Jamie and Taylor, who share a deep commitment to kindness. This shared value strengthens their bond, allowing them to support each other in times of need and celebrate together in times of joy. Through these values-based connections, we build a supportive social circle, enhancing our relationships and enriching our lives.

Beyond the conventional markers of success—material wealth, status, or accolades—personal values offer a more profound and fulfilling metric for measuring our achievements. They remind us that true success is not about the external accolades we accumulate but about living a life that is true to our deepest selves. Picture Ella, who values creativity and independence more than financial success. For Ella, choosing a career as an independent artist, despite the financial uncertainties, represents a true success because it aligns with her core values. Her life, rich in creative satisfaction and autonomy, exemplifies fulfillment that transcends traditional measures of success.

In this life narrative, where each character navigates their unique journey, the underlying values carve out the storyline. These values—be they honesty, kindness, creativity, or independence—shape the choices we make and the legacy we leave behind. They are the essence of our character, the foundation of our interactions, and the true measure of our success. By understanding and living according to our values, we craft a life story that is meaningful and fulfilling and a true reflection of who we are.

It's crucial to build a solid foundation with the strategies outlined in the first 11 weeks of this self-help guide before embarking on defining your values. This is because our perception of values can be significantly influenced by cognitive distortions and negative thinking patterns. If we attempt to identify our values while under the influence of these negative cognitions, we risk endorsing values that lead us astray, reinforcing the cycle of confirmation bias where our subconscious aligns our actions with our perceived worldview, regardless of its positivity or negativity. This phenomenon was explored earlier in this book, highlighting the subconscious's role in seeking congruency within our beliefs and actions. Therefore, approach the value identification process with awareness, ensuring your values truly reflect your authentic self, free from the distortion of negative thought patterns.

Living Your Values

Living your values transcends mere acknowledgment; it is the art of weaving these core principles into your daily existence. This journey from understanding to integration is where the essence of a truly meaningful life unfolds. Imagine your values as the threads of your life's tapestry, each color representing a different principle that is important to you. When you live by your values, you actively choose each thread, ensuring that the overall picture reflects the beauty and depth of your true self.

Consider the simple acts of your day: how you choose to spend your morning, the words you use in conversation, the way you respond to a challenge at work or even the manner in which you engage with strangers. Each of these moments offers an opportunity to express your values. For instance, if kindness is a value you hold dear, a morning might begin with sending a thoughtful message to a friend or choosing to be patient in a moment of frustration during your commute. At work, it might mean offering support to a colleague or approaching conflicts with empathy and understanding.

Integrating your values into daily life also means making conscious choices that align with your principles, even when faced with decisions that test your commitment to those values. It's the courage to choose authenticity over convenience and do what's right rather than easy. This might look like standing up for a colleague in a situation where it would be simpler to stay silent or opt for sustainability in your lifestyle choices, even if it requires more effort or expense.

As your values become the heartbeat of your life, they guide your actions and shape your perceptions and interactions. You start to see the world through the lens of your values, and this perspective influences how you interpret and respond to situations around you. It's like having a personal filter that highlights what truly matters, helping you to focus on what aligns with your inner self and to let go of what doesn't.

Living by your values is a dynamic process; it evolves as you grow and as your understanding of yourself and the world deepens. It requires mindfulness, commitment, and, sometimes, the willingness to make difficult choices. Yet, the rewards of this alignment are immeasurable. It brings a sense of integrity, purpose, and fulfillment to your life, transforming how you live and experience the world. By making your values the heartbeat of your existence, you create a life that is meaningful and rewarding and a true reflection of who you are at your core.

The Process of Identifying Personal Values

Identifying personal values is a process that requires introspection, honesty, and a willingness to dive deep into the chambers of one's heart and mind. This exploration begins in the quiet moments of reflection, where you're invited to sift through your memories and experiences to uncover the moments that truly define you.

Imagine sitting quietly, allowing the noise of the world to fade away as you turn your focus inward. You recall the times you've felt a profound sense of pride, fulfillment, or peace. Perhaps it was a moment of overcoming a significant challenge, a time when you helped someone in need or a quiet afternoon spent in nature. As you relive these moments, you start to notice the common threads that link them—were you acting out of compassion, striving for excellence, or seeking connection? These threads are the values that have silently guided your actions and decisions.

With these insights, you're encouraged to let your mind wander to visualize the life you yearn for. Picture your ideal day, the work that gives you a sense of purpose, and the relationships that bring you joy. Notice the elements that make these scenarios shine—maybe it's the freedom to express yourself creatively, the thrill of achievement, or the warmth of genuine connections. These elements are like beacons, illuminating the values beneath your desires' surface.

Armed with these revelations, the next step is to lay them out and compile a list of values that resonate with your soul. This list may be long, yet the essence of this journey lies in distillation—sifting through the many to identify the few that are non-negotiable, the values that form the bedrock of your identity.

This process of prioritization is not without its challenges. It asks you to examine your life as it is now, to hold it up against the backdrop of your identified values. This scrutiny can reveal areas of congruence and discrepancy, shedding light on aspects of your life that might need reevaluation or change to better reflect what you truly value.

Finally, the journey culminates in the act of definition. Giving language to your values, describing what each means to you personally, transforms abstract concepts into tangible guides. This step is crucial, for it is in the naming that values become real, serving as beacons that can illuminate your path forward, making them an integral part of your daily existence.

Through this narrative of discovery you are mapping out the terrain of your inner landscape, charting a course that aligns with the essence of who you are. This process is both the journey and the destination, leading to a life with intention, purpose, and deep fulfillment.

Integrating Values into Daily Life: The essence of personal values becomes most potent when they used in our daily lives. It's a transformative process where values transition from abstract ideals to tangible forces guiding every decision, action, and interaction. This integration is intentional and deliberate, requiring mindfulness and commitment to align our day-to-day existence with the core principles we hold dear.

Consider the process of setting goals, for instance. When these goals are rooted in our values, they carry a deeper significance and motivation. Imagine someone who values learning and growth setting a goal to read one book related to their field every month. This goal isn't just a task to be checked off; it's a reflection of their commitment to continuous improvement and knowledge expansion. It's about making choices that resonate with who we are at our core, ensuring that our pursuits and achievements are not just milestones but expressions of our deepest selves.

Decision-making becomes a more conscious endeavor when guided by our values. Each choice presents an opportunity to affirm these guiding principles. When faced with a career decision, for example, someone who places a high value on work-life balance might prioritize job opportunities that offer flexibility or proximity to home over those that promise higher pay but longer hours. This alignment between values and choices ensures that our lives are lived authentically, fostering satisfaction and well-being.

Navigating conflicts and challenges through the lens of our values also offers a pathway to a resolution that remains true to our integrity. When disagreements arise, approaching the situation with a value like respect or empathy can lead to more constructive and understanding dialogues. It means striving to see the other person's perspective, seeking common ground, and responding in ways that uphold our values, even in the face of adversity.

Challenges and Growth: Exploring personal values is like navigating a river continually changing its course. Just as the landscape shapes the river's journey, it traverses our journey through life and shapes and reshapes our values. This dynamic process of reflection and growth is not a task to be checked off but an ongoing dialogue with oneself that evolves as we do.

As we journey through different phases of life, our experiences can profoundly influence our perspectives and priorities. What we valued in our youth may shift as we encounter new challenges, relationships, and insights. The process of personal growth involves acquiring new knowledge and experiences and letting go of beliefs and values that no longer serve us. It's a process of shedding old skins to reveal new layers of our identity, each more refined and aligned with our evolving self.

Revisiting and reassessing our values, therefore, becomes an essential practice. It's an invitation to pause, reflect, and take stock of where we are and where we're headed. This periodic reassessment helps to ensure our values resonate with our current self. It's about asking, "Do these values still represent who I am and, more importantly, who I aspire to be?"

Imagine that garden again. Just as the gardener must periodically assess the health of the plants, prune the overgrown, and nurture the new growth, we, too, must tend to the garden of our values. We must identify the values that have strengthened us, recognize those that have served their purpose, and be open to new values that emerge from our experiences. This process of pruning and nurturing ensures that our garden remains vibrant, reflective of our journey, and true to the person we are becoming.

The challenges we face in this process are as varied as they are valuable. They prompt us to confront our fears, question our assumptions, and grow in wisdom and depth. This continuous reflection and growth journey enriches our lives, making our values not just a compass but a map that evolves with us.

The Importance of Character and Morals: When seeking meaning and purpose, the role of character and morals cannot be overstressed. This exploration is beyond the actions we take but about the person we choose to become, choose to be. Our character imbues our existence with depth, richness, and authenticity. The qualities of integrity, kindness, courage, and compassion serve as ideals to aspire to and as the very essence of a life lived fully and meaningfully.

The philosophy at the heart of this exploration posits that our most enduring legacy is the character we cultivate. Unlike the fleeting nature of achievements and accolades, the essence of who we are endures, influencing our path and the lives of those we touch. This chapter aims to guide you through a journey of self-discovery and reflection, encouraging you to delve into your character's nuances, celebrate your strengths, and confront your weaknesses with honesty and courage.

Through personal anecdotes, we'll see how the virtues of integrity, kindness, courage, and compassion have transformed lives, not just in grand, heroic acts but in the quiet, everyday moments that define our humanity. These stories serve as mirrors, reflecting our potential to lead lives of profound impact and meaning simply by being our best selves.

Reflective exercises offer a framework for this introspection, providing a space to pause and examine our character. These exercises invite you to consider questions like: What principles guide my decisions?

How do I act under pressure? What does kindness mean to me, and how do I express it in my daily life? Through these questions, we begin to uncover the core of our moral compass, identifying areas where we shine and areas ripe for growth.

Setting intentions for personal development is the natural progression of this exploration. It's about moving beyond recognition to action, committing to nurturing those qualities that we value most. Whether practicing patience, fostering an open mind, or cultivating a spirit of generosity, each intention is a step closer to becoming the person we aspire to be.

Unpacking Value Systems: Our value systems life the roots of a tree, grounding us and providing the nourishment needed to grow and thrive. They are shaped by experiences, beliefs, and societal messages we've absorbed throughout our lives. However, just as roots can sometimes become entangled, leading to the tree's distress, our value systems can also become cluttered with contradictions and distortions that lead us away from our authentic selves.

The journey of unpacking our value systems involves delving into this complex web, identifying the strands that support our growth and those that hinder it. It's about recognizing that while our values have the power to guide us toward fulfilling lives, they can also be the source of cognitive distortions—those misleading thoughts and beliefs that cloud our judgment and lead us astray.

For instance, societal messages about success and worth can often infiltrate our value systems, leading us to equate our self-worth with external achievements or material possessions. This distortion can drive us to pursue goals that don't align with our intrinsic values, leaving us feeling unfulfilled and disconnected from our true selves.

By engaging in a thoughtful examination of our value systems, we can start to identify these distortions. We ask ourselves critical questions: Which beliefs truly resonate with me, and which have I adopted from external influences? Do these beliefs support the person I want to be, or do they hold me back?

This process is not about discarding our entire value system but refining it. It's about holding each belief to the light and assessing its origin and impact on our lives. This scrutiny allows us to challenge and let go of the beliefs that no longer serve us, clearing the way for a value system that is more aligned with our authentic selves.

Cognitive Distortions and Value Systems

Our minds are powerful storytellers, often weaving narratives that significantly impact our perceptions of worth and purpose. However, when cognitive distortions color these narratives, they can lead us astray from our true selves and the values we hold dear. Cognitive distortions such as black-and-white thinking, overgeneralization, and self-criticism can cloud our judgment and skew our self-perception, holding us back from realizing our full potential.

This exploration into cognitive distortions and value systems is paramount for self-awareness and personal growth. By identifying and challenging these distortions, we embark on a path to a more authentic and fulfilling life.

Black-and-white thinking, for example, forces us into a rigid mindset of absolutes, where life's complexities are unfairly simplified into categories of "all good" or "all bad." This distortion can lead us to judge ourselves and others unfairly, often disregarding the nuanced realities that define our existence. By recognizing this pattern, we can appreciate the shades of gray in our lives, understanding that perfection is an unrealistic standard and that growth often comes from our struggles and imperfections.

Overgeneralization, another common distortion, sees us drawing broad conclusions from a single event. If we fail at a task, we might think, "I'm always going to fail." This mindset can prevent us from seeing each experience as a unique opportunity for learning and growth rather than a definitive statement of our capabilities. Learning to view each experience in isolation as a stepping stone rather than a stumbling block can significantly alter our self-narrative.

Self-criticism, perhaps the most personal distortion, involves being overly harsh and unforgiving. It's a voice that magnifies our flaws and minimizes our strengths. We can foster a kinder relationship with ourselves by challenging this inner critic and replacing it with a more compassionate and understanding voice. This shift enhances our self-esteem and aligns our self-perception with our core values of kindness and compassion.

Confronting these cognitive distortions as we did in previous chapters requires continued mindfulness and a willingness to always question our automatic thoughts. Strategies such as cognitive restructuring, mindfulness meditation, and self-compassion exercises can be invaluable tools in this journey. These practices help us to pause, reflect, and choose responses that reflect our true values rather than reacting out of habit or distorted thinking.

As we navigate this path, we gain a clearer, more compassionate perspective on our lives. We learn to value our journey, with all its imperfections, as a meaningful expression of our authentic selves.

Becoming a Better Person

Personal improvement transcends the mere pursuit of self-enhancement. It is a holistic endeavor that enriches not only our own lives but also the broader constructs of society. This exploration of becoming a better person is deeply intertwined with the aspiration to contribute positively to the world around us. It's a recognition that our growth impacts our relationships, our communities, and, ultimately, the legacy we leave behind.

Striving to be a better person serves as a catalyst for elevating self-esteem and recognizing our inherent value. It is a process that encourages us to reflect on our actions, beliefs, and impact on others, urging us to cultivate qualities such as empathy, kindness, and resilience. These attributes enhance our sense of well-being and allow us to forge deeper, more meaningful connections with those around us.

As we embark on this path of personal growth, we discover that improving ourselves can lead to a ripple effect, inspiring and uplifting those we interact with. Our efforts to become more understanding and compassionate can strengthen our relationships, fostering a sense of mutual respect and support. Moreover, by actively contributing to our communities—whether through volunteering, advocacy, or simply lending a listening ear—we embody the change we wish to see in the world.

Setting personal growth goals is a practical step for realizing our potential to be better individuals. These goals should be specific, measurable, achievable, relevant, and time-bound (SMART), ensuring that they are both challenging and attainable. For example, a goal to enhance empathy might involve committing to one act of kindness each day or seeking to understand rather than judge in difficult conversations.

Taking actionable goal steps requires commitment and flexibility. It involves regularly assessing our progress, celebrating our successes, and learning from setbacks without self-judgment. Practical exercises, such as journaling reflections on daily interactions, practicing mindfulness to enhance self-awareness, or engaging in community service, can serve as valuable tools in this journey.

Ultimately, the quest to become a better person is a lifelong journey of exploration and reflection. It is a path marked by continuous learning, adaptation, and an unwavering commitment to embodying the values we hold dear. As we navigate this journey, we enrich our lives and contribute to a more compassionate, understanding, and connected world.

The Joy of an Authentic Life

Living a truly authentic life aligned with one's values and purposes is in essence sailing on a voyage where the compass is one's heart. The pursuit of authenticity brings with it an unparalleled sense of joy and fulfillment. It is a path that allows individuals to exist and live fully. It allows us to embrace every facet of being and reflecting authenticity in all that is done.

Consider the story of Maya, who, after years of climbing the corporate ladder, realized that her true passion lay in environmental advocacy. Making the bold decision to leave her job, she embraced a path that resonated deeply with her sustainability and conservation core values. Today, Maya finds satisfaction in her work, knowing that every effort she makes is a positive step.

Then there's Nick, who always felt pressured to conform to societal norms and expectations. It wasn't until he embraced his identity and began to live openly and authentically that he experienced true joy. Nick's journey to authenticity brought personal fulfillment and inspired those around him to embrace their truths.

These stories highlight the transformative power of living in alignment with one's values and purposes. Authenticity is about being true to oneself and creating a life rich in meaning and satisfaction. Envisioning your path to an authentic and purpose-driven life involves introspection and a willingness to ask hard questions. The answers to these questions serve as a blueprint for a life that is both true to oneself and deeply fulfilling.

Living authentically is a courageous act of defiance against the pressures to conform. It's a journey marked by challenges, growth, and, ultimately, a deep sense of satisfaction. As you embark on this path, remember that the pursuit of an authentic life is a destination but a continuous journey of becoming, a journey that is as rewarding as it is profound.

This chapter transcends the boundaries of a mere instructional guide; it stands as a steadfast companion along the winding path of self-discovery and personal evolution. Through thoughtful engagement with the exercises and reflections presented within these pages, you embark on a profound journey to clarity and understanding. This process helps to uncover what lies at the heart of your values and purpose and point the way to a life that is a true reflection of those deep-seated truths. As you turn the pages and engage in the self-help guide, do it with diligence and purpose. Your depression-free life awaits.

Week 12 Self-Help Guide

Welcome to living a life defined by what truly matters. Embarking on a journey to a value-driven life is a transformative process that goes beyond mere self-improvement. It will help to discover what truly matters to you and aligning your life with those core principles. This seven-day self-help guide is designed as your compass, guiding you through the introspective and practical steps necessary to identify, understand, and live by your values.

Week 12 Day 1

Objective: To explore and identify personal values that bring a sense of fulfillment and alignment in your life.

Information: Understanding our values helps to illuminate the aspects of our lives that bring us the most joy, fulfillment, and a sense of purpose. This initial exercise aims to delve into your past experiences to uncover these values, providing a foundation for living more authentically.

Instructions:

1. **Preparation:** Find a quiet, comfortable space where you can reflect without interruptions. Have a notebook or digital document ready to journal your thoughts.
2. **Reflection Exercise:** Spend 20 minutes thinking about a time in your life when you felt truly fulfilled, happy, or at peace. Try to recall specific details:
    - What were you doing at the time?
    - Who were you with?
    - What aspects of this experience made it so fulfilling?
3. **Journaling:** Write down your reflections, focusing on the emotions you felt and the values that were being honored in these moments. If you struggle to name specific values, consider qualities like connection, creativity, freedom, or service as starting points.

Reflection: After completing the exercise, reflect on what you've written for a few moments. Ask yourself:

- Were there any surprises in what I identified as fulfilling?
- Do I see a pattern in the types of values that are important to me?

Integration:

- **Daily Observation:** For the next week, carry a small notebook or use a notes app on your phone. Jot down any moments when you feel a sense of joy or fulfillment, no matter how small. Try to identify which of your values are being honored in these moments.
- **Discussion:** Consider sharing your reflections with a trusted friend or family member. Discussing your values with others can provide additional insights and reinforce your commitment to integrating these values into your daily life.

Week 12 Day 2

Objective: To visualize and articulate aspects of your ideal life that reflect your core values, enhancing clarity on your life's direction.

Information: Visualization is a powerful tool for aligning your present life with your deepest values and goals. By imagining your ideal day, work environment, or relationships, you can uncover the elements that resonate most deeply with your core values. This process not only provides inspiration but also serves as a guide for making life choices that are in harmony with your true self.

Instructions:

1. **Visualization Preparation:** Choose a quiet time and place to relax without interruptions. Use a journal or digital device for notes.
2. **Ideal Life Visualization:**
   - Close your eyes and take a few deep breaths to center yourself.
   - Visualize your ideal day from when you wake up to when you go to bed. Imagine the activities you would engage in, the people you would interact with, and the environments you find yourself in.
   - Shift your focus to your ideal work environment. Consider the tasks you're performing, the culture of the workplace, and how you feel throughout the day.
   - Lastly, envision your ideal relationships. Imagine interacting with a partner, family, or friends. Focus on the feelings and connections experienced during these interactions.

3. **Journaling:** After completing each visualization, write down what you observed. Focus on the elements that made each scenario fulfilling. Identify the values these elements represent (e.g., creativity, community, autonomy).

Reflection: Reflect on the visualization process by considering the following questions:

- Which aspects of my ideal life are currently present, and which are missing?
- How do the values identified align with those discovered on Day 1?

Integration:

- **Element Incorporation:** Choose one element from your visualization currently lacking in your life. Develop a small, actionable plan to incorporate this element into your daily or weekly routine.
- **Vision Board:** Consider creating a vision board representing the key elements of your ideal life identified during the visualization. Place it somewhere you will see it daily as a reminder of your values and goals.
- **Community Sharing:** Share your vision of an ideal life with a trusted friend or family member. Discussing your aspirations can offer new insights and strengthen your resolve to integrate these elements into your life.

This exercise bridges the gap between your present reality and the future you aspire to, guided by your core values. By visualizing and reflecting on your ideal life, you're taking a significant step toward making that vision a reality, empowered by a deeper understanding of what truly matters to you.

Week 12 Day 3

Objective: To prioritize and affirm your most significant values, ensuring they are at the forefront of your life's decisions and actions.

Information: After identifying and exploring your values, the next crucial step is to prioritize them. This process helps clarify which values are non-negotiable and should guide your major life decisions. By prioritizing your values, you create a hierarchy that helps you navigate life's complexities more authentically, ensuring that your actions and decisions are in alignment with what matters most to you.

Instructions:

1. **Listing Values:**
   - Begin by listing all the values you've identified as important to you over the past two days. Include values uncovered through reflection, visualization, and any other exercises.

2. **Prioritization Exercise:**
   - Review your list of values, and for each, ask yourself, "Could I live a fulfilled life if this were missing?" If the answer is "no," this value is a core value for you.
   - Rank these core values in order of importance. While this may be challenging, aim to identify the values that you feel are most essential to your sense of self and fulfillment.

3. **Affirmation Creation:**
   - For your top five values, create a short affirmation or statement that encapsulates why each value is important to you and how it shapes your life.

Reflection: Reflect on the prioritization process by asking yourself:

- How did it feel to rank my values in order of importance?
- Were there any surprises or insights gained from affirming why each top value is important to me?

Integration:

- **Daily Reminders:** Set daily reminders of your top values. This could be through alarms, notes placed in visible areas, or digital notifications containing your value affirmations.
- **Decision-Making:** For the next week, consciously refer to your list of top values when faced with big and small decisions. Note any differences in how you feel about the decisions made when your values guide you.
- **Community Engagement:** Share the experience of prioritizing your values with someone close to you. Discuss how this process might influence your relationship or shared activities.

This day's exercise is pivotal in solidifying your commitment to living a life guided by your most cherished values. It not only aids in making more authentic decisions but also serves as a constant reminder of the principles you wish to embody. You lay a solid foundation for a purpose-driven life by prioritizing and affirming your values.

Week 12 Day 4

Objective: To evaluate the alignment between your current lifestyle and prioritized values, identifying areas for realignment.

Information: This step in your journey is crucial for bringing your day-to-day life into harmony with your core values. Often, there's a disconnect between what we value and how we live, whether due to external pressures, old habits, or simply a lack of awareness. By examining your life through the lens of your prioritized values, you can identify discrepancies and take steps to address them. This process ensures that your actions and choices are congruent with what truly matters to you, leading to a more authentic and fulfilling life.

Instructions:

1. **Alignment Assessment:**
   - Reflect on your daily routines, habits, and the choices you've made recently. Consider your relationships, career, and personal growth activities.
   - For each area of your life, ask yourself, "Does this reflect my top values?" Take notes on where you see alignment and where there are gaps.

2. **Identify Discrepancies:**
   - Highlight the areas where there's a significant gap between your values and your current lifestyle.
   - Choose one area where aligning your life with your values could have the most meaningful impact.

3. **Action Plan Development:**

○ Develop a specific, actionable plan for addressing the gap identified. This plan should include small, manageable steps that can be taken to bring this area of your life closer to aligning with your values.

Reflection: After completing the alignment assessment and action plan, reflect on the following:

- What emotions or thoughts arose during this exercise?
- How do I feel about the possibility of making changes to better align my life with my values?

Integration:

- **Implement the Action Plan:** Begin implementing the first step of your action plan. Keep a journal of your progress, noting any challenges and successes.
- **Regular Review:** Schedule a monthly review of your alignment with your values. Use this time to adjust your action plan, celebrate progress, and identify new areas for improvement.
- **Community Involvement:** Discuss your experience and insights with a trusted friend or community group. Sharing your journey can provide additional support and motivation for both you and others.

Day 4's exercise is a vital step for living a life that is not only aligned with your values but also rich in authenticity and purpose. By identifying and addressing discrepancies between your values and your lifestyle, you pave the way for profound personal growth and fulfillment.

Week 12 Day 5

Objective: To deepen your understanding and connection to your top values by defining them in your own words, making them more tangible and actionable in your life.

Information: Defining your values in your terms is a transformative exercise that moves values from abstract concepts to practical guides for living. This personal definition process illuminates the unique significance of each value in your life, clarifying how they influence your decisions, actions, and overall life direction. By articulating what each value truly means, you create a personal blueprint that can guide your behavior and choices more effectively.

Instructions:

1. **Value Definition:**
   - Select your top five prioritized values from Day 3. For each, write a detailed definition in your own words. Include why each value is important to you and how it influences your life. Aim for clarity and depth, making each definition personal and meaningful.

2. **Illustrative Examples:**
   - For each defined value, think of a recent time when you lived according to that value or when you wish you had. Write a brief narrative or bullet points about these instances to illustrate each value in action.

3. **Value Statements:**
   - Craft a concise value statement for each of your top values based on your definitions and examples. These statements

should encapsulate the essence of each value and how you intend to embody them in your life.

Reflection: Reflect on the process of defining and illustrating your values by considering:

- How did articulating my values in my own words change my understanding or perception of them?
- Which examples of living according to my values am I most proud of? Why?

Integration:

- **Visual Reminders:** Create visual reminders of your value statements, such as a small card to carry with you or a post-it note on your mirror.
- **Daily Check-ins:** Incorporate a daily check-in with yourself to assess how well your actions that day aligned with your value statements. Note any insights or adjustments needed.
- **Value-based Decision Making:** Moving forward, use your value statements as a filter for making decisions. Before making a choice, ask yourself which option best aligns with your value statements.

Day 5's exercise is pivotal in making your values a living part of your daily existence. By defining your values in your own words and creating actionable statements, you equip yourself with a clear guide for embodying these values in all aspects of your life. This enhances your sense of authenticity and purpose and strengthens your ability to live in alignment with what truly matters to you.

Week 12 Day 6

Objective: To set specific, actionable goals that are deeply aligned with your top personal values, fostering personal growth and greater life satisfaction.

Information: Setting goals based on your values is a powerful way to ensure that your pursuits and achievements are meaningful and contribute to your overall well-being and happiness. This alignment between values and goals ensures that your efforts are directed toward activities that truly resonate with your core self, enhancing motivation and fulfillment.

Instructions:

1. **Goal Identification:**
   - Reflect on your top five values defined in Day 5. Consider areas of your life where you can further embody these values through specific actions or changes.
   - Identify three personal growth goals that are directly aligned with your values. Ensure these goals are Specific, Measurable, Achievable, Relevant, and Time-bound (SMART).

2. **Action Plan Creation:**
   - For each goal, create a detailed action plan that outlines the steps you will take to achieve it. Include timelines, resources needed, and how you will measure progress.

3. **Commitment Statement:**
   - Write a commitment statement for each goal, expressing your dedication to pursuing this goal in alignment with

your values. This statement should reflect your understanding of why the goal is important and how it contributes to your value-driven life.

Reflection: Reflect on the goal-setting process by asking yourself:

- How do these goals reflect my values?
- What challenges do I anticipate in pursuing these goals, and how can my values guide me in overcoming them?

Integration:

- **Visual Tracking:** Create a visual representation of your goals and action plans, such as a chart or board, that you can display in a frequently seen place. This serves as a constant reminder of your commitments.
- **Weekly Review:** Schedule a weekly review of your goal progress. Use this time to adjust your action plans, celebrate achievements, and reflect on any new insights gained.
- **Value Alignment Check-ins:** Regularly check in with yourself to ensure that your efforts continue to align with your values. Adjust your goals as needed to reflect changes in your values or life circumstances.

Day 6's exercise empowers you to take actionable steps. Setting goals that are in harmony with your values lays the groundwork for a life of authenticity, growth, and fulfillment.

Week 12 Day 7

Objective: To actively embody one of your top values throughout the day, enhancing your connection to this value and integrating it more deeply into your daily life.

Information: Living your values consciously and intentionally is the essence of a fulfilling life. By focusing on embodying a specific value for an entire day, you create a powerful opportunity to understand and appreciate its impact on your actions, decisions, and interactions. This focused approach allows you to see firsthand how aligning with your values can enhance your sense of purpose and satisfaction.

Instructions:

1. **Value Selection:**
   - Choose one of your top five values that you feel particularly drawn to focus on today. This value should be something you wish to integrate more fully into your daily experience.

2. **Intention Setting:**
   - Start your day by setting a clear intention to embody this value in all your actions and interactions. Write down a few sentences about how you plan to do this, including specific behaviors or mindset shifts you will adopt.

3. **Value Embodiment:**
   - Throughout the day, actively look for opportunities to demonstrate this value. This could be through your work, relationships, or even moments of solitude. Be creative and intentional in finding ways to live out this value.

4. **Journaling Prompts:**
   - At the end of the day, take time to journal about your experience. Reflect on the following questions:
     - How did focusing on this value influence my actions and decisions today?
     - In what moments did I feel most aligned with this value?
     - What challenges did I encounter in trying to embody this value, and how did I address them?

Reflection: Reflect on the overall experience of dedicating a day to living out one of your core values. Consider how this focused practice made you feel and what it taught you about the importance of aligning your daily life with your values.

Integration:

- **Repeat the Focus:** Consider rotating through your top values, dedicating a day to each. This will help deepen your understanding and appreciation of each value.
- **Long-Term Implementation:** Based on your experiences, identify ways to continue to consistently embody this value in your life. Set actionable steps for integration.
- **Community Engagement:** Share your experience of living a value-focused day with a friend or family member. Discuss how your values influence your life and explore ways you can support each other in living according to your values.

Day 7's exercise is a capstone to your week's journey, offering a practical and impactful way to bring the insights you've gained into your daily life. By choosing to live in alignment with your values, even just for a day, you take a significant step toward a more authentic and purpose-driven existence.

Bridge Week 12

As you approach the concluding week of our self-help journey, it's time for a profound reflection on the path you've traversed. This moment marks a significant milestone, not just in terms of this guide but in your ongoing journey toward well-being. Envision the bridge that has symbolized your progress—each section representing steps taken toward a more balanced state of mind.

Reflect Deeply on Your Journey:

- **Starting Point:** Recall where you began, acknowledging the challenges and feelings that initially surrounded you.
- **The Path Traveled:** Reflect on the key moments of change, growth, and realization that have shaped your journey.
- **Challenges Overcome:** Think about the obstacles you've faced and how you navigated through them, recognizing your resilience.
- **Growth Experienced:** Acknowledge the personal growth you've achieved, both in understanding yourself and in developing coping strategies.

Marking Your Current Position: For the final time in this program, update your marker on the bridge. Place it where you currently find yourself, considering how far you've come from the start. Allow this marker to represent not just an end but a waypoint on your much larger journey of self-discovery and healing.

If you find yourself not quite ready to step off the bridge, that's perfectly okay. Healing and growth operate on their own unique timelines for each individual. If you feel that you are still on the journey across the bridge, remember that this guide and its 12-week program are designed to be revisited and re-engaged with as many times as necessary. The strategies, exercises, and reflections provided here can be explored repeatedly, each cycle through the guide potentially offering new insights and deeper healing. There's no rush in this process, and there's strength in recognizing when you need more time. Allow yourself the grace to continue working through the guide, using its resources to support your journey until you're ready to take that final step off the bridge. This journey is yours, and moving at the pace that feels right for you is not just acceptable—it's encouraged.

Looking Beyond the Bridge: As you step off this metaphorical bridge, understand that life is a series of bridges—each with its challenges and victories. The path ahead will unfold with new landscapes to explore and new bridges to cross. Remember, the insights and strategies you've gained from this guide equip you with the tools to navigate these future journeys.

A Lifelong Companion: The knowledge and practices encapsulated in this book remain with you, timeless in their relevance. Whenever you find yourself on the precipice of a new bridge, revisit these pages. The reflections, exercises, and insights will continue to serve as a beacon, guiding you towards resilience, understanding, and well-being.

Embrace the journey ahead with the wisdom of past experiences and the knowledge that every bridge crossed strengthens your ability to face what lies beyond. The journey doesn't end here—it evolves, with this guide as a continual source of support and inspiration.

PART III

Moving Forward

18

Embracing a
Depression-Free Life

As our shared journey unfolds to its next chapter, we arrive at a moment of reflection and anticipation. This moment marks a pivotal transition—a gateway to sustaining the progress you've achieved and living fully in the light of a depression-free existence. The path you've walked as you've read these pages has been one of profound transformation, learning, and growth. Yet, the journey toward well-being is continuous. This chapter, therefore, is dedicated to equipping you with strategies for identifying and managing potential triggers and early warning signs of depression, reinforcing the importance of ongoing commitment to your mental health.

Understanding your triggers—those emotional, situational, or environmental factors that can precipitate a return to depressive states—is crucial. To manage these triggers effectively, maintaining a journal can be a profound tool. It serves as a mirror to your experiences, reflecting the triggers as they emerge alongside the thoughts, feelings, and circumstances that accompany them. Developing strategies to navigate these triggers is essential, whether that involves seeking support, engaging in self-care, or employing the coping techniques that have become part of your arsenal.

Equally important is the recognition of early warning signs of depression. These signs, which can include changes in sleep patterns, appetite, mood, and energy levels, are the sentinels alerting you to take action. Engaging in mindfulness and reflective practices helps maintain a connection with your inner landscape, allowing for early recognition of these signs. Should they arise, reaching out for support promptly can significantly alter the course, preventing a deeper slide into depression.

The conclusion of the 12-week self-help guide is not the end but a prompt for continued growth and self-care. The journey ahead calls for revisiting lessons learned, repeating exercises to reinforce their benefits, and an openness to ongoing learning. Your positivity journal, a repository of gratitude and hope, remains vital for nurturing a positive outlook.

Seeking professional help, a step taken with courage and self-compassion, is essential when challenges arise. Whether facing a depression relapse or overwhelming triggers, professional guidance offers tailored strategies and unwavering support, reinforcing your resilience and capacity for recovery.

Living a depression-free life is ongoing and marked by dedication, self-awareness, and an unwavering commitment to growth. It's a path that acknowledges setbacks as part of the human experience, viewing them not as failures but as opportunities for deeper learning and resilience. As you continue to apply the strategies learned, stay connected with your support network, and celebrate each step forward, remember that this journey is yours. It's a journey filled with hope, resilience, and the promise of brighter days.

This chapter aims to empower you to maintain your progress and embrace the continuous journey of self-discovery and healing. The path to a life free from depression is paved with ongoing work, reflection, and self-compassion. You are not alone in this journey; together, we walk toward a future illuminated by well-being and freedom from depression.

19

A Message of Hope

As we draw the curtains on this journey together, I want to leave you with a message that I hope will echo in your heart for days, months, and years to come—a message of hope. The road to recovery from depression is as unique as you are, filled with its own set of challenges and triumphs. But remember, recovery is possible. You have within you the strength, resilience, and courage needed to navigate this path.

One of the most powerful tools at your disposal is self-compassion. It's a gentle reminder that you are doing your best with what you have. It's the understanding that healing is not a linear process; there will be times of progress and there will be setbacks. And that's okay. Treat yourself with the kindness and patience you would offer a dear friend in distress. Remember, self-compassion is not self-indulgence or self-pity but a way to empower yourself to manage life's challenges gracefully.

Perseverance is your beacon of light in moments of darkness. It's the quiet voice that encourages you to take one more step when you feel you can't go on. Your journey through depression has undoubtedly tested your limits, but it has also shown you your incredible capacity to endure and overcome. Keep moving forward, even if it's just a small daily step. Every effort counts, and with time, these efforts will accumulate into significant strides toward recovery.

Recovery from depression is not a destination but a continuous journey. It's an ongoing process of learning, growing, and adapting. Along the way, you'll discover more about yourself, your strengths, your vulnerabilities, and how to navigate life that aligns with your well-being. There may be setbacks, but they do not define your journey— they are merely part of the process. Embrace the journey with an open heart and mind, ready to receive the lessons and blessings it offers.

Perhaps the most important thing to remember is that you are not alone. Countless others are walking this path alongside you, each with a story of struggle and resilience. When you need it, lean on the support of friends, family, and mental health professionals. There is strength in community; sometimes, sharing your journey can lighten the load and bring unexpected joy and connection.

As we part ways in this book, remember that the darkness of depression does not last forever. There is light, hope, and joy in life, even after the deepest despair. Your journey towards healing is a testament to your strength and a beacon of hope for others. Remember, your story isn't over yet; it's just beginning a new chapter where you are the author of your healing and happiness.

Thank you for allowing me to be a part of your journey. May you carry forward the lessons, the growth, and the hope you've gathered here into every aspect of your life. Here's to your continued journey toward a life filled with light, love, and endless possibilities. Remember, recovery is not just a hope; it's a possibility that you are turning into a reality, one day at a time.

PART IV

APPENDIX

Cognitive Distortions

Defense Mechanisms

Depression FAQ

Resource Guide

Common Cognitive Distortions

Cognitive distortions are like optical illusions of the mind. They're patterns of thinking that twist and distort reality, leading us to perceive situations inaccurately and react in unhelpful ways. Imagine wearing glasses with lenses that subtly warp everything you see - that's what cognitive distortions do to our thoughts.

Recognizing these distortions can be tricky because they often feel like truth rather than errors in perception. However, there are signs to watch out for. If you catch yourself engaging in black-and-white thinking (seeing only extremes), catastrophizing (assuming the worst), or constantly blaming yourself or others, chances are you're experiencing cognitive distortions.

These distortions can wreak havoc on our lives. They fuel anxiety, depression, and relationship problems. Picture someone who always jumps to conclusions - they might avoid social situations out of fear of being judged, leading to loneliness and isolation. Or consider the perfectionist who never feels good enough - they may procrastinate on important tasks or give up altogether, stalling their personal and professional growth.

Overcoming cognitive distortions starts with awareness. By learning to recognize these thinking patterns, we can begin to challenge them. This involves questioning our automatic thoughts and examining evidence objectively. For instance, instead of assuming the worst about a situation, we can ask ourselves, "What evidence supports this belief? What evidence contradicts it?"

Cognitive-behavioral therapy offers practical strategies for overcoming cognitive distortions. Therapists help clients identify and challenge distorted thinking patterns, replacing them with more balanced and realistic perspectives. Techniques such as cognitive restructuring and mindfulness can also be helpful in breaking free from the grip of cognitive distortions.

Ultimately, overcoming cognitive distortions requires practice and patience. It's like retraining our brains to see the world more clearly - it takes time, effort, and a willingness to challenge our own assumptions. But the payoff is worth it. By breaking free from these mental traps, we can experience greater peace of mind, healthier relationships, and a more fulfilling life.

Below is a list of 60 common cognitive distortions

1. **All-or-Nothing Thinking (Black and White Thinking):** Seeing things in extremes without considering any middle ground. For example, believing that if you're not perfect at something, you're a total failure.
2. **Always Being Right:** Insisting on being right in every situation, even at the expense of relationships or personal growth. For example, refusing to consider another person's perspective in an argument.
3. **Assumed Constraints:** Believing that you are limited by factors that may not actually exist, such as age, gender, or past experiences. For example, assuming that you can't pursue a new career because you're "too old" or "not qualified enough."
4. **Attentional Bias:** Paying disproportionate attention to negative or threatening stimuli, while overlooking positive or neutral information. For example, noticing and dwelling on criticism from a single coworker while disregarding praise from others.
5. **Attribution Errors:** Making inaccurate attributions about the causes of events or behaviors, leading to misunderstandings and miscommunication. For example, attributing someone's criticism to their inherent personality flaws rather than considering situational factors.

6. **Belief Perseverance:** Clinging to a belief even in the face of contradictory evidence, often due to emotional attachment or cognitive dissonance. For example, continuing to believe in a conspiracy theory despite overwhelming evidence debunking it.

7. **Blaming:** Holding others responsible for your negative emotions or outcomes without considering your own role. For example, blaming a coworker for your own procrastination.

8. **Catastrophizing:** Exaggerating the negative aspects of a situation and expecting the worst possible outcome. For example, believing a small mistake will lead to complete failure.

9. **Cognitive Rigidity:** Difficulty adapting your thoughts or beliefs in response to new information or changing circumstances. For instance, insisting that your political views are correct and refusing to consider alternative perspectives.

10. **Comparative Suffering:** Minimizing or dismissing your own struggles or pain by comparing them to others who you perceive as worse off. For instance, telling yourself that you have no right to feel sad because there are people in the world facing much greater hardships.

11. **Comparing Apples and Oranges:** Making invalid comparisons between two unrelated things or situations. For example, comparing your artistic abilities to a professional painter's without considering differences in skill level or experience.

12. **Comparing Emotional States:** Comparing different emotions as if they were mutually exclusive, rather than recognizing that it's normal to experience a range of emotions. For example, believing that feeling anxious means you can't also feel happy or content.

13. **Comparing with Imagined Realities:** Comparing your current reality to an idealized version of what could have been or what should be, rather than accepting what is. For instance, imagining a perfect relationship and feeling dissatisfied with your own because it doesn't meet those unrealistic standards.

14. **Comparison to Unattainable Standards:** Comparing yourself or your life to unrealistic or unattainable standards, leading to feelings of inadequacy or dissatisfaction. For example, measuring your body image against airbrushed models in magazines and feeling inadequate as a result.

15. **Confirmation Bias:** Seeking out information that confirms your existing beliefs or hypotheses while ignoring or discounting evidence that contradicts them. For instance, only reading news sources that align with your political views and dismissing alternative perspectives.

16. **Control Fallacies:** Believing you have complete control over external events or that you have no control over your own actions and reactions. For example, feeling responsible for someone else's happiness or believing that external factors determine your success entirely.

17. **Discounting the Positive:** Ignoring or downplaying positive experiences or qualities. For example, dismissing compliments by thinking they're insincere or irrelevant.

18. **Egocentric Bias:** Viewing situations and events from a self-centered perspective, often overestimating your own role or importance in them. For example, assuming that someone's behavior is directly related to you or influenced by your actions when it may have nothing to do with you at all.

19. **Emotional Amplification:** Exaggerating the significance or intensity of your emotions in response to a situation. For example, feeling devastated by a minor criticism or setback.

20. **Emotional Reasoning:** Allowing emotions to dictate reasoning and decision-making, rather than objectively evaluating evidence. For example, believing something is true because it feels true emotionally, regardless of factual evidence to the contrary.

21. **Emotional Reasoning:** Believing that your feelings are facts. For instance, feeling anxious about a situation and assuming it must be dangerous.

22. **Externalization:** Attribute negative outcomes or events to external factors, such as other people, circumstances, or luck, rather than taking personal responsibility. For example, blaming your failure to meet a deadline on your coworker's incompetence rather than acknowledging your own procrastination.

23. **Fallacy of Change:** Expecting others to change to suit your needs or expecting to change others. For instance, believing that if someone truly cared about you, they would change their behavior.

24. **Fallacy of Fairness:** Believing that life should be fair and that any unfairness or injustice experienced is intolerable. For example, feeling resentful because you believe you deserve better treatment than what you've received.

25. **False Consensus Effect:** Assuming that others share your beliefs or opinions, leading to overestimation of the prevalence of your perspective. For example, believing that everyone must feel the same way about a controversial issue because your immediate social circle agrees with you.

26. **Fatalistic Thinking:** Believing that outcomes are predetermined and that efforts to change them are futile. For example, assuming that nothing you do will make a difference because "it's just meant to be."

27. **Favorable Comparison:** Comparing yourself only to others who are perceived as worse off, leading to a false sense of superiority or complacency. For instance, feeling good about yourself because you believe you're better than someone else rather than focusing on personal growth.

28. **Forecasting Errors:** Making inaccurate predictions about future events, often assuming the worst-case scenario without considering alternative outcomes or probabilities. For instance, predicting that a job interview will go poorly and catastrophizing about the potential consequences.

29. **Heaven's Reward Fallacy:** Believing that if you suffer enough or sacrifice enough, you will eventually be rewarded. For instance, staying in a toxic relationship because you believe your dedication will eventually be recognized and rewarded.

30. **Hindsight Bias:** Viewing past events as more predictable or inevitable than they actually were, often after learning the outcome. For example, believing that you knew all along that a relationship would end badly, even though you were optimistic about it at the time.

31. **Imposter Syndrome:** Believing that your achievements are undeserved and fearing being exposed as a fraud or incompetent, despite evidence of your competence. For example, attributing your success to luck or other external factors rather than acknowledging your own abilities and efforts.

32. **In-group Bias:** Favoring members of your own group over those outside of it, leading to prejudice or discrimination. For instance, showing preference for colleagues from your department and being dismissive of those from other departments.

33. **Inability to Disconfirm:** Rejecting evidence that contradicts your beliefs, leading to a closed-minded approach and reinforcing existing biases. For example, dismissing scientific evidence that challenges your religious beliefs.

34. **Judgment Focus:** Focusing excessively on making judgments or evaluations about yourself, others, or situations, rather than simply observing or experiencing them. For example, constantly critiquing your appearance or performance in social situations.

35. **Jumping to Conclusions:** Making assumptions without evidence. This can be either mind reading (believing you know what others are thinking) or fortune telling (predicting the future negatively without evidence).

36. **Just World Fallacy:** Believing that the world is inherently fair and that people get what they deserve, leading to victim blaming or overlooking systemic injustices. For example, assuming that

someone who experiences misfortune must have done something to deserve it.

37. **Labeling:** Generalizing a person or situation based on a single characteristic or event. For example, labeling yourself as a failure because you made a mistake.

38. **Magnification and Minimization (also known as "Binocular Trick"):** Exaggerating the importance of negative events and minimizing the significance of positive ones. For example, focusing solely on a minor criticism while ignoring numerous compliments.

39. **Memory Bias:** Recalling past events in a way that reinforces your current beliefs or emotions, rather than accurately remembering what happened. For example, remembering a past failure as more significant or devastating than it actually was.

40. **Memory Filtering:** Selectively remembering only those events or details that confirm your existing beliefs or biases, while disregarding contradictory information. For instance, recalling only the negative aspects of a past relationship while overlooking the positive moments.

41. **Memory Misattribution:** Incorrectly attributing a memory to the wrong source, leading to false beliefs or conclusions. For instance, recalling a conversation with a friend that never actually happened because you heard a similar story from someone else.

42. **Mind Reading:** Assuming you know what others are thinking or feeling, usually in a negative way. For instance, believing someone doesn't like you without any evidence.

43. **Need for Approval:** Seeking validation and approval from others to feel worthy or competent, and feeling distressed or inadequate when it's not received. For example, feeling devastated by rejection or criticism because it threatens your sense of self-worth.

44. **Out-group Homogeneity:** Perceiving members of a different group as more similar to each other than they actually are. For

example, assuming that people from a different culture all share the same values or characteristics.

45. **Overgeneralization:** Drawing broad conclusions based on limited evidence. For instance, if you fail at one task, you believe you'll fail at everything.

46. **Perfectionism:** Setting excessively high standards for yourself or others and experiencing distress or dissatisfaction when those standards are not met. For example, feeling like a failure because you didn't achieve a perfect score on a test, despite scoring well above average.

47. **Personalization:** Taking responsibility for events that are out of your control or blaming yourself for external factors. For instance, believing a friend's bad mood is your fault.

48. **Predicting the Future:** Making dire predictions about future events without considering more likely or positive outcomes. For instance, assuming that a minor mistake will lead to catastrophic consequences.

49. **Regret Avoidance:** Engaging in behaviors or decision-making aimed at avoiding or minimizing regret, even if it means sacrificing potential benefits or opportunities for growth. For example, avoiding taking risks or trying new things out of fear of regretting the outcome.

50. **Selective Attention (or Filtering):** Focusing only on certain aspects of a situation while ignoring others. For example, dwelling on a single negative comment in a conversation and overlooking the positive feedback.

51. **Selective Memory:** Recalling past events or information in a way that supports your existing beliefs or biases, while conveniently forgetting contradictory evidence. For instance, remembering past successes as evidence of your competence while ignoring past failures.

52. **Self-Blame:** Assuming personal responsibility for negative outcomes or events, even when they are beyond your control. For

example, blaming yourself for a car accident that was caused by someone else's reckless driving.

53. **Self-Serving Attribution Bias:** Attributing positive outcomes to internal factors such as ability or effort, while attributing negative outcomes to external factors such as luck or circumstance. For instance, taking credit for a successful project at work but blaming a failed project on lack of support from colleagues.

54. **Self-Serving Bias:** Interpreting information in a way that maintains or enhances your self-esteem, while attributing negative outcomes to external factors and positive outcomes to internal factors. For instance, taking credit for successes but blaming failures on circumstances beyond your control.

55. **Semantic Slanting:** Using language in a way that presents information in a biased or misleading manner to influence perception. For example, describing a political opponent's policies as "radical" or "extreme" to evoke negative emotions.

56. **Should Statements:** Putting undue pressure on yourself or others with "should," "must," or "ought to" statements. For example, thinking, "I should always be productive," or "They should know what I need without me saying it."

57. **Social Comparison:** Constantly comparing yourself to others, often leading to feelings of inferiority or superiority. For example, feeling inadequate because a friend has a more successful career or feeling superior because you believe you're more physically attractive than someone else.

58. **Temporal Discounting:** Valuing immediate rewards more than future rewards, leading to impulsive decision-making and procrastination. For example, choosing to indulge in immediate gratification like watching TV instead of studying for an exam.

59. **Tunnel Vision:** Focusing exclusively on a single aspect of a situation while ignoring broader context or alternative perspectives. For instance, becoming fixated on one potential solution to a problem and disregarding other viable options.

60. **Unfair Comparison:** Comparing yourself to others who are perceived as better off, leading to feelings of inadequacy or inferiority. For example, feeling inadequate because you don't have the same success as someone else without considering the differences in circumstances or opportunities.

Common Defense Mechanisms

Psychological defense mechanisms are ways in which individuals protect themselves from anxiety or distress. Here's a list of 60 common defense mechanisms along with brief descriptions and simple examples:

1. **Avoidance of Accountability**: Evading responsibility or deflecting blame for one's own actions or choices, often by shifting focus onto external factors or circumstances. For example, blaming traffic or bad luck for being late to an appointment instead of acknowledging poor time management.

2. **Avoidance**: Deliberately avoiding thoughts, feelings, or situations that are perceived as threatening or anxiety-provoking. An example would be avoiding social gatherings because of fear of rejection or embarrassment.

3. **Avoidance**: Intentionally steering clear of situations, thoughts, or emotions that evoke anxiety or distress. For instance, avoiding discussing feelings of inadequacy to prevent discomfort.

4. **Avoidant Coping**: Employing avoidance strategies or behaviors to cope with stressful or challenging situations, rather than facing them directly. For example, procrastinating on important tasks to delay dealing with anxiety or fear of failure.

5. **Behavioral Addictions**: Developing compulsive behaviors or habits, such as gambling, shopping, or excessive exercise, as a way to cope with stress, anxiety, or emotional pain.

6. **Catastrophizing**: Exaggerating the potential negative consequences of a situation or event, often leading to increased anxiety

or distress. For instance, imagining the worst possible outcome of a minor mistake or setback.

7. **Compartmentalization**: Segregating conflicting thoughts, feelings, or behaviors into separate mental compartments to avoid cognitive dissonance. For example, rationalizing unethical behavior by compartmentalizing it from one's moral values.

8. **Compartmentalization**: Separating conflicting thoughts or feelings into separate compartments to avoid cognitive dissonance. An example is a person who cheats on their partner but convinces themselves that their actions are justified because they still love their partner.

9. **Compensation**: Overemphasizing or overachieving in one area to make up for shortcomings in another. An example would be someone who feels inadequate in social situations but excels in academic or professional pursuits.

10. **Compensation**: Overemphasizing strengths or achievements in one area to compensate for perceived shortcomings in another. For example, someone who feels insecure about their appearance may excel in academics or sports.

11. **Conversion**: Transforming emotional distress or psychological conflict into physical symptoms without organic cause. For instance, experiencing blindness or paralysis as a result of unresolved trauma.

12. **Defensive Pessimism**: Adopting a pessimistic outlook or expecting the worst as a way to protect oneself from disappointment or failure. For instance, someone may constantly anticipate negative outcomes to avoid being caught off guard by setbacks.

13. **Denial**: Refusing to accept or acknowledge reality, especially when it's unpleasant or distressing. For example, someone with a drinking problem may deny that they have a problem despite evidence to the contrary.

14. **Displacement**: Redirecting one's emotions or impulses from the original source toward a less threatening target. For example,

being angry with one's boss but yelling at a family member instead.

15. **Dissociation**: Detaching oneself from reality or the physical body as a way to cope with overwhelming emotions, trauma, or distressing experiences. For example, feeling as though one is watching themselves from outside their body during a traumatic event.

16. **Distortion**: Perceiving or interpreting reality in a way that aligns with one's desires, beliefs, or expectations, often ignoring contradictory evidence. For example, seeing a romantic interest as flawless despite evidence of their imperfections.

17. **Ego Defense Mechanisms**: Employing various tactics to protect the ego from threats to self-esteem or self-concept. Examples include denial, projection, and rationalization.

18. **Emotional Detachment**: Creating emotional distance or aloofness in relationships as a way to protect oneself from vulnerability, rejection, or intimacy. For example, avoiding deep conversations or emotional expression in order to maintain control or independence.

19. **Emotional Eating**: Using food as a way to cope with or soothe difficult emotions, such as stress, sadness, or boredom. For example, turning to ice cream or chocolate when feeling upset or lonely.

20. **Emotional Inhibition**: Suppressing or inhibiting the expression of emotions, particularly negative or uncomfortable ones, to maintain composure or avoid vulnerability. For example, suppressing tears or anger during a difficult conversation.

21. **Emotional Numbing**: Blocking or numbing oneself to emotional experiences as a way to avoid pain or discomfort. For example, shutting down emotionally after experiencing repeated rejection or trauma.

22. **Emotional Overcontrol**: Exerting excessive control or restraint over one's emotions, often out of fear of losing control or

appearing vulnerable. For example, suppressing tears or anger even in situations where it would be healthy or appropriate to express them.

23. **Emotional Scapegoating**: Using emotions, particularly negative ones, as a scapegoat for problems or conflicts within oneself or in relationships with others. For example, blaming anger or jealousy for relationship difficulties instead of addressing underlying issues or communication problems.

24. **Emotional Suppression**: Burying or suppressing one's emotions, particularly negative or distressing ones, in order to appear strong, composed, or in control. For instance, forcing oneself to smile and act cheerful despite feeling sad or upset inside.

25. **Emotional Volatility**: Experiencing extreme fluctuations in mood or emotional intensity, often in response to perceived threats, stressors, or triggers. For example, experiencing sudden and intense mood swings in reaction to minor frustrations or disappointments.

26. **Escapism**: Avoiding reality or unpleasant emotions by immersing oneself in distractions or fantasies. For example, binge-watching television shows or playing video games to avoid dealing with stress or anxiety.

27. **Exaggeration**: Magnifying or embellishing one's achievements, talents, or virtues as a way to boost self-esteem or gain approval from others. For instance, exaggerating one's role in a group project to appear more competent.

28. **External Validation**: Seeking validation or approval from external sources, such as peers, authority figures, or social media, to bolster self-esteem or reinforce self-worth.

29. **Externalization**: Blaming external factors or circumstances for one's own problems or shortcomings rather than taking personal responsibility. For instance, blaming traffic for being late to work instead of acknowledging poor time management skills.

30. **Externalizing Blame**: Blaming external factors or circumstances for one's own failures, mistakes, or shortcomings, rather than taking personal responsibility. For instance, attributing poor academic performance to a difficult teacher rather than acknowledging lack of effort or preparation.

31. **False Attribution**: Incorrectly attributing one's own thoughts, feelings, or behaviors to external sources, such as other people, inanimate objects, or fate. For example, believing that a lucky charm is responsible for success, rather than acknowledging personal effort or ability.

32. **Fantasy Bonding**: Creating a false sense of connection or intimacy with others through idealized fantasies or projections, rather than through genuine emotional engagement or vulnerability.

33. **Fantasy**: Creating an imaginary world or scenarios to escape from reality. For example, someone who is unhappy with their job may spend a lot of time daydreaming about winning the lottery and never having to work again.

34. **Humor**: Using humor to cope with difficult or uncomfortable situations. For example, making jokes about a stressful event to lighten the mood and reduce tension.

35. **Hypochondriasis**: Exaggerating or obsessing over minor physical symptoms as a way to avoid dealing with emotional distress. For instance, someone experiencing anxiety may constantly worry about having a serious illness.

36. **Idealization**: Seeing someone or something as perfect, admirable, or flawless to avoid facing reality. For example, idolizing a celebrity despite not knowing them personally.

37. **Identification with the Aggressor**: Adopting the attitudes or behaviors of an aggressor or oppressor as a means of coping with feelings of powerlessness or fear. For example, a victim of abuse may begin to identify with the abuser's mindset or values.

38. **Identification**: Associating with or imitating someone admired or respected in an attempt to enhance self-esteem. For example, a child may idolize a famous athlete and try to emulate their behavior on and off the field.

39. **Identification**: Emulating or aligning oneself with individuals or groups perceived as powerful or esteemed to bolster self-esteem or reduce anxiety. For example, adopting the mannerisms and beliefs of a celebrity role model.

40. **Identity Distortion**: Distorting or exaggerating aspects of one's identity, such as personality traits, accomplishments, or experiences, in order to gain attention, admiration, or sympathy from others.

41. **Intellectual Displacement**: Redirecting emotional conflicts or anxieties into intellectual pursuits or academic endeavors. For example, burying oneself in books or research to avoid dealing with personal relationship issues.

42. **Intellectual Rationalization**: Using logical or rational explanations to justify or excuse irrational or emotionally-driven behaviors or decisions. For example, rationalizing impulsive spending as "retail therapy" or self-care.

43. **Intellectualization**: Focusing excessively on abstract or intellectual aspects of a situation while avoiding the emotional aspects. For instance, discussing the technicalities of a breakup rather than acknowledging the pain.

44. **Isolation**: Disconnecting thoughts or emotions from their associated feelings, often through intellectualization or rationalization. For example, discussing a traumatic event in a detached, matter-of-fact manner without expressing any emotional distress.

45. **Magical Thinking**: Believing in supernatural or irrational connections between thoughts, actions, or events, often as a way to exert control or alleviate anxiety. For instance, believing that wearing lucky socks will guarantee success in a job interview.

46. **Maladaptive Daydreaming**: Engaging in excessive, elaborate daydreaming or fantasy as a way to escape from reality or cope with distressing emotions. For example, creating intricate imaginary worlds to avoid dealing with real-life problems.

47. **Minimization**: Downplaying the significance of one's thoughts, feelings, or actions. An example is someone who drinks heavily but insists they "only have a few drinks" each night.

48. **Obsessive-Compulsive Personality**: Rigid adherence to rules, routines, or rituals as a way to exert control over one's environment or alleviate anxiety. For example, meticulously organizing belongings or following strict daily schedules to manage uncertainty or fear.

49. **Overidentification with Victimhood**: Exaggerating or perpetuating one's own sense of victimization or persecution as a way to gain sympathy, attention, or validation from others. For example, constantly dwelling on past injustices or hardships to justify present behavior or attitudes.

50. **Passive Acceptance**: Resigning oneself to unfavorable circumstances or situations without taking proactive steps to change them. For instance, accepting mistreatment in a relationship without asserting boundaries or seeking help.

51. **Passive Observation**: Observing or analyzing one's own thoughts, feelings, or behaviors from a detached or passive perspective, rather than actively engaging with or addressing them.

52. **Passive Resistance**: Exhibiting passive behaviors to resist demands or expectations, often without openly expressing opposition. For example, deliberately procrastinating on tasks assigned by a supervisor.

53. **Passive-aggressiveness**: Indirectly expressing hostility or resentment through nonverbal behaviors, such as sarcasm, procrastination, or intentional inefficiency. An example would be giving someone the silent treatment instead of directly addressing an issue.

54. **Perfectionism**: Setting excessively high standards for oneself or others and becoming overly critical or self-critical when those standards are not met. For example, obsessively striving for flawlessness in academic, professional, or personal endeavors.

55. **Projection of False Beliefs**: Imposing one's own beliefs, values, or expectations onto others and assuming that they share the same perspective. For example, assuming that everyone values success and ambition as much as oneself does.

56. **Projection of Hostility**: Attributing one's own hostile or aggressive impulses or intentions onto others, often leading to suspicion, mistrust, or conflict in relationships. For example, assuming that others are out to get you because you secretly harbor hostile feelings toward them.

57. **Projection**: Attributing one's own unacceptable thoughts, feelings, or desires to others as a way of avoiding self-awareness or responsibility. For instance, accusing a partner of being jealous while denying one's own jealousy.

58. **Psychological Displacement**: Redirecting emotions or impulses from their original source to a less threatening target. For example, venting frustration on inanimate objects or pets instead of confronting the actual source of anger.

59. **Psychological Filtering**: Selectively attending to or focusing on information or experiences that confirm preexisting beliefs, biases, or expectations, while ignoring or discounting contradictory evidence. For instance, interpreting compliments as insincere or dismissing positive feedback as irrelevant.

60. **Psychological Withdrawal**: Retreating into one's own mind or inner world to escape from external stressors or conflicts. For instance, daydreaming or mentally checking out during boring or uncomfortable situations.

61. **Psychosomatic Symptoms**: Experiencing physical symptoms that are rooted in psychological distress or unresolved emotional

conflicts. For instance, developing headaches or stomachaches in response to stress.

62. **Rationalization**: Creating logical explanations or justifications for behaviors or thoughts that are otherwise unacceptable. For instance, someone might rationalize their excessive drinking by saying they're just "enjoying life."

63. **Reactive Formation**: Adopting beliefs or behaviors that are the opposite of one's true feelings or desires in response to anxiety or guilt. For instance, someone experiencing same-sex attraction may vehemently oppose LGBTQ rights due to internalized homophobia.

64. **Regression**: Reverting to an earlier stage of development in the face of stress. For instance, an adult may start sucking their thumb during times of extreme anxiety.

65. **Repression**: Unconsciously blocking disturbing or threatening thoughts, feelings, or memories from awareness. For instance, someone who experienced trauma as a child may have no memory of the event.

66. **Rumination**: Persistently dwelling on negative thoughts, feelings, or memories without finding resolution or relief, often leading to increased distress and anxiety. For instance, replaying past mistakes or failures in one's mind repeatedly.

67. **Scapegoating**: Blaming others or external circumstances for one's own mistakes or problems. For instance, blaming a co-worker for a project's failure instead of acknowledging one's own contribution to the problem.

68. **Selective Association**: Choosing to associate only with individuals or groups who share similar beliefs, values, or perspectives, thereby avoiding exposure to dissenting opinions or challenging ideas.

69. **Selective Attention**: Focusing only on certain aspects of a situation while ignoring others, particularly those that provoke

discomfort or conflict. For instance, ignoring evidence that contradicts one's political beliefs.

70. **Selective Forgetting**: Choosing to remember only certain aspects of a situation while conveniently forgetting others. For instance, forgetting the negative aspects of a past relationship while romanticizing it.

71. **Selective Memory**: Remembering only certain aspects of past events while conveniently forgetting or distorting others. This can serve to protect oneself from painful or uncomfortable memories.

72. **Selective Perception**: Filtering or distorting incoming information to fit preexisting beliefs, biases, or expectations. For example, interpreting ambiguous social cues as confirmation of one's negative self-image.

73. **Self-Deception**: Deluding oneself into believing falsehoods or rationalizations to maintain a positive self-image or avoid facing uncomfortable truths. For example, convincing oneself that a toxic relationship is healthy or that one is happier than they truly are.

74. **Self-Handicapping**: Creating obstacles or excuses to avoid putting forth effort or taking responsibility for failure. For instance, procrastinating on studying for an exam and then blaming a low grade on lack of preparation.

75. **Self-Isolation**: Withdrawing from social interactions or cutting oneself off from others as a way to avoid rejection, judgment, or emotional pain. For example, avoiding social gatherings or events out of fear of being criticized or ridiculed.

76. **Social Comparison**: Evaluating one's own abilities, opinions, or accomplishments in relation to those of others as a way to boost self-esteem or cope with feelings of inadequacy. For example, feeling better about oneself by comparing oneself to others who are perceived as less successful or fortunate.

77. **Spiritual Bypassing**: Using spiritual beliefs or practices to avoid addressing unresolved emotional or psychological issues. For instance, believing that positive affirmations alone can heal deep-seated traumas without seeking professional help.

78. **Splitting**: Viewing situations, people, or things as either all good or all bad, with no middle ground. For instance, someone may see a friend as either perfect or completely flawed, depending on their recent interactions.

79. **Sublimation**: Channeling unacceptable impulses or emotions into socially acceptable activities. For example, someone with aggressive tendencies might become a successful athlete.

80. **Substitution**: Redirecting unacceptable impulses or emotions into more socially acceptable outlets. For instance, channeling aggression into intense workouts or competitive sports.

81. **Suppression**: Consciously pushing unwanted thoughts, emotions, or memories out of awareness. For example, intentionally avoiding thinking about a traumatic event to prevent distress.

82. **Symbolic Substitution**: Substituting symbolic or superficial actions or behaviors for deeper, more meaningful expressions of emotion or connection. For example, giving someone a gift as a way to show affection or apology, rather than expressing genuine remorse or love.

83. **Undoing**: Engaging in actions or rituals to negate or counteract feelings of guilt or anxiety stemming from previous behaviors. An example is volunteering for charitable causes after behaving selfishly.

84. **Withdrawal**: Retreating from social interactions or avoiding responsibilities to cope with stress or anxiety. For example, isolating oneself from friends and family during periods of depression.

Depression FAQ

Are antidepressants necessary for treating depression? While not everyone needs medication, antidepressants can be an effective part of treatment for moderate to severe depression.

Are there different types of depression? Yes, including Major Depressive Disorder, Persistent Depressive Disorder (dysthymia), Seasonal Affective Disorder (SAD), and others.

Can a lack of vitamin D contribute to depression? Yes, low levels of vitamin D have been linked to depression, although the exact relationship is still being studied.

Can alcohol or drug use worsen depression? Yes, substance use can exacerbate depression symptoms and interfere with treatment outcomes.

Can changing my diet really help with depression? Yes, certain dietary changes can support mental health. Diets rich in fruits, vegetables, lean protein, and omega-3 fatty acids can potentially reduce symptoms of depression.

Can children and adolescents get depressed? Yes, depression affects all age groups, including children and adolescents, though symptoms may differ.

Can creative activities like art or music therapy help with depression? Yes, engaging in creative activities can provide an emotional outlet, reduce stress, and offer a sense of accomplishment.

Can depression affect memory and concentration? Yes, depression can lead to difficulties with concentration, decision-making, and memory.

Can depression be a side effect of medication? Some medications can have side effects that include depression, so it's important to discuss any changes in mood with a healthcare provider.

Can depression be a symptom of other medical conditions? Yes, conditions like thyroid disorders, vitamin deficiencies, and other chronic illnesses can have depression as a symptom.

Can depression be completely cured? While depression can be effectively managed and symptoms can be significantly reduced, some individuals may experience episodes of depression throughout their lives.

Can depression be treated? Absolutely. Depression is treatable with a combination of psychotherapy, medication, lifestyle changes, and other methods.

Can depression go away on its own? While some people may experience temporary improvement, professional treatment is often necessary to fully address depression.

Can depression lead to suicide? Yes, depression is a major risk factor for suicide, highlighting the importance of early treatment and support.

Can depression make other illnesses worse? Depression can exacerbate the symptoms of other chronic illnesses by affecting one's ability to manage their health effectively.

Can exercise really help with depression? Yes, regular physical activity has been shown to have a positive effect on mood and can reduce symptoms of depression.

Can hormonal imbalances contribute to depression? Yes, hormonal changes and imbalances, such as those related to thyroid problems, menopause, or postpartum, can contribute to depressive symptoms.

Can lifestyle changes affect depression? Yes, lifestyle changes such as regular exercise, a healthy diet, and adequate sleep can positively impact depression symptoms.

Can major life events trigger depression? Yes, events such as the loss of a loved one, divorce, or job loss can trigger depression in susceptible individuals.

Can meditation replace medication or therapy for depression? While meditation can be a beneficial component of treatment, it should not replace professional medical advice or therapies for depression.

Can meditation replace therapy or medication for depression? While meditation can be a valuable tool for managing symptoms, it should complement, not replace, traditional treatments like therapy and medication for most individuals.

Can pets help with depression? Yes, pets can provide companionship, reduce stress and anxiety, and increase opportunities for exercise and socialization.

Can stress cause depression? Chronic stress can lead to depression by affecting brain function, mood, and thought processes.

Can technology help in managing depression? Yes, digital tools like mood tracking apps and teletherapy can complement traditional treatments for depression.

Can volunteering or helping others impact depression? Engaging in altruistic activities can boost mood, increase social interaction, and provide a sense of purpose and fulfillment.

Can yoga be beneficial for depression? Yes, yoga combines physical movement, meditation, and breathing exercises, which can reduce stress and improve mood.

Does depression affect physical health? Yes, depression can impact physical health, leading to issues like changes in appetite, sleep disturbances, and chronic pain.

How can I differentiate between grief and depression? While grief involves feelings of emptiness and loss following a significant loss, depression includes persistent sadness and the inability to experience pleasure in activities one used to enjoy.

How can I differentiate between grief and depression? While grief involves feelings of loss, it typically decreases in intensity over time. Depression involves persistent sadness and hopelessness that doesn't necessarily tie to a specific event.

How can I encourage a loved one to seek help for depression? Offer support, share information about depression, and gently suggest professional evaluation and treatment options, emphasizing that depression is a common and treatable condition.

How can I find affordable treatment for depression? Look into community mental health centers, sliding-scale fee clinics, online therapy platforms, and mental health apps for more affordable options.

How can I find the right mental health professional for my depression? Look for professionals with experience in treating depression, ask for referrals from trusted sources, and consider scheduling initial consultations to find a good fit.

How can I help a teenager dealing with depression? Be supportive, listen without judgment, encourage open communication, and seek professional help if necessary.

How can I maintain my social life while dealing with depression? Start with small gatherings, communicate your feelings with friends, and engage in activities that you enjoy and find meaningful.

How can I maintain treatment gains after feeling better? Continue practicing coping skills, maintain a healthy lifestyle, and have a plan in place for managing stressors or triggers.

How can I motivate myself to exercise when I'm depressed? Start small with activities you enjoy, set manageable goals, and gradually increase intensity. Remember, any movement is better than none.

How can I rebuild my life after depression? Set small, achievable goals, rebuild your routine gradually, and seek support from friends, family, and professionals as you navigate your recovery journey.

How can I support someone with depression? Offer empathy, listen without judgment, encourage them to seek professional help, and stay informed about depression.

How can I tell if I have depression? If you've experienced symptoms like persistent sadness, loss of interest in activities, changes in appetite or sleep, and feelings of worthlessness for more than two weeks, it may be depression.

How can journaling help with depression? Journaling offers a way to express thoughtsand feelings, reflect on experiences, and track mood changes over time.

How can mindfulness and meditation help with depression? Mindfulness and meditation can reduce stress, improve emotional regulation, and decrease symptoms of depression.

How do cultural factors influence the perception of depression? Cultural beliefs and norms can significantly impact how depression is perceived, discussed, and treated, with some cultures more open to acknowledging mental health issues than others.

How do I balance treatment for depression with maintaining privacy at work? You are not obligated to share your mental health status with your employer, but you may discuss accommodations or support you need without disclosing specific details.

How do I know if therapy is working for my depression? Signs of progress include improved mood, increased motivation, better sleep patterns, and a more positive outlook on life.

How do light therapy lamps work for Seasonal Affective Disorder? Light therapy mimics natural sunlight, which can help regulate mood, improve sleep, and reduce symptoms of SAD.

How do support groups help with depression? Support groups provide a safe space to share experiences, offer mutual support, and decrease feelings of isolation.

How does depression affect sleep patterns? Depression can lead to both insomnia and hypersomnia, affecting one's ability to fall or stay asleep, or causing excessive sleeping.

How does depression differ from occasional sadness? Unlike temporary sadness, depression is persistent, affecting individuals most of the day, nearly every day, for at least two weeks.

How does depression impact daily life and relationships? Depression can affect one's ability to work, study, eat, sleep, and enjoy life, often straining personal and professional relationships.

How does depression influence one's thought patterns? Depression can lead to negative, self-critical thoughts, a pessimistic view of the future, and a distorted perception of oneself and others.

How does exposure to nature impact depression? Spending time in nature has been shown to reduce stress, improve mood, and enhance mental wellbeing, contributing to depression relief.

How does exposure to sunlight affect depression? Exposure to sunlight can increase serotonin levels, improving mood and helping to alleviate symptoms of Seasonal Affective Disorder (SAD).

How does nutrition impact depression? Nutritional deficiencies, such as low levels of omega-3 fatty acids, vitamin D, and B vitamins, can influence mood and contribute to depression.

How does one build resilience against depression? Building resilience involves developing coping skills, fostering strong relationships, and maintaining a positive outlook on challenges.

How does sleep affect depression? Poor sleep can exacerbate depression symptoms, while healthy sleep patterns can improve mood and well-being.

How does sunlight exposure help with depression? Sunlight exposure increases the production of serotonin in the brain, which can boost mood and help regulate sleep.

How important is social support in treating depression? Strong social support is vital, as it provides emotional comfort, reduces feelings of isolation, and can encourage treatment-seeking behavior.

How is depression diagnosed? Diagnosis typically involves a comprehensive evaluation by a mental health professional, including interviews and sometimes physical exams or questionnaires.

Is depression genetic? Depression can run in families, suggesting a genetic link, but environmental and psychological factors also play critical roles.

Is depression more common in any specific gender or age group? Depression can affect anyone, though rates are higher in women and young adults.

Is it common to experience depression during pregnancy or postpartum? Yes, perinatal depression includes depression that occurs during pregnancy (antenatal) or after childbirth (postpartum).

Is it normal to feel depressed after a major life change? Yes, it's common to experience depressive symptoms during significant life transitions or stress, but prolonged feelings may indicate depression.

Is it possible to prevent depression? While not all cases can be prevented, managing stress, building resilience, and maintaining healthy lifestyle choices can reduce the risk.

Is there a connection between gut health and depression? Emerging research suggests a link between gut health and mood disorders, including depression, due to the gut-brain axis.

Is there a link between gut health and depression? Emerging research suggests a significant connection between gut health and mood. The gut-brain axis can influence depression, with probiotics and a healthy diet being potentially beneficial.

What are defense mechanisms, and how do they relate to depression? Defense mechanisms are psychological strategies used unconsciously to protect oneself from anxiety or distress, which can sometimes mask or exacerbate depression.

What are some common misconceptions about depression? Misconceptions include the belief that depression is just a lack of willpower, it can be snapped out of, or it's not a real illness.

What are some common side effects of antidepressants? Side effects vary by medication but can include nausea, weight gain, decreased libido, dry mouth, and sleep disturbances.

What are some mindfulness exercises for depression? Mindfulness exercises include focused breathing, body scans, mindful eating, and walking meditation, all aimed at bringing attention to the present moment.

What are some strategies for coping with depression at work? Strategies include setting realistic goals, breaking tasks into smaller steps, seeking support from HR or a trusted colleague, and practicing stress-reduction techniques.

What are some strategies for dealing with negative thoughts? Cognitive-behavioral techniques like challenging negative thoughts, practicing gratitude, and reframing thoughts can be effective.

What are the risks of untreated depression? Untreated depression can lead to worsening symptoms, significant impairment in daily life, and an increased risk of suicide.

What causes depression? Depression can result from a combination of genetic, biological, environmental, and psychological factors.

What if I don't feel better after starting treatment for depression? It's not uncommon to need adjustments in treatment plans. Communicate openly with your healthcare provider about your concerns.

What is 'smiling depression,' and how is it recognized? "Smiling depression" refers to individuals who appear happy or content outwardly while suffering from depression internally, making it challenging to recognize.

What is a depressive episode, and how long can it last? A depressive episode is a period characterized by symptoms of major depression lasting for at least two weeks, but episodes can last for several months or longer without treatment.

What is acceptance and commitment therapy (ACT), and how does it treat depression? ACT helps individuals accept their thoughts and feelings rather than fighting them, committing to actions that align with their values despite the presence of depression.

What is bipolar disorder, and how is it related to depression? Bipolar disorder is characterized by mood swings ranging from depressive lows to manic highs, with periods of depression being one phase of the disorder.

What is cognitive distortion, and how does it relate to depression? Cognitive distortions are irrational thought patterns that can contribute to depression, such as all-or-nothing thinking or overgeneralization.

What is depression? Depression is a common but serious mood disorder that affects how you feel, think, and handle daily activities.

What is dysthymia? Dysthymia, or Persistent Depressive Disorder, is a chronic form of depression with less severe but longer-lasting symptoms than major depression.

What is electroconvulsive therapy (ECT), and when is it used? ECT is a medical treatment most commonly used for severe depression that has not responded to other treatments. It involves brief electrical stimulation of the brain while the patient is under anesthesia.

What is psychodynamic therapy, and how can it help with depression? Psychodynamic therapy explores unconscious processes and past experiences to understand and alleviate depressive symptoms.

What is Seasonal Affective Disorder (SAD)? SAD is a type of depression related to changes in seasons, often worsening in winter months.

What is the first step in treating depression? The first step is often acknowledging the problem and seeking professional help from a healthcare provider or therapist.

What is the impact of social media on depression? Excessive or negative social media use can increase feelings of inadequacy, loneliness, and depression, though it can also provide support and connection if used positively.

What is the link between depression and chronic illnesses? Depression is more common among individuals with chronic illnesses due to the stress and limitations these conditions can impose on one's life.

What is transcranial magnetic stimulation (TMS) for depression? TMS is a non-invasive procedure that uses magnetic fields to stimulate nerve cells in the brain to improve symptoms of depression.

What is treatment-resistant depression? This term describes depression that doesn't respond to traditional treatment methods, such as medication and psychotherapy.

What role does self-compassion play in recovery from depression? Practicing self-compassion can reduce self-criticism and promote healing by encouraging a kind and understanding attitude towards oneself.

What role does sleep play in managing depression? Quality sleep is essential for emotional and physical well-being, with poor sleep often exacerbating depression symptoms.

What role does therapy play in treating depression? Therapy, such as cognitive-behavioral therapy (CBT) or interpersonal therapy (IPT), is crucial for addressing the underlying issues and thought patterns contributing to depression.

What should I do if I have thoughts of harming myself or others? It's crucial to seek immediate help from a mental health professional, call a crisis hotline, or visit an emergency room if you're experiencing these thoughts.

What should I do if I'm having thoughts of suicide? Seek help immediately from a mental health professional, call a suicide hotline, or reach out to a trusted individual.

What's the connection between anxiety and depression? Many individuals experience both anxiety and depression, as the two conditions often co-occur and can influence each other.

What's the difference between psychotherapy and counseling? Psychotherapy is generally a longer-term treatment focusing on deeper issues, while counseling may address more immediate, situational problems.

What's the impact of social media on depression? Excessive social media use can increase feelings of inadequacy, loneliness, and anxiety, potentially worsening depression.

What's the role of mindfulness in preventing relapse into depression? Mindfulness can help you become aware of early warning signs of relapse, manage stress more effectively, and break cycles of negative thinking.

National Resources for Depression and Suicide Prevention

1. National Suicide Prevention Lifeline

- **Description**: A national network of local crisis centers that provides free and confidential emotional support to people in suicidal crisis or emotional distress 24 hours a day, 7 days a week.
- **Contact**: 1-800-273-TALK (1-800-273-8255)
- **Website**: suicidepreventionlifeline.org

2. Crisis Text Line

- **Description**: Free, 24/7 support for those in crisis, connecting people in crisis to trained Crisis Counselors.
- **Contact**: Text HOME to 741741
- **Website**: crisistextline.org

3. National Alliance on Mental Illness (NAMI)

- **Description**: The nation's largest grassroots mental health organization dedicated to building better lives for the millions of Americans affected by mental illness.
- **Contact**: 1-800-950-NAMI (1-800-950-6264)
- **Website**: nami.org

4. American Foundation for Suicide Prevention

- **Description**: Provides resources and support to those affected by suicide, funding scientific research, and offering educational programs to increase awareness about mental health and suicide prevention.
- **Contact**: Find local chapters
- **Website**: afsp.org

5. SAMHSA's National Helpline

- **Description**: The Substance Abuse and Mental Health Services Administration's (SAMHSA) National Helpline is a free, confidential, 24/7, 365-day-a-year treatment referral and information service (in English and Spanish) for individuals and families facing mental and/or substance use disorders.
- **Contact**: 1-800-662-HELP (1-800-662-4357)
- **Website**: samhsa.gov/find-help/national-helpline

6. Mental Health America

- **Description**: A leading community-based nonprofit dedicated to addressing the needs of those living with mental illness and promoting the overall mental health of all Americans.
- **Website**: mhanational.org

7. Depression and Bipolar Support Alliance (DBSA)

- **Description**: Provides hope, help, support, and education to improve the lives of people who have mood disorders.
- **Website**: dbsalliance.org

8. Veterans Crisis Line

- **Description**: Provides 24/7, confidential support to all veterans, service members, National Guard and Reserve members, and their families and friends.

- **Contact**: 1-800-273-8255 and Press 1, Text 838255
- **Website**: veteranscrisisline.net

9. The Trevor Project

- **Description**: Offers crisis intervention and suicide prevention services to lesbian, gay, bisexual, transgender, queer & questioning (LGBTQ) young people under 25.
- **Contact**: 1-866-488-7386, Text START to 678678
- **Website**: thetrevorproject.org

10. Trans Lifeline

- **Description**: A grassroots hotline and microgrants 501(c)(3) non-profit organization offering direct emotional and financial support to trans people in crisis – for the trans community, by the trans community.
- **Contact**: 1-877-565-8860 (USA)
- **Website**: translifeline.org

11. Teen Line

- **Description**: A teen-to-teen hotline with community outreach services, providing a safe, non-judgmental space for teenagers to talk about their problems and concerns.
- **Contact**: Text "TEEN" to 839863 (6pm-9pm PST) or call 310-855-4673
- **Website**: teenlineonline.org

12. Anxiety and Depression Association of America (ADAA)

- **Description**: Offers information on prevention, treatment, and symptoms of anxiety, depression, and related conditions.
- **Website**: adaa.org

13. Child Mind Institute

- **Description**: An independent, national nonprofit dedicated to transforming the lives of children and families struggling with mental health and learning disorders.
- **Website**: childmind.org

14. The Jed Foundation (JED)

- **Description**: Works to prevent suicide for teens and young adults and to protect emotional health by partnering with high schools and colleges to strengthen their mental health, substance misuse, and suicide prevention programs and systems.
- **Website**: jedfoundation.org

15. National Institute of Mental Health (NIMH)

- **Description**: The lead federal agency for research on mental disorders. Offers comprehensive information on mental disorders, a range of related topics, and the latest mental health research.
- **Website**: nimh.nih.gov

16. Active Minds

- **Description**: The leading nonprofit organization that empowers students to speak openly about mental health in order to educate others and encourage help-seeking.

- **Website**: activeminds.org

About Dr. Dave

Dr. Dave Ferruolo is the founder, president, and operational director of LifeWorks Counseling Associates, PLLC. He brings a lifetime of entrepreneurial experience, business ownership and leadership to the company. Dr. Dave strives for excellence in everything he does, with a vision for LifeWorks to be a premier counseling agency in New Hampshire and a leader and innovator with the delivery of online TeleHealth counseling services. Each LifeWorks Clinician is hand-picked from literally dozens of qualified applicants, with qualities that align with the core values and high standards expected of a LifeWorks Clinician.

Dr. Dave ran his first business at 15 years-old, and after high school he served our country as a U.S. Navy SEAL. His highly competitive nature aligns with his core character of achieving excellence and continual improvement in all life endeavors. As a lifelong entrepreneur, Dr. Dave has had his share of success and failures, from which he has learned and continues to evolve. His education includes: a technical school certificate in music theory and performance; a Bachelors in Business; a Bachelor in Psychology; a Masters in Clinical Social Work; and a Doctorate of Education in Leadership with a dissertation focus on veteran mental health and reintegration issues. He is an Licensed Independent Clinical Social Worker (LICSW) and Master Licensed Alcohol and Drug Counselor (MLADC). Dr. Dave brings his over 40 years of acquired knowledge, skills, education, experience, and wisdom to *DEPRESSION FREE.*

Certified in various therapeutic modalities-including cognitive-behavioral therapy, mindfulness, trauma-focused therapies, and psychedelic-assisted therapies, Dr. Dave leverages his extensive knowledge to empower those struggling with depression toward liberation.

References

American Psychiatric Association. (2013). *Diagnostic and Statistical Manual of Mental Disorders (5th ed.)*. Washington, DC: American Psychiatric Publishing.

Anderson, F. G., Sweezy, M., & Schwartz, R. C. (2017). *Internal Family Systems Skills Training Manual: Trauma-Informed Treatment for Anxiety, Depression, PTSD & Substance Abuse*. PESI Publishing & Media.

Bannink, F. P. (2007). Solution-focused brief therapy. *Journal of contemporary psychotherapy, 37*(2), 87-94.

Bannink, F. P. (2015). *1001 solution-focused questions: Handbook for solution-focused interviewing*. New York, NY: Norton & Company.

Barlow, D., & Durand, V. (2009). Abnormal psychology; An integrative approach (5ed.). New York, NY: McGraw-Hill.

Bateman, A., & Fonagy, P. (2016). *Mentalization-based treatment for personality disorders: A practical guide*. Oxford, UK: Oxford University Press.

Beck, A. T., Rush, A. J., Shaw, B. F., & Emery, G. (1979). *Cognitive Therapy of Depression*. New York: Guilford Press.

Beck, J. S. (2011). *Cognitive behavior therapy: Basics and beyond* (2nd ed.). New York, NY: Guilford Press.

Bell, A. C., & D'Zurilla, T. J. (2009). Problem-solving therapy for depression: a meta-analysis. *Clinical psychology review, 29*(4), 348-353..

Blonna, R. (2017). *ACT on life not on anger: The new Acceptance and Commitment Therapy guide to problem anger*. New Harbinger Publications.

Brach, T. (2016). *Radical acceptance: Embracing your life with the heart of a Buddha*. New York, NY: Bantam Books.

Brackett, M. A. (2019). *Permission to feel: Unlocking the power of emotions to help our kids, ourselves, and our society thrive*. New York, NY: Celadon Books.

Brackett, M. A., Rivers, S. E., & Salovey, P. (2011). Emotional intelligence: Implications for personal, social, academic, and workplace success. *Social and Personality Psychology Compass, 5*(1), 88-103.

Burns, D. D. (1999). *The Feeling Good Handbook*. New York: Plume.

Butler, A. C., Chapman, J. E., Forman, F. M., & Beck, A. T. (2006). The empirical status of cognitive-behavioral therapy: A review of meta-analyses. Clinical Psychology Review, 26 (1), 17-31.

Capuzzi, D., & Stauffer, M. D. (Eds.). (2016). *Counseling and Psychotherapy: Theories and Interventions*. American Counseling Association.

Chand, S., Ravi, C., Chakkamparambil, B., Prasad, A., & Vora, A. (2018). CBT for depression: What the evidence says. *Current Psychiatry*, *17*(9), 14-23.

Chödrön, P. (2016). *When things fall apart: Heart advice for difficult times*. Boston, MA: Shambhala Publications.

Clear, J. (2018). *Atomic habits: An easy & proven way to build good habits & break bad ones*. New York, NY: Avery.

Codd III, R. T. (2018). *Effective Techniques for Dealing with Highly Resistant Clients*. PESI Publishing & Media.

Corcoran, J. (2006). Cognitive-behavioral methods for social workers: A workbook. Boston, MA: Allyn & Bacon.

Corcoran, J., & Pillai, V. (2018). *Social workers' desk reference* (3rd ed.). Oxford, UK: Oxford University Press.

Creswell, J. D. (2017). *Mindfulness interventions*. Annual Review of Psychology, 68, 491-516.

Cudzik, M., Soroka, E., & Olajossy, M. (2019). The impact of emotional intelligence level on the depression vulnerability. *Current Problems of Psychiatry*, *20*(3), 179-186.

Cuijpers, P., Quero, S., Noma, H., Ciharova, M., Miguel, C., Karyotaki, E., ... & Furukawa, T. A. (2021). Psychotherapies for depression: a network meta-analysis covering efficacy, acceptability and long-term outcomes of all main treatment types. *World Psychiatry*, *20*(2), 283-293.

Dahl, J., Wilson, K. G., & Nilsson, A. (2015). Acceptance and Commitment Therapy and the treatment of persons at risk for long-term disability resulting from stress and pain symptoms: A preliminary randomized trial. *Behavior Therapy, 35*(4), 785-801.

Davidson, R. J., & Begley, S. (2012). *The emotional life of your brain: How its unique patterns affect the way you think, feel, and live--and how you can change them*. New York, NY: Hudson Street Press.

De Shazer, S. (1985). *Keys to solution in brief therapy*. New York, NY: Norton.

Dillon, C. (2003). *Learning from mistakes*. Belmont, CA: Brooks/Cole

Dindo, L., Van Liew, J. R., & Arch, J. J. (2017). Acceptance and Commitment Therapy: A transdiagnostic behavioral intervention for mental health and medical conditions. *Neurotherapeutics, 14*(3), 546-553.

Doran, J. M. (2015). *The Theory and Practice of Experiential Dynamic Psychotherapy.* Karnac Books.

Driessen, E., Cuijpers, P., de Maat, S. C., Abbass, A. A., de Jonghe, F., & Dekker, J. J. (2010). The efficacy of short-term psychodynamic psychotherapy for depression: a meta-analysis. *Clinical psychology review, 30*(1), 25-36.

Duckworth, A. (2016). *Grit: The power of passion and perseverance.* New York, NY: Scribner.

Duhigg, C. (2016). *Smarter faster better: The secrets of being productive in life and business.* New York, NY: Random House.

Ellis, A. (1962). *Reason and emotion in psychotherapy.* New York, NY: Lyle Stuart.

Fava, G. A., & Tomba, E. (2019). *Increasing psychological well-being in clinical and educational settings: Interventions and cultural contexts.* Dordrecht, Netherlands: Springer.

Feldman, C., & Kuyken, W. (2019). *Compassion in the landscape of suffering.* Contemporary Buddhism, 20(1), 143-155.

Flaxman, P. E., Blackledge, J. T., & Bond, F. W. (2016). *Acceptance and Commitment Therapy: Distinctive features.* Routledge.

Folke, F., Parling, T., & Melin, L. (2012). Acceptance and Commitment Therapy for Depression: A Preliminary Randomized Clinical Trial for Unemployed on Long-Term Sick Leave. *Cognitive and Behavioral Practice, 19*(4), 583-594.

Fonagy, P., & Allison, E. (2014). The role of mentalizing and epistemic trust in the therapeutic relationship. *Psychotherapy, 51*(3), 372-380.

Forsyth, J. P., & Eifert, G. H. (2016). *The Mindfulness and Acceptance Workbook for Anxiety: A Guide to Breaking Free from Anxiety, Phobias, and Worry Using Acceptance and Commitment Therapy*, Second Edition. New Harbinger Publications.

Franklin, C., Trepper, T. S., Gingerich, W. J., & McCollum, E. E. (Eds.). (2016). *Solution-focused brief therapy: A handbook of evidence-based practice.* Oxford, UK: Oxford University Press.

Fredrickson, B. L. (2013). *Love 2.0: Finding happiness and health in moments of connection.* New York, NY: Penguin Books.

Freud, A. (1936). *The Ego and the Mechanisms of Defense.* London: Hogarth Press and Institute of Psycho-Analysis.

Gabbard, G. O. (2017). *Gabbard's treatments of psychiatric disorders* (5th ed.). Arlington, VA: American Psychiatric Association Publishing.

Gallagher, M. W., Zvolensky, M. J., Long, L. J., Rogers, A. H., & Garey, L. (2019). *The impact of acceptance and commitment therapy on positive psychological outcomes: A systematic review and meta-analysis.* Journal of Contextual Behavioral Science, 14, 379-395.

Gerber, A. J., & Piers, C. (2019). *Neuropsychodynamic psychiatry.* New York, NY: Springer.

Germer, C. K. (2019). *The mindful path to self-compassion: Freeing yourself from destructive thoughts and emotions.* New York, NY: Guilford Press.

Gilbert, P. (2019). *Compassion: Concepts, research and applications.* London, UK: Routledge.

Gingerich, W. J., & Peterson, L. T. (2013). Effectiveness of solution-focused brief therapy: A systematic qualitative review of controlled outcome studies. *Research on Social Work Practice, 23*(3), 266-283.

Goleman, D. (1995). *Emotional intelligence.* New York, NY: Bantam Books.

Goleman, D., & Senge, P. (2014). *The triple focus: A new approach to education.* Florence, MA: More Than Sound.

Grant, A. (2016). *Originals: How non-conformists move the world.* New York, NY: Viking.

Grant, A. M., & Greene, J. (2018). *Solution-focused coaching: Managing people in a complex world.* New York, NY: Routledge.

Greenberg, L. S. (2015). *Emotion-focused therapy: Coaching clients to work through their feelings* (2nd ed.). Washington, DC: American Psychological Association.

Gross, J. J. (Ed.). (2007). *Handbook of Emotion Regulation.* New York: Guilford Press.

Haddock, S. A., Weiler, L. M., Trump, L. J., & Henry, K. L. (2017). The efficacy of internal family systems therapy in the treatment of depression among female college students: A pilot study. *Journal of marital and family therapy, 43*(1), 131-144.

Haidt, J. (2012). *The righteous mind: Why good people are divided by politics and religion.* New York, NY: Pantheon Books.

Hanson, R. (2015). *Hardwiring happiness: The new brain science of contentment, calm, and confidence.* New York, NY: Harmony.

Hanson, R. (2018). *Resilient: How to grow an unshakable core of calm, strength, and happiness.* New York, NY: Harmony Books.

Harris, R. (2019). *ACT Made Simple: An Easy-To-Read Primer on Acceptance and Commitment Therapy* (2nd ed.). New Harbinger Publications.

Hasler, G. (2010). Pathophysiology of depression: do we have any solid evidence of interest to clinicians? *World Psychiatry, 9*(3), 155-161.

Hayes, S. C., & Hofmann, S. G. (Eds.). (2018). *The third wave of cognitive behavioral therapy and the rise of process-based care.* Guilford Press.

Hayes, S. C., & Lillis, J. (2012). *Acceptance and Commitment Therapy.* Washington, DC: American Psychological Association.

Hayes, S. C., Levin, M. E., Plumb-Vilardaga, J., Villatte, J. L., & Pistorello, J. (2013). Acceptance and commitment therapy and contextual behavioral science:

Examining the progress of a distinctive model of behavioral and cognitive therapy. *Behavior Therapy, 44*(2), 180-198.

Hayes, S. C., Strosahl, K. D., & Wilson, K. G. (1999). *Acceptance and Commitment Therapy: An Experiential Approach to Behavior Change.* New York, NY: Guilford Press.

Herbine-Blank, T., Kerpelman, D. C., & Sweezy, M. (2016). *Intimacy from the Inside Out: Courage and Compassion in Couple Therapy.* Routledge.

Hofmann, S. G., & Gómez, A. F. (2017). Mindfulness-based interventions for anxiety and depression. *Psychiatric Clinics of North America, 40*(4), 739-749.

Hofmann, S. G., Asmundson, G. J. G., & Beck, A. T. (2018). *The science of cognitive behavioral therapy.* San Diego, CA: Academic Press.

Hofmann, S. G., Asnaani, A., Vonk, I. J., Sawyer, A. T., & Fang, A. (2012). The efficacy of cognitive behavioral therapy: A review of meta-analyses. *Cognitive Therapy and Research, 36*(5), 427-440.

Hollon, S. D., Thase, M. E., & Markowitz, J. C. (2002). Treatment and prevention of depression. *Psychological Science in the Public Interest, 3*(2), 39-77.

Holmes, T. R. (2015). *Parts Work: An Illustrated Guide to Your Inner Life.* Winged Heart Press.

Honyashiki, M., Furukawa, T. A., Noma, H., Tanaka, S., Chen, P., Ichikawa, K., ... & Caldwell, D. M. (2014). Specificity of CBT for depression: a contribution from multiple treatments meta-analyses. *Cognitive therapy and research, 38*, 249-260.

Kabat-Zinn, J. (1990). *Full Catastrophe Living: Using the Wisdom of Your Body and Mind to Face Stress, Pain, and Illness.* New York: Delta.

Kabat-Zinn, J. (1994). *Wherever you go, there you are: Mindfulness meditation in everyday life.* New York, NY: Hyperion.

Kabat-Zinn, J. (2016). *Mindfulness for beginners: Reclaiming the present moment—and your life.* Boulder, CO: Sounds True.

Kabat-Zinn, J., & Davidson, R. J. (Eds.). (2019). *The Mind's Own Physician: A Scientific Dialogue with the Dalai Lama on the Healing Power of Meditation.* New Harbinger Publications.

Karrouri, R., Hammani, Z., Benjelloun, R., & Otheman, Y. (2021). Major depressive disorder: Validated treatments and future challenges. *World journal of clinical cases, 9*(31), 9350.

Katz, M., Hilsenroth, M. J., Gold, J. R., Moore, M., Pitman, S. R., Levy, S. R., & Owen, J. (2019). Adherence, flexibility, and outcome in psychodynamic treatment of depression. *Journal of Counseling Psychology, 66*(1), 94.

Keltner, D., Oatley, K., & Jenkins, J. M. (2019). *Understanding emotions* (4th ed.). Hoboken, NJ: Wiley.

Kendler, K. S., Gatz, M., Gardner, C. O., & Pedersen, N. L. (2006). A Swedish national twin study of lifetime major depression. *American Journal of Psychiatry, 163*(1), 109-114.

Kim, J. S. (2008). Examining the effectiveness of solution-focused brief therapy: A meta-analysis. *Research on Social Work Practice, 18*(2), 107-116.

Kim, J. S. (2015). *Solution-focused brief therapy: A multicultural approach.* Thousand Oaks, CA: SAGE Publications.

Kirsch, I., Moore, T. J., Scoboria, A., & Nicholls, S. S. (2002). The emperor's new drugs: An analysis of antidepressant medication data submitted to the U.S. Food and Drug Administration. *Prevention & Treatment, 5*(1), 23.

Knox, J. (2015). *Self-Agency in Psychotherapy: Attachment, Autonomy, and Intimacy.* Norton & Company.

Koorankot, J., Moosa, A., Froerer, A., & Rajan, S. K. (2022). Solution focused vs problem focused questions on affect and processing speed among individuals with depression. *Journal of Contemporary Psychotherapy, 52*(4), 347-353.

Lebow, J., Chambers, A., Christensen, A., & Johnson, S. M. (Eds.). (2019). *Encyclopedia of couple and family therapy.* Switzerland: Springer International Publishing.

Lemma, A. (2016). *Introduction to the practice of psychoanalytic psychotherapy* (2nd ed.). Chichester, UK: Wiley Blackwell.

Linehan, M. M. (1993). *Cognitive-behavioral treatment of borderline personality disorder.* New York, NY: Guilford Press.

Lloyd, J., & Hertlein, K. M. (2015). *The complete systemic therapist: Integrating systemic approaches in psychotherapy.* Boston, MA: Cengage Learning.

Lopes, P. N., Salovey, P., & Straus, R. (2017). Emotional intelligence, personality, and the perceived quality of social relationships. *Personality and Individual Differences, 107,* 212-218.

López-López, J. A., Davies, S. R., Caldwell, D. M., Churchill, R., Peters, T. J., Tallon, D., ... & Welton, N. J. (2019). The process and delivery of CBT for depression in adults: a systematic review and network meta-analysis. *Psychological medicine, 49*(12), 1937-1947.

Luoma, J. B., Hayes, S. C., & Walser, R. D. (2017). *Learning ACT: An Acceptance and Commitment Therapy skills-training manual for therapists* (2nd ed.). New Harbinger Publications.

Lutz, A. B. (2017). *Learning solution-focused therapy: An illustrated guide.* Washington, DC: American Psychiatric Association Publishing.

Lutz, W., Schiefele, A. K., Wucherpfennig, F., Rubel, J., & Stulz, N. (2016). Clinical effectiveness of cognitive behavioral therapy for depression in routine care: A propensity score based comparison between randomized controlled trials and clinical practice. *Journal of affective disorders, 189,* 150-158.

Luyten, P., Mayes, L. C., Fonagy, P., Target, M., & Blatt, S. J. (2015). Handbook of psychodynamic approaches to psychopathology. New York, NY: Guilford Press.

Lyubomirsky, S. (2013). *The myths of happiness: What should make you happy, but doesn't, what shouldn't make you happy, but does.* New York, NY: Penguin Press.

MacCann, C., & Roberts, R. D. (2008). New paradigms for assessing emotional intelligence: theory and data. *Emotion, 8*(4), 540.

MacLearn, C. (2008). Use of self in cognitive behavioral therapy. Clinical Social Work Journal , 36 (3), 245-253.

Maguire, L. (2002). Clinical social work: Beyond generalist practice with individuals, groups, and families. Pacific Grove, CA: Brooks/Cole.

Manber, R., Kraemer, H., Arnow, B., Trivedi, M., Rush, A., Thase, M., et al. (2008). Faster remission of chronic depression with combined psychotherapy and medication than with each therapy alone. Journal of Counseling and Clinical Psychology , 76 (3), 459-476.

Mansell, W., Harvey, A., Watkins, E., & Shafran, R. (2019). Conceptual foundations of the transdiagnostic approach to CBT. *Journal of Cognitive Psychotherapy, 33*(1), 14-33.

Manson, M. (2016). *The subtle art of not giving a f*ck: A counterintuitive approach to living a good life*. New York, NY: HarperOne.

McGinn, L. K. (2000). Cognitive behavioral therapy of depression: theory, treatment, and empirical status. *American journal of psychotherapy, 54*(2), 257-262.

McGonigal, K. (2015). *The upside of stress: Why stress is good for you, and how to get good at it.* New York, NY: Avery.

McKergow, M., & Korman, H. (2017). *Inbetween: Neither inside nor outside the therapy room.* London, UK: Solutions Books.

McWilliams, N. (2016). *Psychoanalytic diagnosis: Understanding personality structure in the clinical process* (2nd ed.). New York, NY: The Guilford Press.

Mikolajczak, M., Gross, J. J., & Roskam, I. (2019). Parental emotional regulation: The wider impact on family life. *Emotion Review, 11*(3), 230-243.

Miller, W. R., & Rollnick, S. (2002). Motivational interviewing: Preparing people for change (2nd ed.). New York: Guilford Press.

Neff, K. (2011). *Self-compassion: The proven power of being kind to yourself.* New York, NY: William Morrow.

Neff, K., & Germer, C. (2018). *The Mindful Self-Compassion Workbook: A Proven Way to Accept Yourself, Build Inner Strength, and Thrive.* The Guilford Press.

Nelis, D., Quoidbach, J., Mikolajczak, M., & Hansenne, M. (2011). Increasing emotional intelligence: (How) is it possible? *Personality and Individual Differences, 50*(1), 56-61.

Newport, C. (2016). *Deep work: Rules for focused success in a distracted world*. New York, NY: Grand Central Publishing.

Nezu, A. M., Nezu, C. M., & D'Zurilla, T. J. (2013). *Problem-solving therapy: A treatment manual*. New York, NY: Springer Publishing Company.

Oud, M., De Winter, L., Vermeulen-Smit, E., Bodden, D., Nauta, M., Stone, L., ... & Stikkelbroek, Y. (2019). Effectiveness of CBT for children and adolescents with depression: A systematic review and meta-regression analysis. *European psychiatry, 57*, 33-45.

Raes, F., & Williams, J. M. G. (2019). *The power of mindfulness: Mindfulness meditation training in sport (MMTS)*. New York, NY: Springer.

Ratner, H., George, E., & Iveson, C. (2012). *Solution focused brief therapy: 100 key points and techniques*. New York, NY: Routledge.

Ruiz, F. J. (2010). A review of Acceptance and Commitment Therapy (ACT) empirical evidence: Correlational, experimental psychopathology, component and outcome studies. *International Journal of Psychology and Psychological Therapy, 10*(1), 125-162.

Ryan, R. M., & Deci, E. L. (2017). *Self-determination theory: Basic psychological needs in motivation, development, and wellness*. New York, NY: Guilford Press.

Salzberg, S. (2017). *Real love: The art of mindful connection*. New York, NY: Flatiron Books.

Schultz, D. P., & Schultz, S. E. (2008). *Theories of personality* (9. ed.). Belmont, CA: Wadsworth.

Schwartz, R. C. (1995). *Internal family systems therapy*. New York, NY: Guilford Press.

Schwartz, R. C., & Sweezy, M. (2019). *Internal Family Systems Therapy*, Second Edition. New York, NY: Guilford Press.

Segal, Z. V., Williams, J. M. G., & Teasdale, J. D. (2002). *Mindfulness-based cognitive therapy for depression: A new approach to preventing relapse*. New York, NY: Guilford Press.

Seligman, M. E. P. (2018). *The hope circuit: A psychologist's journey from helplessness to optimism*. New York, NY: Public Affairs.

Shedler, J. (2010). The efficacy of psychodynamic psychotherapy. *American Psychologist, 65*(2), 98-109.

Shulman, L. (2012). The skills of helping: Individuals, groups, and communities (7 ed.). Belmont, CA: Thomson Brooks/Cole.

Siegel, D. J. (2016). *Mind: A journey to the heart of being human*. New York, NY: W. W. Norton & Company.

Sinek, S. (2019). *The infinite game*. New York, NY: Portfolio/Penguin.

Smock Jordan, S., Froerer, A. S., & Bavelas, J. B. (Eds.). (2019). *SFBT conversations: The art and practice of solution-focused brief therapy.* New York, NY: Routledge.

Stahl, J. V., Hill, C. E., Jacobs, T., Kleinman, S., Isenberg, D., & Stern, A. (2009). When the shoe is on the other foot: A qualitive study of intern-level treinees' preceived learning from clients. Psychotherapy: Theory, Research, Practice, Training , 46 (3), 376-38

Stevens, M., Lieschke, J., Cruwys, T., Cárdenas, D., Platow, M. J., & Reynolds, K. J. (2021). Better together: How group-based physical activity protects against depression. *Social science & medicine, 286,* 114337.

Stockton, D., Kellett, S., Berrios, R., Sirois, F., Wilkinson, N., & Miles, G. (2019). Identifying the underlying mechanisms of change during acceptance and commitment therapy (ACT): A systematic review of contemporary mediation studies. *Behavioural and cognitive psychotherapy, 47*(3), 332-362.

Stoddard, J. A., & Afari, N. (Eds.). (2014). *The big book of ACT metaphors: A practitioner's guide to experiential exercises and metaphors in acceptance and commitment therapy.* Oakland, CA: New Harbinger Publications.

Strosahl, K., Robinson, P. J., & Gustavsson, T. (2015). *Brief interventions for radical change: Principles and practice of focused acceptance and commitment therapy.* New Harbinger Publications.

Summers, F. (2016). *Transcending the legacies of childhood abuse: A psychodynamic view.* New York, NY: Guilford Press.

Sweezy, M., & Ziskind, E. L. (Eds.). (2016). *Innovations and Elaborations in Internal Family Systems Therapy.* Routledge.

Trivedi, M. H., Rush, A. J., Wisniewski, S. R., Nierenberg, A. A., Warden, D., Ritz, L., Norquist, G., Howland, R. H., Lebowitz, B., McGrath, P. J., Shores-Wilson, K., Biggs, M. M., Balasubramani, G. K., & Fava, M. (2006). Evaluation of outcomes with citalopram for depression using measurement-based care in STAR*D: implications for clinical practice. *American Journal of Psychiatry, 163*(1), 28-40.

Twohig, M. P., & Levin, M. E. (2017). Acceptance and Commitment Therapy as a treatment for anxiety and depression: A review. *Psychiatric Clinics of North America, 40*(4), 751-770.

Twomey, C., O'Reilly, G., & Byrne, M. (2015). Effectiveness of cognitive behavioural therapy for anxiety and depression in primary care: a meta-analysis. *Family practice, 32*(1), 3-15.

Vago, D. R., & Silbersweig, D. A. (2012). Self-awareness, self-regulation, and self-transcendence (S-ART): A framework for understanding the neurobiological mechanisms of mindfulness. *Frontiers in Human Neuroscience, 6,* 296.

Van Dam, N. T., van Vugt, M. K., Vago, D. R., Schmalzl, L., Saron, C. D., Olendzki, A., Meissner, T., Lazar, S. W., Kerr, C. E., Gorchov, J., Fox, K. C. R., Field, B. A.,

Britton, W. B., Brefczynski-Lewis, J. A., & Meyer, D. E. (2018). *Mind the hype: A critical evaluation and prescriptive agenda for research on mindfulness and meditation.* Perspectives on Psychological Science, 13(1), 36-61.

Van Dijk, S. (2018). *DBT made simple: A step-by-step guide to dialectical behavior therapy.* Oakland, CA: New Harbinger Publications.

Wallerstein, R. S. (2015). *Forty-two lives in treatment: A study of psychoanalysis and psychotherapy.* New York, NY: Routledge.

Walser, R. D., & Westrup, D. (2017). *Acceptance & Commitment Therapy for the treatment of post-traumatic stress disorder & trauma-related problems.* New Harbinger Publications.

Wenzel, A., Brown, G. K., & Karlin, B. E. (2011). *Cognitive behavioral therapy for depression in veterans and military servicemembers: Therapist manual.* Washington, DC: U.S. Department of Veterans Affairs.

Westen, D., Gabbard, G. O., & Blagov, P. (2015). *Psychodynamic diagnostic manual: PDM-2.* Silver Spring, MD: Alliance of Psychoanalytic Organizations.

Williams, M., & Penman, D. (2015). *Mindfulness: An eight-week plan for finding peace in a frantic world.* New York, NY: Rodale Books.

World Health Organization. (2017). *Depression and Other Common Mental Disorders: Global Health Estimates.* World Health Organization.

Wrzesniewski, A., Dutton, J. E., & Debebe, G. (Eds.). (2013). *Research in organizational behavior: Vol. 33. Purpose and meaning in the workplace.* Bingley

Xue, Y. (2023). Family System and Depression: Theoretical Perspectives and Intervention. *Journal of Education, Humanities and Social Sciences, 22,* 523-530.

Young, J. E., Klosko, J. S., & Weishaar, M. E. (2003). *Schema Therapy: A Practitioner's Guide.* New York: Guilford Press.

Zettle, R. D. (2015). Acceptance and commitment therapy for depression. *Current Opinion in Psychology, 2,* 65-69.

www.ingramcontent.com/pod-product-compliance
Lightning Source LLC
Chambersburg PA
CBHW070859120626
46546CB00001B/63